DATE DUE

MAR 1 3 2009			
MAR 1 3 2009			
AUG 1 9 2009			
SEP 2 4 2010			
OCT 1 5 2011			
OCT 1 6 2013			
APR 2 5 2014			
GAYLORD		PRINTED IN U.S.A.	

D0972929

Other Titles in the Smart Pop Series

THE MAN FROM KRYPTON

THE MAN FROM KRYPTON

A CLOSER LOOK AT SUPERMAN

EDITED BY
GLENN YEFFETH

BENBELLA BOOKS, INC.
Dallas, Texas

"Previous Issues" © 2005 by Lawrence Watt-Evans
"A History of Violence" © 2005 by David Hopkins
"You Will Believe a Man Can Walk: Christopher Reeve's Part in the Superman Myth" © 2005 by Sarah Zettel
"Jewel Mountains and Fire Falls: The Lost World of Krypton" © 2005 by Monkeybrain, Inc.
"Man of Steel, Woman of Kleenex" © 1971 by Larry Niven, reprinted from *All the Myriad Ways*
"Actor and Superactor" © 2005 by Keith R. A. DeCandido
"A Tale of Two Orphans: The Man of Steel vs. the Caped Crusader" © 2005 by Lou Anders
"God, Communism and the WB" © 2003 by Gustav Peebles, reprinted from *The Believer*
"Supermyth!" © 2005 by Steven Harper
"Six Things that Plain Don't Make any Sense about Superman" © 2005 by Adam-Troy Castro
"Is Superman a Superman?" © 2005 by Adam Roberts
"The Mirror of Gilgamesh: The Foe Superman Fears the Most and the Ally He Can't Do Without" © 2005 by John G. Hemry
"The Golden Shield: Image as Superman's Greatest Power" © 2005 by Paul Lytle
"Superman by Moonlight: Can Clark and Lois Break the Curse?" © 2005 by Yvonne Jocks
"Speeding Bullets and Changing Lanes" © 2005 by Joseph McCabe
"A Word of Warning for Brandon Routh" © 2005 by Lou Anders
"Superman's Moral Evolution" © 2005 by Peter B. Lloyd
"Brain Versus Brawn: The Many Lives (and Minds) of Lex Luthor, the World's Greatest Villain" © 2005 by Bob Batchelor
"Superman, Patriotism and Doing the Ultimate Good: Why the Man of Steel Did So Little to Stop Hitler and Tojo" © 2005 by Paul Levinson
"This Is a Job For..." © 2005 by Larry Dixon

BenBella Books, Inc.
6440 N. Central Expressway, Suite 617
Dallas, TX 75206
www.benbellabooks.com
Send feedback to feedback@benbellabooks.com

Printed in the United States of America
10 9 8 7 6 5 4 3 2 1

Library of Congress Cataloging-in-Publication Data

The man from Krypton : a closer look at Superman / edited by Glenn Yeffeth.
    p. cm.
  ISBN 1-932100-77-6
  1. Superman (Fictitious character) I. Yeffeth, Glenn, 1961–

PN6728.S9M33 2006
741.5'973—dc22

2006005980

Proofreading by Jessica Keet and Stacia Seaman
Cover design by Todd Michael Bushman
Cover art by Paul Gilligan
Text design and composition by John Reinhardt Book Design
Printed by Victor Graphics, Inc.

Distributed by Independent Publishers Group
To order call (800) 888-4741
www.ipgbook.com

For special sales contact Yara Abuata at yara@benbellabooks.com

Contents

PREVIOUS ISSUES

FASTER THAN A speeding bullet, more powerful than a locomotive—Superman is undeniably a symbol of power. What's more, he fights for truth, justice and the American way; he's an icon of power used for good, power handled responsibly. It may be Spider-Man who actually said, "With great power comes great responsibility," but The Big Blue Boy Scout was living it twenty years before Spidey spun his first web.

Superman has powers and abilities far beyond those of mortal men; he can make himself ruler of the world, take anything he wants or kill anyone who gets in his way—but he doesn't. He's a good guy, the *ultimate* good guy, because he apparently isn't even *tempted* to abuse his powers. He's wholesome and noble and selfless. His foster parents raised him that way, and he's true to his upbringing.

It's long been recognized that this is part of what makes him boring sometimes, or at least hard to write good stories about; he's *too* powerful, *too* perfect. No menace can really endanger him—he's invulnerable. His moral choices are never really difficult; the Kents gave him so strong a sense of right and wrong that there's not much room for self-doubt. DC's editorial powers have more than once tried to make things easier for their scripters by cutting him back to a more human scale, but it never really sticks, because he's *Superman*. If he isn't power incarnate *and* a moral paragon, he's not the same iconic character.

What makes him Superman is that he's practically perfect in every way.

At least, on the outside.

But even though he's Superman, he has issues that are implicit in his background. He's kept them concealed all these years, but if you know where to look, you can find them. Especially if you look at the version of the character I grew up with, the so-called "Silver Age" or "pre-Crisis" Superman that existed from about 1955 to 1985.

A starting point to show you what I mean is his clothes. They say clothes make the man, and certainly part of what makes Superman the icon he is, is that familiar outfit of blue tights, red shorts, red boots, yellow belt and flowing red cape. He always wears it—and I do mean *always*.

In those pre-Crisis years, Superman's costume was indestructible. He *needed* an indestructible costume when he was out there getting blasted by ray guns, or strolling unscathed through nuclear explosions, or taking a swim through the sun's photosphere. So where did that costume, so much a part of the Superman legend, come from?

Well, as any long-time DC reader can tell you, Ma Kent (Martha Clark Kent, to give her full name) made it for him by sewing together the blankets that were wrapped around him in the rocket that sent him from Krypton to Earth. He wears it under his street clothes, in order, he says, to be ready to change to Superman at an instant's notice.

That very recognizable costume was at the heart of a good many stories back in the Silver Age; people tried to steal it, it showed through Clark Kent's torn clothing at inconvenient times and so forth. It's always been a major part of Superman's life.

And it must be inconvenient. Think about it: Clark Kent can't open his shirt collar on a hot day because that dumb suit would show. Wearing shorts when it's 95 degrees and everyone else is in cut-offs is a major decision that probably costs him a lot of worry, because fitting in means he has to take off the long johns. (The heat doesn't bother him, of course, but Clark Kent's reputation for eccentricity mustn't get out of hand.)

Now, some other superheroes may have some justification for wearing a super-suit under their clothes, but this is a man who can move faster than light and has clothes that can be stretched or compressed almost infinitely. The Flash used to keep his super-suit in a ring—Supes could surely do the same, and would no longer need to worry about ray guns or moths putting holes in his clothes and revealing that telltale red and blue. He could leave the suit in his Fortress, or even in orbit, and still reach it and change clothes and get to anywhere on the face of the Earth in a seventh of a second. So why doesn't he?

Well, remember where that suit came from. It's not made from ordinary fabric, but from Kryptonian blankets—that's how it survives all the abuse it gets.

In fact, it's made from the very blankets that were wrapped around him when he was an infant. The blankets he slept under. The cute little blankets his mother tucked him into.

That's right, friends—the super-suit is Superman's baby blanket. It's his security blanket—not figuratively, but literally. The Last Son of Krypton doesn't just carry a piece of his old baby blanket in his pocket, as some insecure people do; he's *wearing* it.

Told you he has issues.

But hey, we can cut him some slack. Despite being the most powerful being in the world, the guy has a rough life—he saves the universe almost daily, both his parents and his adoptive parents are dead (if we ignore the occasional dumb stories where Jor-El and Lara turn up in the Survival Zone or wherever), he has lots of secrets he can't share with anyone and there's nobody around with whom he can knock back a few beers, get tipsy and arm-wrestle—he can't get tipsy at *all*, so far as I know, without risking very serious trouble. And, going further, could a gin and tonic or a fruity daiquiri even affect the Man of Steel's mind, or is he as impervious to its effects as he is to almost everything else earthly?

That's something that people don't seem to consider. At the end of a long day of rounding up bank robbers and mad scientists, how does Superman relax? Because he is so incredibly powerful, he just can't let himself go—not anywhere inhabited, anyway. He's liable to wreck several square blocks if he tries. He can't kick the furniture to blow off stress—he'll be punting footstools into orbit. He can't slap a friend on the back without either killing him or swatting him all the way to Taiwan. People admire him, they're in awe of him—but they've got to be a little scared, as well, when dealing with someone who can kill them by breathing hard.

Superman lives half his life in an unnatural, assumed role as Clark Kent just so he can deal with people on an equal basis occasionally, and even then, he has to be constantly on guard against doing something superhuman. The guy has got to be lonely and under constant stress.

So is it really surprising that he carries a security blanket?

No, not carries—*wears*. In fact, he *flaunts* it, though of course no one recognizes it for what it is. He stands there, chest out, as the bullets bounce off, and you can just imagine him thinking, *You can't hurt me! I have my blankie!*

This explains why he pretty much never takes it off even when he *is* relaxing. In all of those scenes in the Fortress of Solitude when he's taking it easy, playing chess against his super-robot, writing in his diary by carving Kryptonian words into solid steel plates with his fingernail, or whatever, does he ever slip out of his work clothes and into a dressing gown? When he takes a refreshing dip in a lava pool, does he ever strip down to his shorts to feel that warm tingle on his chest? Nope—the big red "S" stays firmly in place at all times.

That's a little eccentric—as well as unhygienic. Most of us don't wear the same underwear day in and day out, and we have good reasons for that. However, we see that Superman *does* clean his super-suit sometimes—by flying through the sun while wearing it.

That's right, he usually doesn't take it off even to wash it. This guy has it bad. Most people with security blankets at least put them down occasionally.

But then, Superman does have it rough. His home planet blew up; his species is effectively extinct. Yes, humans *look* the same, but we know they *aren't*—we can't clean *our* clothes by flying through the sun. Compared to Superman, we and all our creations are ridiculously fragile; if he ever forgets for even a second just how delicate we are, he could kill dozens of people. He must live his entire life as if he were walking through card houses floored with eggshells. Just cracking his knuckles might shatter windows! He can't belch, he can't fart, without worrying about killing innocent bystanders.

That suit at least gives him *something* he doesn't need to worry about damaging!

And it's something safe and comforting. Remember that there are other bits of his home planet still around—and they're trying to kill him. Kryptonite isn't just a bunch of green meteors to him; it's his *homeland*, his ancestral soil, the old country that sent him to America.

And it's poisonous.

This is a man who *really* can't go home again; his home is gone, and any souvenir he might find is toxic.

Any souvenir, that is, except that silly suit he wears.

And then there's the way he's treated by the people around him. He's an immigrant to our planet, and he's tried his best to fit in. He's done everything he can to be a good person, a good man, a good American, and how do people react to him?

Well, a fair number of the people he meets are trying to kill him. Everyone from street punks to Lex Luthor feels free to take shots at him, with guns and knives and death-rays, and nobody ever takes that seriously. Yes, the bad guys go to jail for robbing banks or trying to conquer the world without a permit, or whatever, but does it ever occur to anyone to file felony assault charges? These guys punch Superman, they shoot at him, stab him, run cars into him, hit him with missiles and energy beams and giant robot fists, and the cops never even *ask* him if he wants to press charges. Sure, he's unhurt, but that's not the *point*! He was still assaulted. Someone could *ask*.

That's his enemies—but what about his friends? They're constantly demanding his help, asking to be rescued, inviting him to help out with charity events, but do they ever just suggest a cup of coffee and a chat? Do they respect his privacy? Lois Lane and Lana Lang spend an absurd amount of time and effort trying to find out his "secret identity"—that's the thanks he gets for saving their lives and admitting to them in the first place that he *has* a secret identity?

Let's face it, for the pre-Crisis Superman, most of his alleged friends aren't so much friends as sycophants. Lois Lane wants him not be-cause she actually knows him, but because he's the ultimate trophy male—brains and brawn beyond human ken, all in a well-built pack-age. She spends more time trying to blackmail him or spy on him than she does just talking to him.

And Jimmy Olsen isn't so much a friend as his Number One Fan, basking in the admiration of his fellow nerds because he's buddies with the demi-god in the blue tights.

The only people who come close to treating Superman as one of their own, rather than as a celebrity, are the other superheroes—and let's face it, hanging out with a guy who dresses up as a giant bat, or a guy in a Robin Hood costume who puts boxing gloves on arrows, is not exactly a healthy social life. These people are freaks, just as much as Superman himself, even if they can't juggle asteroids. Clark Kent grew up wanting to fit in, to be the all-American boy; spending time with these weirdos may be better than nothing, but he's got to feel a little like the captain of the football team forced to eat lunch at the geeks' table.

And, of course, that's why he has his Clark Kent identity, so he can pretend to be normal—but even there, he can't be comfortable. He has to worry constantly about giving himself away. If Superman ac-cidentally leaves a palm-print in solid steel, it's not a big deal; people will just ooh and ahh, and it may wind up as a souvenir somewhere, but it's of no real consequence. If *Clark Kent* accidentally puts a fin-ger through a desktop, though, that's a real problem—someone might put two and two together.

As the TV show *Smallville* has repeatedly pointed out, any time he's out there pretending to be an ordinary human, he's *lying*. He's hiding who he is from his alleged closest friends, keeping secrets from the people he claims to love. That's got to be rough on a guy who wants, more than anything else in the world, to do what's right and be loved for it.

So if you ask me, along with everything else, he wears that suit under his clothes to remind him of who he is—that he's never *real-ly* Clark Kent; he's the freak, the alien, the Superman, who can't let himself go for an instant, who can't trust anyone, who can't let any-one trust *him*, who must always be on guard—but who still has the comforting presence of his baby blanket, reminding him that once, as a baby, he *did* have the unconditional love of two mothers, one who bore him and one who raised him, and the calm certainty that he was safe.

I can't begrudge him that small comfort, I suppose. After all, he's saved the world repeatedly, and is doing everything he can to make it a better place.

But jeez, I wish he washed that thing more often.

LAWRENCE WATT-EVANS is the author of some three dozen novels and over a hundred short stories, mostly in the fields of fantasy, science fiction and horror. He won The Hugo Award for short fiction in 1988 for "Why I Left Harry's All-Night Hamburgers," served as president of the Horror Writers Association from 1994 to 1996 and treasurer of SFWA from 2003 to 2004, and lives in Maryland. He has two kids in college and shares his home with Chanel, the obligatory writer's cat.

David Hopkins

A HISTORY OF VIOLENCE

WHILE OTHER PEOPLE may ponder the loftier subjects of truth and meaning, I've always wondered how Wolverine can bend his wrists when the claws sheath back into his hand. How can the Silver Surfer stay on his board with no noticeable traction or grip tape? Are Dr. Strange and his manservant Wong secret lovers? Why haven't the citizens of Gotham City put two and two together about Batman and Bruce Wayne? How can Flash have any self-respect when he fights a villain named "Rainbow Raider"? If when Billy Batson grows up, he says "Shazam," will that make him younger? And why would the noble Wonder Woman wear star-spangled undies?

I've also wondered how Superman could punch another person and not kill him. Forget a deeper postmodern critique of the superhero as a reconstruction of masculine language systems. I want to know how Superman doesn't kill people when he hits them. How does he not accidentally send a fist straight through the chest of a bank robber or would-be world conqueror? He's Superman, the strongest of the super-powered cape-wearing spandex titans. Even the phrase "more powerful than a locomotive" is an outdated understatement. From my own fanboyish research, I wager this Last Son of Krypton could do lethal damage using only his pinky finger.

I imagined this hypothetical scenario:

Superman playfully whacks Jimmy Olsen upside the head. Jimmy's head wobbles, a dopey grin spreads across his face, his eyes roll toward the back of his head and he falls over. "Oh, Jimmy," Superman laughs heartily. Next issue opens with Lois Lane, Perry White and a guilt-ridden Clark Kent standing over Jimmy's open grave. Pity.

And that's what happens when you're dealing with a guy who can squeeze coal into diamonds (*Action Comics*, No. 115) and throw an uninhabited planet through space (*Superman*, No. 110). However, the wise fanboy will explain that Superman is not only incredibly strong, but he's also completely in control of his power. He is not a bull in a china shop. Superman has the perfect combination of absolute power and absolute restraint. The good citizens of Metropolis need not worry about their hero accidentally sneezing and knocking down four city blocks. He's in control. The man who bends steel can also slap around Jimmy Olsen without cracking the poor kid's skull. If Superman were to punch someone, that bank robber or would-be world conqueror again, he would only hit hard enough to knock out the bad guy. Superman doesn't kill, and he's not carelessly violent. My hypothetical scenario made me wonder about Superman's history of violence and his infallible use of restraint. Should Jimmy Olsen wear a helmet? Would it help?

APPLE PIE AND FASCISM

Within the panels and pages of comic books, this dichotomy of power and restraint works. It works, because Superman's audience believes not only in his greatness, but also in his goodness. His no-kill ethic and commitment to the preservation of life makes him one of the good guys. Arguably, it's simplistic to create an ethical standard where people can be soldiers without killing. For all the heroes throughout history who have had to take a life, somehow Superman's hands stay clean as he fights to defend truth, justice and the American way. Superman is the perfect allegory of America's own idealism toward justifiable force: to be the most powerful and yet the most benevolent.

The superhero genre is all about the use of power and violence to solve problems. Not surprisingly, the superhero icon flourished during World War II, when both Superman and America turned their efforts against the Nazis and the Japanese. Pulitzer Prize-winning author and comic-book guru Michael Chabon makes this observation in the film *Comic Book Superheroes Unmasked*:

> There was a sort of irony in the fact that these characters, many of whom had in that period, in the Golden Age, evolved to fight the Nazis, were themselves very much in the Nazi ideal. The idea that you can solve problems through physical strength, by being stronger and more dominating, more powerful, that is fascism. That's it. That's the essence of fascism. I don't think the creators of superheroes or the kids who were reading at the time were the slightest bit aware of it.

The name "Superman" itself is ironic. Friedrich Nietzsche's Übermensch is commonly translated as "superman," and his philosophy was widely studied and popular among the Nazis. Like the Nazi belief in a super race, the Kryptonians represent a dominant species, a super race themselves. Possibly, as a result, critics forget Superman's use of restraint and compassion. They label him a "fascist" (Seagle 60), a thinly veiled pro-Nazi isolationist on American soil.

HOW VIOLENT IS SUPERMAN?

Amusing as it would be to see Superman cut loose and beat the crap out of his opponents, that's not him, even though one's first assumption is that Superman hits people. It's hard to believe such an American icon wouldn't use his fists more often. After all, John Wayne and Clint Eastwood punch people all the time. When a cowboy enters a bar, a fist fight breaks out. Surely, the Man of Steel has the same spit and grit as these characters. I searched through various media incarnations of Superman to find a trace of gratuitous violence. First, I looked at all the covers of *Action Comics* and *Superman* comics from the '30s and '40s to see if I could discover any seeds of violence.

On the cover of *Action Comics* No. 1, Superman holds a car over his head and smashes it into a nearby boulder. Two gangsters run away in terror, while the gangster closest to Superman is on his hands and knees, staring in shock. It's unclear whether he's staring at Superman or breaking the fourth wall and looking desperately at the reader. His stare asks the obvious question: Who *is* this man? I feel sorry for the poor guy trying to claim insurance. How do you explain that one? However, this car-smashing could hardly prove any violent abandon on Superman's part. His aggression is directed toward the automobile. He doesn't hurt anyone.

In fact, in the '30s and '40s, Superman had some odd issues with several modes of transportation. On the cover of *Action Comics* No. 10, only his third cover appearance, he punches an airplane in mid-flight, knocking off one of the wings. He stops a train on the cover of *Action Comics* No. 13 to save it from a broken bridge and then handles a submarine in issue 15. On the cover of *Action Comics* No. 17, he pushes over a tank. The *Superman* No. 13 cover shows Superman punching a boat. Clearly, the guy doesn't like most forms of automotive transportation, but no people are hurt.

In *Action Comics* No. 36, Superman moves from demolishing vehicles to punching robots. The robot is a step closer to hitting an actual person, but I wouldn't say hitting a robot counts as a true violent act except for the Isaac Asimov sci-fi fan, in which case such a scenario might pose an interesting ethical debate. Three questions must then be asked: Is the robot sentient? Does the robot feel pain? Is Superman aware of the robot's possible artificial intelligence? Technically, the robot is not breaking the first rule of Robotics ("A robot may not harm a human being, or, through inaction, allow a human being to come to harm"), because Superman is not a human being. Thus, we can't hold the robot morally accountable, unless the robot was built on another planet that used more inclusive language in programming its three laws.[1]

Finally, on the cover of *Action Comics* No. 47, Superman punches a person! It's Lex Luthor, of all people, making his first appearance on the cover. It's deliciously violent. Superman punches him through a freakin' brick wall! The dialogue is particularly telling. While Lex flies backward from the force of the blow, he says, "You can hit!" Su-

---

[1] To my dear editor Shanna, that may be the single most geeked-out paragraph I've ever written. I am proud and slightly disturbed.

perman says, "You ought to see me when I really try!" Superman indicates he is *holding back*, which proves my whole scenario about Jimmy needing to wear a helmet around Superman. This cover begs the question, how is Lex still alive after going through a brick wall? After some investigation, I discovered that in this particular story, Lex stole a power gem that made him super strong and invulnerable. Huh. I can't fault Superman for hitting him, knowing it wouldn't hurt or kill Lex. Stupid power gem. The next time Superman punches anyone is all the way in *Action Comics* No. 112, sixty-five issues later. He hits Mr. Mxyzptlk, yet another super-powered person who wouldn't be seriously hurt or killed by Superman's fist. Four issues later, he punches a snowman wearing a top hat (*Action Comics*, No. 116). But I mean, wouldn't you?

For the life of me, I couldn't find a single cover where Superman really hurt someone, acted carelessly or displayed any fascist style of violence. If he hit anyone, it would be a similarly powerful villain (or a snowman) who could take a hit or two from the Man of Steel. In most cases, Superman merely contained the lesser criminal element, bending steel around them, carrying them to the police or, once again, beating up their car. As an interesting side note, on the cover of *Superman* No. 87, he hits *himself* with a sledgehammer—the epitome of "Kids, don't try this at home." Self-inflicted punishment doesn't count, though. Much later, in 1978, Superman fought Muhammad Ali in the ring. Boxing is a violent sport. That does not make the boxers themselves inherently violent or malicious. We might even feel sympathy for Ali having to go toe-to-toe with the mighty Kryptonian, if it weren't for the fact Superman *lost* the fight. He took a tremendous beating. No doubt, many people lost money betting on that one. The upset was partially due to a nasty dose of red sunlight. In the end, the two greats shook hands and all was forgiven.

After looking over the covers, I turned to *Superman: The Movie.* Not once does Superman punch anyone in the film. He catches a helicopter. He spins around and bores through the street. He pushes a nuclear missile into outer space. He stops a school bus from falling, allows a train to pass over his back and prevents a flood when a dam breaks. Leading to his most amazing trick, he flies around the Earth, reverses its rotation and, in doing so, turns back time. All impressive, but no fighting. The only truly violent act might be when Lois recites the lamest poem in the history of human civilization, "Can You Read My Mind?"[2]

However, after the success of the first film, Superman didn't stay such a pacifist. In the 1980 sequel, Superman gets violent against the powerful General Zod, Ursa and Nod. In this blasphemous second movie, Superman breaks the no-kill rule, and without too much hesitation, either. General Zod and his two stooges are stripped of their powers. Instead of flying them to prison in true Superman fashion (as he did with Luthor in the first film), he crushes General Zod's hand and throws him into the Abyss. Lois figures if Superman can do it, she can, too, and playfully pushes Ursa to her death. Nod commits suicide on accident. But don't get me started on the sequel. That movie had so many plot holes. Why would Superman get rid of his powers (especially the ability to *fly*), when he's at the Fortress of Solitude—located in a barren Arctic wasteland approximately 130 miles from the North Pole? My fantasy version of *Superman II* includes an *idiotic* Clark Kent freezing to death, because he didn't anticipate walking home. Roll the credits. And how did he get his powers back? It's never explained. And the end of the film provides another uncharacteristically vicious moment for Superman: He gets even. Clark Kent walks into an Alaskan diner where earlier a local bully named "Rocky" beats the powerless Kent in front of Lois Lane. The fight was over a barstool. Now Kent returns, picks up Rocky and slides him down the bar, sending him crashing into a jukebox. He pays for the damage.

I don't have the energy to look at *Superman III* and *IV*. In my mind, these horrifically bad, "Can You Read My Mind?" bad, movies do not exist. Instead, I turn to *Superman: The Animated Series*, created by Bruce Timm and Paul Dini. This cartoon, which aired on the WB from 1996 to 2000, continued with the same "mini-movie" style of storytelling used in their popular Batman series. The editors decided to pare down Superman's powers to create a greater sense of conflict. There's lots of action. True to the original comics, Super-

---

[2] www.superman.ws/fos/themovie/mind.php (You've been warned!).

man beat up all sorts of vehicles owned by evil people—cars, trains, tanks and boats. He fought a few robots and super-powered people who couldn't be hurt by it (though no snowmen). Superman even punched Lex Luthor once again...in the final episode ("Legacy, Part II"). No, Lex didn't die. His head didn't fly off like some video game fatality. Superman held back.

In my investigation of Superman's history of violence, I wasn't about to read more than 800 issues of *Action Comics* and 600-plus issues of *Superman* comics to find my answers. I'm a dedicated fanboy, but come on. I have a life. Instead, I turned to my friend Doug Hayes. My knowledge of DC Comics pales in comparison to Doug's, and I knew he'd offer some good insight. The e-mail conversation went something like this:

> ME: Hey, Doug, is there any evidence that Kryptonians might be genetically disposed toward violence? (I wondered, because Krypton is always shown as this dispassionate technologically advanced utopia. I thought they must put something in the water.)
>
> DOUG: Not in any iteration that has made it to comic books or movies. It was presented in at least one version of Krypton's past as having been a part of their history, much like the theory of evolution proposes about human beings.

In other words, Krypton had a past filled with war and violence, but over time, it evolved and transcended those petty matters.

Yeah, Doug's a real geek. I thought I'd hit the jackpot. He even added this little bit of trivia:

> DOUG: Also, Doomsday is a product of Kryptonians testing genetic disposition of violence and the genetic ability to get stronger. You know, what doesn't kill you makes you stronger. Except in the Doomsday version, they did keep killing him and cloning him over and over again. All in the name of science and world defense!

Doomsday being the one who killed Superman (*Superman* Vol. 2, No. 75), this comic was violent and a complete slug fest. This led to more questions.

ME: To the best of your knowledge, has Superman ever killed . . . anyone? Ever?

DOUG: Well . . . technically: Yes. He killed the three Phantom Zone criminals from the pocket universe because they threatened to kill all his loved ones. But maybe since it was in another 'verse, it doesn't count?

ME: Maybe so.

Geek.

FREDERIC WERTHAM AND THE PERCEPTION OF THE "SUPERMAN COMPLEX"

When searching for a history of violence, there's no greater Superman critic than Dr. Fredric Wertham. Despite overwhelming evidence contrary to his argument, history proves that the public will believe any brainiac with the title "doctor" in front of his or her name.

In 1954, this child psychologist wrote a book, *Seduction of the Innocent*, on the effect of comics on children. Wertham's critique on the industry fanned the flames of anti-comic hysteria, leading to a Senate hearing on the effect of comic books on juvenile delinquency. During this time, laws were introduced in eighteen states restricting the sale of comic books. Some major cities banned the sales of comics completely. Widespread protests and comic-book burnings took place in front of newsstands and stores. In all, Wertham's crusade nearly sabotaged DC Comics and the entire fledgling industry.[3]

The three most popular superheroes of that time were Superman, Batman and Wonder Woman. According to Wertham, Batman and Robin encouraged homosexual thoughts, because Robin was drawn bare-legged and had an unflinching devotion to Batman. While I have my own theory about Dr. Strange and his manservant Wong, Batman's relationship to Robin was that of a caring surrogate father,

---

[3] For more about Dr. Fredric Wertham, read the Sequart.com essay, "The End of Seduction," by Julian Darius at www.sequart.com/columns/index.php?col=2&column=715. It's a fascinating and thorough account of this man and his impact on the comic-book industry.

not a boyfriend. And Wonder Woman? Wertham believed she was giving young girls the wrong idea about a woman's place in society. Clearly, from Wertham's perspective, if Wonder Woman wanted to fight crime, she would have to do it without leaving the kitchen. As for Superman, the doctor had two complaints. First, according to Wertham, comic books were giving kids wrong ideas about the laws of physics, because Superman could fly. Duly noted. What boy hasn't tied a towel around his neck and jumped off his parent's roof? I consider it a necessary lesson in reality. After I attempted it about five or six times, I, too, came to accept I couldn't fly. That and my wife yelled at me to get off the roof. Second, Wertham coined the term "Superman Complex," a condition where the reader gains pleasure from seeing someone beat the crap out of another person while they themselves remain immune. For example, this complex may explain my insatiable love of *America's Funniest Home Videos*. An unsuspecting dad gets hit in the crotch with a baseball bat, and I don't. Thus my amusement.

When I Googled "Superman Complex," I found most people had no clue about Wertham's version of the term. Instead, a "Superman Complex" was overwhelmingly synonymous with a "Savior Complex," overextending oneself in the pursuit of helping others or doing a good thing. The public just does not see Superman as Wertham does. The Man of Steel is not viewed as a force of violence, but as a savior.

I polled my students in class one day about their opinions on Superman. (Yes, I can do that.) I handed them a sheet of paper with a series of questions about Superman and compiled the information to see their response, motivated by basic curiosity. Wertham had an agenda, but how would the average kid today react to the American icon he was attacking? Out of 125 students, not a single one regarded him as a violent individual. The most common response went like this: "Superman is a guy with powers who saves people." Superman saves. All hail the Prince of Peace. These students were not comic-book fanboys like Doug Hayes or myself; they were just average teenagers, many of who never read a Superman comic in their life or saw *Superman* in the theater, and probably don't even know Asimov's Three Laws of Robotics. Yet they overwhelmingly responded in accord with one another.

The movie *The Iron Giant* also tells us a lot about the overall perception of Superman, once again contrary to Wertham's "Superman Complex." In one scene, Hogarth Hughes shows the Iron Giant his comic book stash and points out Superman:

> HOGARTH: This guy is Superman. Sure, he's famous now, but he started off just like you. Crash-landed on Earth. Didn't know what he was doing. But he only uses his powers for good, never for evil. Remember that.

The Iron Giant understands Superman to be a moral code for powerful people, a Sermon on the Mount. Be good, as Superman is good. The contrasting image is that of gun, a mindless weapon to be exploited by someone else. The Iron Giant wants to save the day, and use his powers responsibly. At the end of the movie, he bravely declares he is not a gun. He's Superman.

The diamond shaped S-symbol itself is a modern piece on a sacred iconography. The meaning has transcended its original purpose. No longer does the "S" really stand for Superman. It has come to communicate a certain value of strength. In January 2004, Egyptian conjoined twins made worldwide news because of their separation surgery in Dallas and their remarkable recovery. The hospital staff nicknamed Mohamed, one of the children, "Superman." I remember seeing the Superman symbol on his helmet in the newspaper. I was deeply touched by how this symbol could be transfigured when worn by a frail child. Mohamed is already a very strong name in the Middle East, and it's ironic the American staff replaced it with our own "Superman" name. Clearly, those who nicknamed the child "Superman" were referencing his strength and courage, not any violent-natured complex.

A HISTORY OF PLAYING THE PART

Superman has the power of a god, and yet he still can and must interact with people on a painfully human level. This task might be easier if he weren't fighting on a daily basis against corrupt villains. Even in those cases, though, he exercises restraint. He's a champion, a fighter, but not violent. His restraint and his power co-exist. Which leads me back to my original question: How could Superman punch another person and not kill him? Shouldn't this be an easy answer?

Yes, but the answer reveals the third part of his nature—one of power, restraint and, finally, theatrics. If Superman punches someone and *doesn't* knock a hole through him, the whole action is excessive. Why not thump them with his pinky (albeit a lethal pinky)? Why bother with the whole act of swinging a fist? Superman would be generous to the villain, giving him the satisfaction of having withstood a punch, when in fact Superman would be holding back so much you couldn't call it a punch at all. From his perspective, it's all staged combat. In this case, Superman doesn't have a history of violence. He has a flair for theatrics. He likes to act, to play the part. This aspect of Superman has been with him since *Action Comics* No. 1—his obsession with the alter ego.

Much of Superman's own hero fantasy must be due to the fact he was raised in Smallville. No doubt, he grew up seeing Errol Flynn movies, thrilling to the exploits of swashbucklers and rogue pirates at the local theater. He read about Tarzan, Doc Savage and Buck Rogers in the pulp magazines. Such characters also enamored his creators Jerry Siegel and Joe Shuster, who endowed their creation with some of the same courageous attributes.

As a child, Superman was still Clark Kent, not the secret alter ego, but the person his adoptive parents named. Ma and Pa Kent took Clark to church every Sunday, and he knew the story of Moses. Even at that age, could he see the parallel? For Superman to wear a cape and fly through the city of Metropolis, he understood it wasn't enough to stop evil. People had to see him *fight* evil, so as to not trivialize the struggle that exists for truth and justice. Clark Kent, the mild-mannered *Daily Planet* reporter, is an act, but, to some degree, so is Superman. Both hold back. Power and violence do not show the true strength or courage of a person, but control and restraint do.

REFERENCES

Boring, Wayne (a). "The Secret of the Superman Trophy." *Superman* No. 110. National Comics Publications (DC Comics): Jan. 1957.

Comic Book Superheroes Unmasked. Dir. Steve Kroopnick. Host Peta Wilson. The History Channel, 23 June 2003.

Coville, Jamie. "The Comic Book Villain, Dr. Fredric Wertham, M.D." Seduction of the Innocents and the Attack on Comic Books. 15 Nov. 2005. <http://www.psu.edu/dept/inart10_110/inart10/cmbk4cca.html>.

Jurgens, Dan (w, p) and Brett Breeding (i). "Dooomsday!" *Superman* Vol. 2 No. 75. DC Comics: Jan. 1993.

"Legacy, Part II." *Superman*. Episode 54, Dir. Dan Riba. WB, 12 Feb. 2000.

O'Neil, Dennis (w), Neal Adams (p), Dick Giordano and Terry Austin (i). *Superman vs. Muhammad Ali*. DC Comics: Fall 1978.

Seagle, Steven T. (w), and Teddy Kristiansen (a). *It's a Bird...* New York: DC Comics, 2004.

Siegel, Jerry (w), and Joe Shuster (a). *Action Comics* No. 1. National Comics Publications (DC Comics): June 1938.

Siegel, Jerry (w), and Joe Shuster (a). "The Cory Town Chain Gang." *Action Comics* No. 10. National Comics Publications (DC Comics): Mar. 1939.

Siegel, Jerry (w), and Joe Shuster (a). "The Cab Protection League." *Action Comics* No. 13. National Comics Publications (DC Comics): June 1939.

Siegel, Jerry (w), and Paul Cassidy (a). "Kidtown." *Action Comics* No. 15. National Comics Publications (DC Comics): Aug. 1939.

Siegel, Jerry (w), and Joe Shuster (a). "The Sabotage of the Clarion." *Action Comics* No. 17. National Comics Publications (DC Comics): Oct. 1939.

Siegel, Jerry (w), Joe Shuster (p), and Wayne Boring (i). "Fifth Columnists." *Action Comics* No. 36. National Comics Publications (DC Comics): May 1941.

Siegel, Jerry (w), and John Sikela (a). "Powerstone." *Action Comics* No. 47. National Comics Publications (DC Comics): Apr. 1942.

Siegel, Jerry (w), Joe Shuster and Leo Nowak (a). "The Machinations of The Light." *Superman* No. 13. National Comics Publications (DC Comics): Nov.–Dec. 1941.

Sikela, John (a). "The Cross-Country Chess Crimes." *Action Comics* No. 112. National Comics Publications (DC Comics): Sep. 1947.

Superman: The Movie. Dir. Richard Donner. Perf. Marlon Brando, Christopher Reeve, Margot Kidder. Warner Bros., 1978.

Superman II. Dir. Richard Lester. Perf. Gene Hackman, Christopher Reeve, Margot Kidder. Warner Bros., 1980.

The Iron Giant. Dir. Brad Bird. Perf. Jennifer Aniston, Harry Connick Jr. Warner Bros., 1999.

Uncredited. "The Wish That Came True." *Action Comics* No. 115. National Comics Publications (DC Comics): Dec. 1947.

Uncredited. "The Wizard of Winter." *Action Comics* No. 116. National Comics Publications (DC Comics): Jan. 1948.

DAVID HOPKINS is a high school English teacher and comic-book writer. His two series, Karma Incorporated and Emily Edison, are both available through Viper Comics. He lives in Arlington, Texas, with his wife, Melissa, and their daughter, Kennedy. David is still waiting for a call from DC Comics, so he can write his "Death of Jimmy Olsen" comic book. Visit David's Web site at www.antiherocomics.com.

Sarah Zettel

YOU WILL BELIEVE A MAN CAN WALK:

CHRISTOPHER REEVE'S PART IN THE SUPERMAN MYTH

OH, NO! NOT Superman!"
This cry rang through a darkened movie theater in suburban Detroit. The film we were watching was *Deathtrap*, and Christopher Reeve had just kissed Michael Caine.

Now, in *Deathtrap* Reeve was playing a homosexual sociopath, and doing a splendid job, may I add, but to me, and evidently a number of other people in the audience, he was still Superman. He was the one who had brought the iconic figure to the big screen, and did it with charm and delight. He went on to play many other characters in his career, but for those of us who are now of a certain age, he would remain Superman in our hearts, even when he could no longer walk, let alone fly.

In all, Christopher Reeve performed the role of Superman in four movies. I remember when the first one came out. It really was a big deal. Yes, there had been Superman movies before, but not since the late '50s. *Superman* was going to be the first modern superhero movie pitched at older adolescents and adults, and, believe it or not, the idea was daring. Comic book heroes were for children, specifically, for boys under fifteen. We were still some years away from the revolution wrought by writers such as Alan Moore, Frank Miller and Neil Gaiman. These men would eventually transform comics into grim, adult tales that needed warning labels about sex and violence.

Leaving aside the cartoons like *Justice League* and *Superboy*, the only live-action Superman I, like many of my generation, was most familiar with was the George Reeves (no relation) series. Now, the demands of TV back in the '50s were fairly light, visually speaking. Reeves flew in profile with a loud wind noise. He fit his costume like a sack of potatoes, and changed clothes without changing manner-isms at all. This is not to disparage George Reeves, but, frankly, he was working on a project for a young audience that would only be seen on a small and blurry screen. Moving the character and its de-mands to a big, modern movie screen presented a number of chal-lenges for the actor. Of course the flying effects were going to have to be as seamless. The movie trailer, after all, was "You will believe a man can fly." Well and good. The SFX boys could take care of that with the still-new processes pioneered by this young Turk named George Lucas. But the actor had to be able to believe that this flying person could *live*, could walk through the city, could care, could be loved and could hide.

When Chris Reeve came to take the role, he had to create not one, but two believable looks. If anybody was going to buy Clark Kent as a secret identity for the physical perfection of Superman, the disguise was going to have to be a good one.

Acting is one of those deceptive professions. With all the talk of "method," interior life and emoting, it is easy to overlook the deeply physical nature of the art. The physical changes developed by Reeve made Kent and Superman seem to be separate people. He was able to show the drama of the transformation as well as the disguise.

As you may have noticed, Reeve was not a small guy, but when he played Kent, you had the feeling he was *too* big. Reeve hunched and slouched, bringing Kent's shoulders up almost to his ears, mak-ing him seem like he had no neck, a look that was enhanced by the buttoned-up collar and tie he always wore. In addition, he filled any scene like an oversized puppy fills a living room, and moved with a clumsiness that veered close to slapstick. Every door was too narrow, every ceiling was too low. By his awkward stance and his continually wry expression, he conveyed the impression of *knowing* that he was too big, but not knowing what to do about it. Reeve portrayed Clark Kent as a big man who felt he ought to be small.

When Reeve transformed into Superman, he didn't just whip open his shirt and toss aside the glasses, his whole physical being changed. His manner of speech, his stance, his facial expressions changed along with his uniform. Oddly, though he stood up straighter as Superman, he seemed smaller, sleeker. Reeve's Superman fit into his own skin because he exuded a physical confidence that was missing from Kent.

The transformation did not end there. As Kent, Reeve tucked his chin way in, which made his face square. As Superman, he lifted that chin, giving us his full movie-star profile. Even Kent's voice was different from Superman's. Superman speaks from the diaphragm like a stage actor. Kent speaks from behind his nose.

All this is important. In that initial film, one of Reeve's most important jobs was making us believe that a group of ordinarily intelligent people, like ourselves, could fail to see the resemblance between the Man of Steel and the Mild-Mannered Reporter.

From the prospect of physical acting, Reeve had an even tougher job in *Superman II*. He had to play Superman without his powers. There's a scene in a diner where he gets beat up by a trucker. It's a good scene, but what's brilliant is the physical ambivalence Reeve pulls off while it's happening. He's dressed as Kent, oversized '70s glasses and all, but he's got his chin out, and his voice goes up and down along with his shoulders, giving the character a sort of half-and-half feel that is extremely awkward, and is supposed to be. He confronts the trucker using Kent's mannerisms and Superman's facial expressions, giving you the clear idea that Kent is the only way he knows how to deal with people when he's not in uniform. And he gets what the puppyish, clownishly polite Kent would have gotten. He gets beat up until he has to deal with the shock of seeing his own blood for the first time in his life. And talk about a wonderful moment of acting. Reeve looks down at his own hand, completely stunned for just a second at this simple thing.

In all fairness, I must acknowledge that Reeve's Superman series was not exactly an exercise in deathless cinema. When I was fourteen, *Superman II* was my absolute favorite film, and I saw it multiple times in the theater. But I was in love, and we do foolish things for love. Looking back across almost thirty years, heaven help me, I see that while this was the first real attempt to make a superhero acceptable for an adult, and mixed-gender viewing audience, the producers and writers could not get away from Hollywood's idea of a comic book. The scripts, especially for *Superman II*, do not make a lot of sense. The villains make no sense at all. Part of this was Hollywood's fault; part of it was the material upon which they had to draw. This was before the revolution in comic-book writing, brought to us courtesy of Alan Moore, Frank Miller and Neil Gaiman. The Watchmen were not going to rework the entire superhero landscape for several years yet, and Batman was not yet a practicing goth. So, of necessity, these were lighter, less substantial films, with a heck of a lot less angst than any superhero movie made since.

But while the angst quotient was much lower than the humor quotient, they did take a risk in making the character at least somewhat vulnerable. Before this, Superman wasn't vulnerable, he was incorruptible. His only weakness was physical (all those pesky colors of Kryptonite that kept popping up). In the George Reeves TV series, neither Superman nor Clark Kent was a vulnerable person. That series was clearly made for young boys, and yes, I do mean boys specifically. He saved the world from organized crime and the occasional supervillain, did guest appearances on things like *I Love Lucy*, and was either your father or your big brother, showing you the way an American male ought to behave. He was forthright, upright and had a twinkle in his eye. He really was, to use Frank Miller's terminology, The Big Blue Boy Scout. But watching incorruptibility for two hours at a stretch gets really boring. In a movie pitched toward an older audience, the pure Boy Scout approach was not going to cut it. Superman had to be uplifting, and he had to be warm on a very human level. In addition to believing the flight, you had to believe a modern woman would fall in love with a guy in tights and a cape.

So, they did something else that had never been done before. They sent Superman on a date. Nice date. Lots of flying, hand-holding and that thousand-watt smile Reeve could flash. We won't talk about the goofy voiceover. But what it did was allow Reeve to show all his capacity to charm. Only as Superman was his smile open, his manner casual, even sophisticated. Lois Lane was a modern, cynical woman who needed to be courted and Reeve's Superman did so, smoothly, gallantly. He grieved deeply and tenderly when he failed to save her. It was all calculated to make the women in the audience fall in love. Our emotions were not taken entirely for granted, and man, when I was twelve, the gambit worked, and in spades. By the time Superman was standing by the wrecked car, grinning in foolish love to see Lois alive again, I was completely, utterly and permanently in love.

What that performance also did, however, was set the stage for all the superhero movies that have followed, up to and including the Batman movies. All superhero portrayals since have been about the vulnerability within the invulnerability, about the hard choices and the fear that the hero must face. Take *Spider-Man 2*, where Peter Parker, like Superman, loses his powers, and must find the strength to re-establish them within himself. Even the hyper-gothic Batman movies owe something to Reeve's Superman. There are flashes of humor and humanity in the modern movie Batman that are a direct outgrowth of the formula Reeve established for the movie superhero. In the comic books, before the revolution, heroes didn't have to make choices, they just had to fight the good fight. After Reeve, every superhero had to face some kind of tough choice, had to face their connection to the world around them and explore the limits that isolation placed on them.

Reeve rose to all the challenges this deceptively light role placed on him, and he did it so well that he ran into the problem all actors who really create a character run into. He got typecast, and not just by the studios. I admit it. I helped. I saw him in *Time Enough for Love* (great little film), and he was still Superman. I saw him in *Death-trap*, and many years later in his supporting role in *The Remains of the Day*, and he was still Superman. That adolescent love was *not* going to go away, even when I saw him with all that silver in his hair. Fond memories of The Big Blue Boy Scout were going to color everything I saw, despite the fact that I knew it was doing Reeve the actor a disservice. It's this kind of thing that tends to drive character actors nuts, and I can't blame them. They want to ply their craft and work in different roles, and despite all his efforts, Reeve was typecast for a very long time. *The Remains of the Day* was his chance to start getting out of it and back into film. Superman was twenty years behind him. A whole new generation of moviegoers had grown up. He had a part in a film that was a box office success. The road back to pictures was open, and Reeve could now hang up the cape, as he showed us Superman must long to do from time to time.

Then came the accident.

In 1995, while competing in a horse race, Reeve's mount refused a jump, and Reeve was thrown. The six-foot-four, two-hundred-twenty-pound man landed on his head.

His spine snapped clean through.

Prompt and complex surgery saved his life, but his spinal cord was severed. From the neck down, he could not move. For all anybody at that time knew, this paralysis was permanent, and it was total.

The accident got wall-to-wall coverage, and in all that coverage, the permanently, brutally injured Reeve was suddenly Superman again. "Best known for his role as Superman," could be heard in every single report. And those of us who did indeed know him best for that role felt oddly sad. I knew this was a man, and I should, and did, feel sorry for him and his family. This was a terrible accident for anybody, but it was worse for an actor. Let's face it, if I lived through breaking my neck, the current state of technology would allow me to be able to continue to practice my profession. I would still be writing novels and odd opinion essays. What was a man who made his living physically becoming other people going to do? Especially with Superman hovering over him as a red-and-blue shadow?

The answer, it turned out, was rise to the occasion.

Yes, I know. Reeve got the care and attention he did because he was a celebrity, and because he was rich. His being white and handsome probably didn't hurt either. There are thousands of quadriplegics, good people with families, who have had horrible accidents or been wounded in war, who do not get anything like this level of care.

But here's the thing: Here's a man whose living was his perfect body, and he was immersed in a culture and a profession where physical imperfection, frankly, is not tolerated. He could have hidden himself. He didn't. He got out in front of it. He became an advocate. Fame can be a tool. It's a blunt tool, like a sledgehammer, but like a sledgehammer, it can be used effectively if you've got an appropriate job. Making noise on behalf of the severely injured is a good job for fame. He endowed programs. He addressed committees. I don't know if I can go so far as to say he led, but he inspired.

And he didn't stop working. He started directing. He continued acting. I'll admit his reworking of *Rear Window* was not up to the original with James Stewart and Grace Kelly, but it had its own special suspense, because you *knew* that Reeve's character could not even crawl away from the murderer in his apartment. He consulted for *The Bone Collector*, in which Denzel Washington plays a quadriplegic detective. He even did an appearance on *Smallville*, giving the young Clark Kent a vital clue as to his true identity.

That appearance on *Smallville* said more clearly than anything else that he didn't resent Superman. It was the lack of bitterness which got to me the most about the real-life heroism Reeve displayed. It would have been easy, even natural, to feel some animosity toward the role. It had dogged his career. It was one piece of far from deathless work he had done as a young man at the peak of his physical perfection. Now he couldn't even walk, and he couldn't have shaken that old part if he wanted to. Only, he didn't seem to want to. He embraced the role of Superman and in the eyes of the rest of us, he built on it. He expanded the notion of heroism far more after the accident than he ever did before it. This, we felt, was how a real super-man behaved. He displayed courage and faith every day. He worked and worked hard. He was not afraid.

I'm sure Reeve had his bad days. How could he not? He was paralyzed from the neck down, for God's sakes! He couldn't even breathe on his own for a long time and a host of little things could have killed him where he lay. I'm sure he yelled and cried and made life miserable for those who were only trying to care for him. What his wife went through trying to remain strong for him and throw herself into his care is beyond imagining. I'm sure he fell off that horse a thousand times and had to fight like hell to get back on it. Knowing that does not diminish what he did in public for one moment. He lived up to the character he had created for the rest of us and he gave the performance of a lifetime, and it was all because of one simple act.

He believed. He was going to walk. He was going to find a way. A little bit at a time, one day at a time. He was going to do this the hard way if he had to, but he was going to do it. Up front and in public, he believed, and he made me believe too. And wasn't that, ultimately, what superheroes were supposed to do? We were supposed to see them struggling to uphold, well, truth, justice and the American way, and be motivated to do the same, or at least believe that it could be done, no matter what the odds.

It worked on me.

I honest to God believed. I believed he was going to walk again. When I had occasion to think about him, like when I saw the interview on *Inside the Actors Studio*, say, or glanced at some glossy magazine in the checkout line, I believed he was going to walk. He'd opened his body up for research and experimentation. He'd regained some small mobility. He could breathe on his own. The constant exercise he put himself through had begun to create new neural pathways. Stem cells were coming along and he was a relatively young man.

I was completely stunned when he died. Completely. Like I said, I believed. When Reeve fell prey to an infected sore, a very common occurrence among paraplegics, I actually sat in silence. I won't say I cried, but I came close. Something brave and good was gone from the world. Superman had gone away, and he wasn't coming back.

So, now they're making a new Superman movie, and there will be a young and handsome actor in the lead, and I'll probably go, and I'll be impressed by the effects and I'm certain the writing will be better, but in the back of my mind, I'll be wondering if this new kid would be able to take this image, this hope, into real life as Christopher Reeve did for all the world to see.

And don't think I can't see the fish-eye some of you are giving this essay. Yes, I am a romantic. I admit this freely. No, I don't particularly like the unrelievedly grim and gritty tone comics have taken since Alan Moore brought in The Watchmen like a storm cloud and The Dark Knight followed as a mighty wind. Frankly, it's been raining on my parade ever since. Angst has become another special effect. Oooo, look, he's *grim*. This isn't kiddie stuff. This is *serious*.

Oh, grow up.

In the words of Ursula Le Guin, "This is the treason of the artist. That only pain is intellectual, only evil interesting." Hope is also worthy, and not all struggle is pointless even if it ends in the appearance of defeat. The good fight has its own merits and not everyone will turn against you for fighting it. Strangers can be kind and there are others out there working for truth, justice and a cure, and so you should be ready for that cure to come. We need the Superman Chris Reeve shared with us after his fall. We need that warm, brave, generous character so that we can remember that in real life it is more important that a man can try than that he can fly.

––––––––––––

SARAH ZETTEL was born in Sacramento, California. Shortly after this she embarked on a wide and varied reading career from ten cities, four states and two countries. This combined to give her a wide and varied range of opinions, some of which are included in this book, and eventually settled her in the life of a science fiction and fantasy author. She is currently at work on her twelfth novel. Sarah lives in Michigan with her husband, Tim, son, Alexander and cat, Buffy the Vermin Slayer.

Chris Roberson

JEWEL MOUNTAINS AND FIRE FALLS:
THE LOST WORLD OF KRYPTON

WHEN FIRST INTRODUCED, Superman's home planet of Krypton was a fairly notional place. It was originally presented in very little detail, and served as little more than a backdrop for the unfolding drama of the lone scientist Jor-El who, unable to prevent the destruction of his world, launches his only son, Kal-El, in a small rocket ship bound for Earth. Readers were shown very little else of the planet, its culture or its history; it was simply a place to be destroyed so that Superman's story could begin.

For many years, Krypton fared no better. It was handled in a haphazard manner by a number of different creators, all working at cross-purposes and without a central unifying vision.

Almost twenty years after the planet was first introduced, though, all of that changed. A strong editorial vision, with an eye toward consistency and invention, led to drastic improvements. Over the course of decades a small number of creators codified the history, culture, language and geography of the fictional planet.

Krypton, which in its first appearance was not even named, in time became a full-blown, well-realized constructed world, one to rival the best science fiction and fantasy worlds. In an act of editorial short-sightedness, this world and its history were completely erased by fiat, and the Superman line of comics has never recovered. But there may still be hope....

WORLD-BUILDING

While the concept has not risen to the attention of *Encyclopedia Britannica* or the *Oxford English Dictionary*, Wikipedia defines a "constructed world" as "a fictional world, often created for a novel, video game, or role-playing game.... A constructed world typically has a number of constructed cultures and constructed languages associated with it." The process of created constructed worlds is often termed "world-building."

> "World-building" stories feature protagonists (humans or aliens) living in environments very different from our own. In general, the story is designed to display the features of that environment. (Stephen Baxter)

One of the best-known constructed worlds is that of Middle-earth, created by J. R. R. Tolkien and featured in his Lord of the Rings trilogy, among others. Tolkien referred to constructed worlds as "Secondary Worlds," and termed the construction of them as an act of "sub-creation."

> To make a Secondary World inside which the green sun will be credible, commanding Secondary Belief, will probably require labour and thought, and will certainly demand a special skill, a kind of elvish craft. Few attempt such difficult tasks. But when they are attempted and in any degree accomplished then we have a rare achievement of Art: indeed narrative art, storymaking in its primary and most potent mode." (J. R. R. Tolkien, "On Fairy-Stories")

The key features of constructed worlds include Maps, Culture, Language, History and Religion. Over the course of years, Krypton was given each of these. When they were stricken from continuity by editorial fiat, though, they were lost forever, and never replaced.

KRYTPON FOUND

The development of Krypton, from its first primitive appearance to its full-blown flowering, can be divided into three distinct stages:

The first, borrowing the terminology of the comics, is the Golden Age of Krypton, which ran from 1934 to 1950. This was a period of Creation, primitive and uncoordinated, which began with the creation of Superman and his home planet of Krypton by Jerry Siegel and Joe Shuster.

The second stage was the Silver Age of Krypton, which began in 1950 with Mort Weisinger's appointment as supervising editor, reached full flower when Jerry Siegel returned as scripter in 1959, and ended in 1970 with Weisinger's retirement. This was a period of Elaboration, inventive and expansive.

The third and final stage was the Bronze Age of Krypton, which began in 1970 with the end of Weisinger's editorial rein, and ended in 1985 with the publication of *Crisis on Infinite Earths*. This was a period of Refinement, in which Krypton was codified and delimited.

GOLDEN AGE OF KRYPTON

Though he first appeared in the comics in 1938, Superman was originally intended by creators Jerry Siegel and Joe Shuster as a newspaper strip, written and drawn in 1934. These strips were later published in newspapers in 1939, after the success of Superman comic books, and provide an intriguing glimpse into the earliest formations of the character. The origin of Superman occupies twelve daily newspaper strips, ten of which are concerned with the destruction of Krypton. We are introduced to scientist Jor-L, his wife Lara, and their infant son Kal-L, all of whom belong to a race of hyper-evolved "supermen."

Krypton, a distant planet so far advanced in evolution that it bears a civilization of supermen—beings which represent the human race at its ultimate peak of perfect development! Mile after mile streaks by as Jor-L, Krypton's foremost scientist, races along at a terrific speed that would out-distance the fastest express train... a great leap carries Jor-

L hundreds of yards into the air to a balcony near the top of his home. (*Superman* newspaper strip)

In Superman's first appearance in *Action Comics* No. 1, the as-then unpublished newspaper strips were cut and pasted into comic form, the origin reduced to a single page, most of which was given over to descriptions of Clark Kent's powers. Of the last days of the planet of supermen, only one panel remained, in which neither Jor-L nor Krypton were named, and Lara was not even mentioned.

As a distant planet was destroyed by old age, a scientist placed his infant son within a hastily devised spaceship, launching it toward earth.

Kent had come from a planet whose inhabitants' physical structure was millions of years advance of our own. Upon reaching maturity, the people of his race became gifted with titanic strength. (*Action Comics* No. 1)

The following year, Superman's origin would be retold again, in the pages of *Superman* No. 1. This time, the "doomed planet" gets a name, though Jor-L remains only an anonymous scientist, and Lara again is passed over. Superman's powers are, once again, explained as the benefit of evolution, the birthright of every Kryptonian.

Just before the doomed planet, Krypton, exploded to fragments, a scientist placed his infant son within an experimental rocket ship, launching it toward Earth.

Superman came to Earth from the planet Krypton, whose inhabitants had evolved, after millions of years, to physical perfection. The smaller size of our planet, with its slighter gravity pull, assists Superman's tremendous muscles in the performance of miraculous feats of strength. (*Superman* No. 1, 1939)

In 1945, Superman's origin is retold yet again, in the first installment of *Superboy*, the adventures of Superman as a boy. In this retelling, Krypton is still a planet of super-science, but no longer it seems one of supermen. Jor-L, now named Jor-El, is a brilliant scientist, but appears to be no more super than his Earthly counterparts. The intimation is that all of Superman's abilities now stem from the fact that he is a Kryptonian on Earth, and not because all Kryptonians had been supermen (though they were, the narration stresses, quite attractive!).

> Once, in the outer reaches of infinite space, there existed a great planet which glowed like a green star in the limitless firmament. This was the planet Krypton! There was life on planet Krypton—human beings of high intelligence and great physical beauty.... The force of gravity on Krypton was far greater than that on Earth....
> [FIRST MAN]: —then a Kryptonian, on planet Earth, could take an ordinary step and leap over the tallest building!
> [SECOND MAN]: In fact he could almost defy gravity entirely! (*More Fun Comics* No. 101)

Interestingly, while Jor-El and Lara are named, their infant son is not, referred to only as "the babe."

Though it had been a keystone of his story since the beginning, Superman is unaware of his extraterrestrial origins, or the source of his powers, for more than a decade. It isn't until 1949 that Superman encounters a strange meteorite, whose presence makes him weak. Tracing the meteorite's trajectory and flying so quickly he travels backward in time (!), he locates their origin as a planet "far outside Earth's solar system."

> Landing, Superman sees an advanced civilization, and people of great intelligence and physical perfection!
> [KRYPTONIAN WOMAN]: I'm worried! Though junior is past five, he does not yet know his engineering! (*Superman* No. 61)

Superman, invisible and intangible, follows a man who resembles him closely, who proves to be Jor-El, a scientist. Jor-El explains to his wife, Lara, that their planet is about to explode, and that there is just enough room in his model spaceship for her and their child. She chooses to stay at his side, sending their unnamed child alone "into the void." Superman, watching helplessly, thinks to himself, *The death of a world! I wonder if this infant will survive? I've got to know!* In his intangible state, he follows the small craft, all the way toward Earth, where it is found by an elderly couple, who Superman immediately recognizes as his "foster parents."

"Now I understand why I'm different from Earthmen! I'm not really from Earth at all—I'm from another planet—the planet Jor-El called Krypton!!"

Handily deducing that the troublesome meteorites are particles of Krypton, or Kryptonite, he returns to the present day.

Throughout this Golden Age, Krypton is presented in only the most cursory fashion, with contradictory details. The reader is given very little sense of it as a living planet with a culture of its own.

SILVER AGE OF KRYPTON

In 1950, Mort Weisinger was hired as supervising editor of the Superman line. For much of the following decade he served as story editor on the television series *The Adventures of Superman*, and it was not until after the series was cancelled in 1957 that Weisinger would turn his full attention to the comics. Beginning the following year, though, his hand at the tiller can be felt, as the Superman line began to change. He brought Jerry Siegel, who had been away from the comics industry for some time, back as a scripter for the comics line, and together they created something new.

> Weisinger took a different approach for Superman. He gave his character a history and a family, providing kids a fictional world to enter and discover. In the process, he and Jerry Siegel discovered what had lain in plain view for twenty years but had never been explored: the pain at the heart of the orphan exile from another world. (Jones)

The first hints of this new approach, this "fictional world," can be seen in the pages of *Action Comics* No. 242. This issue introduces Brainiac, an alien villain who travels from world to world, shrinking cities. When he arrives on Earth, intent on shrinking Paris and the other capitals of the world, Superman discovers on his spaceship the shrunken city of Kandor, once capital of Krypton. Touring Kandor, Superman is shown robotic farmhands, metal-eating moles kept in glass cases and even an artificial sun that provides light and heat. After defeating Brainiac, Superman places the bottle city of Kandor in his Arctic Fortress of Solitude. Kandor arguably presents a clearer picture than the reader had received to date of the culture of Krypton, and it was one which Superman could visit again and again in the years to follow.

The following year, readers learned the fate of another Kryptonian city. *Action Comics* No. 252 introduces Superman's cousin Kara Zor-El, better known as Supergirl, whose family survived the destruction of Krypton when, "By sheer luck, a large chunk of the planet was hurled away intact, with people on it...." Later to be named Argo City, this "chunk" would in later retellings pick up a dome over the city, to account for the ability of the inhabitants to survive in open space.

But it was in 1960 that Siegel and Weisinger would turn their attentions to Krypton itself, and the planet which would become familiar to generations of comics readers was born. In *Superman* No. 141, through misadventure, Superman accidentally travels back in time to Krypton, shortly before its destruction. Mistaken for an extra in a science-fiction film, *The Space Explorers*, he travels to the city, where he comes upon his parents, Jor-El and Lara, entering the Palace of Marriage.

> Like all Kryptonian married couples, the bride and groom don marriage bracelets of a color variation all their own, which no other couple is allowed to duplicate.... (*Superman* No.141)

Superman meets and falls in love with Lyla Lerrol, Krypton's "most famous emotion-movie actress." Taking a position as Jor-El's research assistant, he works to find a way to prevent the destruction of Krypton. Naturally, his plans are doomed to failure, and in the end Superman returns to his own time.

In the story, Krypton's red sun is contrasted with Earth's yellow sun, which itself is identified as the source for all of Superman's abilities, without any mention of genetics or Krypton's heavy gravity. This was to remain the explanation for Superman's abilities from this point onwards.

In addition, key aspects of Kryptonian geography are introduced in *Superman* No. 141, including the Rainbow Canyon, the Jewel Mountains, the Hall of Worlds, Gold Volcano, and Meteor Valley, and reference is made to Kandor, and its abduction by Brainiac.

By 1961, all of the pieces were in place. *Superman* No. 146 presents a new retelling of Superman's origin, with subtle but significant differences. With only two pages devoted to Krypton, we're presented not with a race of supermen, jumping over buildings, but with a people every bit like middle-class Americans, living in a technological utopia. Weather Control Towers to blow away smog and purify the air, and Metal Maids to do their housework. The Metal-Eaters in their glass cages reappear, and the Council of Scientists refuse to believe Jor-El's predictions of doom when their Cosmic Clock tells them everything is fine.

In a matter of only years, under the guidance of Mort Weisinger, Krypton came quickly into focus. The general map laid out in these few stories would remain unaltered for nearly three decades, but it would fall to other hands in the following years to fill in the details.

BRONZE AGE OF KRYPTON

In 1970, Mort Weisinger resigned. Julius Schwartz took over the title of supervising editor, though the duties were shared by a team of editors, one of whom was E. Nelson Bridwell, Weisinger's former assistant editor. Also a writer, in his capacity as editor or scripter Bridwell was responsible for several key texts of the Bronze Age. Originally a fan, Bridwell was reportedly a devotee of the trivia and minutiae of Superman's fictional universe. He scoured the comics, making copious notes, reconciling the disparate stories and claims of the Silver Age into one unified history.

In the pages of *Superman*, a series of back-up stories ran throughout the early '70s, devoted to the history of Krypton. Entitled "The Fabulous World of Krypton," the writers of the series included Bridwell, Cary Bates, Elliot S! Maggin, Marv Wolfman and Denny O'Neil. These stories, running just a few pages in length, each spotlighted a different aspect of Kryptonian culture and history, beginning with the planet's colonization in prehistory by two stranded space travelers (Kryp and Tonn, naturally), through the barbarous generations as their descendants slid backward into savagery, and documenting their slow climb back toward civilization and technology. Stories featured the legends of culture heroes like Hex-Le (who with his enemy Kya-Ta was responsible for giving the former-ly non-rotating planet a rotation) and Rik-Ar (who led the slaves in revolt against the tyrant Taka-Ne, and in honor of whom all Kryp-tonian men wear headbands). Others presented Jor-El's personal dia-ries (complete with references to the Kryptonian calendar), filling in gaps in the story of Superman's parents.

In *The Amazing World of Superman*, readers were presented a re-telling of Superman's origin. Streamlined and refined, it is a distilla-tion of all the previous versions, using the 1961 retelling as its basis, but incorporating elements from earlier versions, as well.

It is in the miniseries *The World of Krypton* that Krypton comes into complete focus. The three issues constitute a reworking of the majority of the extant stories featuring Jor-El and Lara, incorporat-ing stories from "The Fabulous World of Krypton," and including cameos by every Kryptonian survivor (Kandorians included) who ever told Superman, "I knew your father." Even Superman himself makes an appearance, as we are shown the events of *Superman* No. 141 from Jor-El's point of view.

In the opening, Superman's grandfather provides a capsule his-tory of the planet, echoing themes introduced throughout the Silver Age.

Planet Krypton was born over 6 billion time cycles ago from a gaseous mass flung off by our giant red sun, yet until only 10,000 years ago (*18 Kryptonian years equal approximately 25 Earth years. –ENB) Krypton was a primitive wilderness—but in those 100 centuries a race of intellectual supermen evolved, and a scientific empire was born! It is a world of awesome beauty—with such wonders as the Jewel Mountains—monstrous peaks of pure crystal...formed of the skeletons of giant Crystal Birds which filled the skies of prehistoric Krypton. But men dared challenge this world's often brutal nature, successfully carving their cities into the harsh wastes of Krypton's poles, creating the dazzling splendor of Antarctic City. Thus the great-est civilization in the history of our world came to be—for never have the people of Krypton hesitated in facing the unknown—nor have we turned from any question for knowledge which could bring us even greater glory as a people. (*The World of Krypton* No. 1)

Kryptonian super-science, too, is presented in greater detail than ever before. We are shown young Jor-El's first day at school, where students are instructed with thought-transfer helmets, through which "information is electronically implanted directly onto the brain, and working in conjunction with computers the student is taught how to actively apply that new knowledge." But these are only for beginning students. "More advanced students are taught through RNA training! Information is introduced into the body through a genetically coded messenger—RNA—and permanently implanted in the brain by additional subliminal training!"

The narrative of *The World of Krypton* makes full use of all of the elements of Kryptonian culture introduced over the years (and one can almost see the fingerprints of Bridwell compiling and synthesizing dozens of casual references into a unified culture). These include the months of the Kryptonian calendar, units of time measurement, titles and forms of address, funeral customs, wedding services, and a naming-ceremony (though adherents to science, the Kryptonians revere their sun, Rao).

Even more detail about Kryptonian culture was presented in the pages of the miniseries *Krypton Chronicles*. More properly the history of the House of El, this miniseries reworked and synthesized a number of older stories about Superman's ancestors, going as far back as Erok, the "First Bethgar of Urrika," a culture hero who founded both the house of El and the first Kryptonian city. Much like the better-known constructed worlds of science fiction, like Frank Herbert's *Dune, Krypton Chronicles* comes complete with appendices, detailed glossaries of Kryptonian words and phrases, a detailed map of Krypton, and an annotated family tree ranging from the earliest recorded Kryptonian history to Superman himself. We learn that the Kryptonian alphabet is made up of 118 characters, that plurals are formed by adding an "o" suffix, and that there are 11 characters in the Kryptonian numerical system (zero through ten).

By this point fully mapped, delineated and codified, Krypton served as the basis for some of the most memorable Superman stories of this era. Chief among them was a story created by Alan Moore and Dave Gibbons, the team responsible soon after for *Watchmen*, which stands as one of the best respected superhero stories in the history of the comics medium. The story, "For the Man Who Has Everything," appeared in *Superman Annual* No. 11. Caught in a hallucination by the villain Mongul, Superman experiences the life he would have led, had Krypton not exploded. Married to former actress Lyla Lerrol, Kal-El is unable to reconcile with his father Jor-El, who had been disgraced when his predictions of Krypton's doom proved false. Trying to reclaim the spotlight, Jor-El becomes embroiled in the Old Krypton Movement of the Sword of Rao sect, while Kal-El's cousin Kara is hospitalized after being attacked by Anti-Phantom Zone activists. Kal-El finds himself in the empty vastness of Kandor Crater, with his son Van-El, when he comes to the inescapable conclusion that everything around him is an illusion.

"For the Man Who Has Everything" is arguably the most powerful portrait of the psychology of loss at the heart of Superman's character ever attempted, and it owes its narrative weight to the constant evocation of the minutiae of Krypton's invented history and culture. The map laid out by Weisinger and Siegel in the Silver Age, and limned by E. Nelson Bridwell in the Bronze Age, the sense of a three-dimensional fictional world that readers could enter and discover, lends an air of verisimilitude to Kal-El's story that otherwise wouldn't have been possible. This story strikes at the heart of the sense of loss, the pain of an orphan from an unknown world, that was the driving narrative engine behind the Silver Age, but without its fully realized setting, that pain and loss would have rung hollow.

Unfortunately, that same year, plans were already in the works that would forever change the face of Krypton, and cut Superman loose from his roots.

KRYPTON LOST

The origins of the decision which led to the erasure of Krypton lie, arguably, outside the bounds of the comic-book medium entirely, with the Krypton of the silver screen. But it was not the commercial success of *Superman: The Movie* which was the cause, but instead its influence on a single creator.

OTHER KRYPTONS

Krypton had been portrayed on the small and large screens before, but in previous versions, such as in the original Fleischer animated shorts and the Kirk Alyn film serials, the presentations had hewed closely to those of the Golden Age comics. In the television series, *The Adventures of Superman* (1952), viewers were presented with an alien world that was familiar, in more ways than one. The Krypton of the series, seen in the premier episode, was that of the Golden Age comics, but lensed through the secondhand props, costumes and sets of old black-and-white film serials (the costume worn by Jor-El, in fact, was originally worn by Buster Crabbe in *Flash Gordon Conquers the Universe*).

With the release of *Superman: The Movie* (1978), viewers were presented with another Krypton entirely. John Barry, a British production designer whose credits included *A Clockwork Orange* and *Star Wars*, brought Krypton to the silver screen. But Barry's Krypton was not one comic readers had seen before. No longer a middle-class utopia of super-science, or even a home of genetic supermen, this Krypton was a cold, impersonal world of crystal and ice.

John Barry's Krypton would become the gold standard for the filmed and televised versions of the planet, referenced in the subsequent Superman films, including *Supergirl: The Movie* (1984), and in *Lois and Clark: The New Adventures of Superman* (1993). And while the television series *Smallville* (2001) has yet, at the time of this writing, to visit Krypton itself, Kryptonian artifacts and architecture abound, and while these are often adorned by the Kryptonian alphabet originally developed for the Post-Crisis Superman comics in 2000, the "look and feel" is evocative of the Krypton envisioned by John Barry for *Superman: The Movie*.

POST-CRISIS KRYPTON

In 1985, DC Comics launched an ambitious miniseries entitled *Crisis on Infinite Earths*. Designed to streamline and simplify the continuity of the DC Universe, the series was released with the tagline "Worlds will live. Worlds will die. And the universe will never be the same again." The "worlds" in question were the parallel Earths of the DC Multiverse, reduced in the course of *Crisis* to a single Earth, a single history, and a single future. But also on the chopping block was the world of Krypton.

Crisis offered DC the opportunity to relaunch, or "reboot" the Superman line, starting over from the ground up. Superman's origin was retold, as though it were happening for the first time. And the Krypton readers were presented with was not one they had read about before.

The job of retooling Superman fell to John Byrne, who had developed a large fan following on Marvel titles such as *The Uncanny X-Men* and *Fantastic Four*. Marv Wolfman, who was given the task of scripting one of the relaunched Superman titles, reportedly had some input on the character of Lex Luthor, but otherwise Byrne was given free rein with the franchise. In late 1986, shortly after Alan Moore was given the opportunity to write one last two-part story featuring the Superman of the Silver and Bronze ages, DC published Byrne's *The Man of Steel*, a six-issue miniseries which retold Superman's origins, beginning with the last days of Krypton.

Seeming to draw inspiration more from John Barry's Krypton than that of Jerry Siegel, Mort Weisinger, or E. Nelson Bridwell, in *The Man of Steel* John Byrne presented readers a Krypton that was sterile, antiseptic and unfeeling. This is a Krypton in which skin-to-skin contact is unthinkable, and face-to-face communication is rare. Jor-El is still a scientist, still unable to convince the establishment that Krypton is doomed to explode, but Lara is no longer his loving wife, but instead is his intended bride, whom he has loved from afar, but who does not return his affection. Their infant son, in fact, is the product not of their love but of the commingling of their genetic material in the "gestation chambers."

However, readers were given only a glimpse of this new Krypton in the pages of *The Man of Steel*, eight pages which feature only Jor-El, Lara and a pair of robot servitors. It would not be until the following year, with the publication of the four-issue miniseries *The World of Krypton* (1987, John Byrne, Mike Mignola, Rick Bryant), that Byrne would reveal more of this new world. In *The World of Krypton*, Byrne showed readers the new history of Krypton, but it is nothing like the storied past readers had come to know in the Bronze Age. Instead, this is a dark, sinister history, dominated by millennia-long civil war that left the survivors isolated from one another, perpetually armored against the elements as well as their own emotions.

In an interview Peter Sanderson conducted with Byrne at the time of the relaunch, the creator made clear his intentions for Krypton.

"When I showed the first issue to Richard and Wendy Pini, Wendy said I'd created a Krypton that deserved to blow up," recalls Byrne. "And that was my intent. I don't want nostalgia for that place. It's very clear in that first issue that Superman is lucky to have come here." Eventually, when Superman learns he is from Krypton, he will declare, 'I'm a human being,' because he doesn't want to be Kryptonian. Krypton is anathema to him.'" (Sanderson)

Byrne succeeded. After *The World of Krypton*, though Kryptonian artifacts and the occasional survivor might make an appearance in Superman comics, the planet itself—its history, geography and culture—was rarely if ever seen in those pages again. If Superman found Krypton anathema, it seemed he wasn't alone.

KRYPTON REGAINED?

Superman, cut loose from his trappings and mythology, is little more than a flying strongman in a blue-and-red suit. And a key part of the Superman mythos, as it was defined and refined in the Silver and Bronze ages, is the world of Krypton. The Superman with whom readers have been presented since *The Man of Steel* has been, in a very real sense, a man without a planet.

But could Superman's roots be transplanted? Could the constructed world which was the cornerstone of the best Superman stories ever published be regained? It seemed unlikely, but in recent years there have been the signs of hope. Ironically, given the negative impact of the Superman films on the franchise, the first hopeful glimmers came not from the comics, but from another media entirely.

In 1996 *Superman: The Animated Series* premiered. Created by Bruce Timm and Paul Dini, this was a new vision of Superman, informed and influenced by all of the previous versions, but its own creation, nevertheless. It represents a synthesis of previous incarnations, and in that respect resembles E. Nelson Bridwell's reworked origin from *The Amazing World of Superman*. The first episode of the series is set entirely on Krypton, and while it is not precisely that from the Pre-Crisis comics, neither is it the sterile, unfeeling world of John Barry and John Byrne. Instead, it is a warm, inviting planet of super-science, strange creatures and brilliant scientists. The most brilliant of scientists, of course, is Jor-El, and he and his loving wife, Lara, dote on their son, Kal-El. This is not Mort Weisinger's Krypton, but if his Superman had been transported here, he would have found it hauntingly familiar.

For some time, even after the success of the animated series, the comics stayed the course, continuing to present the cold, antiseptic, unappealing Krypton of *The Man of Steel*. By the turn of the decade, though, there came a sea-change. There began to be editorial pressure to reclaim more of the ground lost in the Post-Crisis reboot (arguably inspired by Alan Moore's *Supreme*, a Superman-homage that skillfully used elements Mort Weisinger would have found familiar to create a nuanced, subtle, evocative landscape for superheroics). These pressures culminated in a storyline which began in the pages of *Superman* Vol. 2 No. 166, written by Jeph Loeb and published in 2001.

An attempt to return to the "pre-Crisis" Krypton, Loeb's storyline introduces the claim that the sterile Krypton of Byrne's *The Man of Steel* was all some sort of illusion, a fiction of the doomed planet, designed to be as unappealing as possible so as to help young Kal-El adapt to life on his adopted homeworld. This "continuity implant," though, introduced more problems that it solved. It accomplished none of the resonance of Alan Moore's *Supreme*, or even the frisson of recognition of Dini and Timm's animated series, and came across as a fairly cynical ploy to appeal to nostalgia.

It is hardly surprising, then, that the next reworking of Krypton and Superman's origin would come only two years later. Without any mention of the Loeb storyline, or of Byrne's *The Man of Steel*, for that matter, DC launched a new twelve-issue miniseries, *Rebirth* (2003), with scripts by Mark Waid and art by Leinil F. Yu and Gerry Alanguilan. A new reinterpretation of Superman and his origin, *Re-*

birth draws inspirations from sources as disparate as the comics of the Silver Age as well as the Post-Crisis *The Man of Steel*, and *Superman: The Animated Series* as well as the live-action *Smallville*. While not a literal return to any previous incarnation, from the few glimpses we're given of the world and its history, the Krypton of *Rebirth* seems to share more in common with the Krypton of Weisinger and Bridwell than that of Barry and Byrne.

In 2006, DC launched a new series, *All Star Superman*, written by Grant Morrison, with art by Frank Quitely. Of all the creators working in mainstream comics today, none produces work closer in spirit to that of Mort Weisinger than Grant Morrison. Morrison understands that central to the character of Superman is not his strength, or his flight, but the "mad ideas" which inform his world. If any creator was to offer hope of a return to the kind of rich, detailed landscape which was the Pre-Crisis Krypton, Morrison would be the best contender. At the time of this writing, though, only two issues of the series have been published, which include only brief glimpses of Krypton and its culture. It is worth noting, though, that Morrison manages to top even Jerry Siegel and Joe Shuster's *Action Comics* No. 1, by distilling the entire origin of Superman to a single page of four panels and eight words:

Doomed Planet.
Desperate Scientists.
Last Hope.
Kindly Couple. (*All Star Superman* No. 1)

REFERENCES

Baxter, Stephen. "Building Worlds: Construction and Influences." *The Bulletin of the Science Fiction and Fantasy Writers of America*. Fall 1995. <http://www.sfwa.org/bulletin/articles/baxter.htm>.

Finger, Bill (w) and Al Plastino (a). *Superman* No. 61. National Comics Publications (DC Comics): 1949.

Jones, Gerard. *Men of Tomorrow: Geeks, Gangsters, and the Birth of the Comic Book*. New York: Basic Books, 2004.

Kuperberg, Paul (w), Howard Chaykin (p), Murphy Anderson (i), E. Nelson Bridwell (ed.). *The World of Krypton*. DC Comics: 1979.

Morrison, Grant (w), Frank Quitely (a). "...Faster..." *All Star Superman* No. 1. DC Comics: Jan. 2006.

Sanderson, Peter. John Byrne Interview. *Amazing Heroes* No. 96, June 1986.

Siegel, Jerry (w), Joe Shuster (a). *Superman* newspaper strip. 1939.

Siegel, Jerry (w), Joe Shuster (a). *Action Comics* No. 1. National Comics Publications (DC Comics): 1938.

Siegel, Jerry (w), Joe Shuster (a). *Superman* No. 1. National Comics Publications (DC Comics): 1939.

Siegel, Jerry (w), Wayne Boring (a). *Superman* No.141. National Comics Publication (DC Comics): 1960.

Tolkien, J. R. R. "On Fairy Stories." *Essays Presented to Charles Williams.* Oxford University Press, 1947.

Uncredited. *More Fun Comics* No. 101. National Comics Publications (DC Comics): 1945.

CHRIS ROBERSON'S short fiction can be found in the anthologies *Live Without a Net* (Roc, 2003), *The Many Faces of Van Helsing* (Ace, 2004), *FutureShocks* (Roc, 2006) and *Forbidden Planets* (Daw, 2006). His novels include *Here, There & Everywhere* (Pyr, 2005), *The Voyage of Night Shining White* (PS Publishing, 2006) and *Paragaea: A Planetary Romance* (Pyr, 2006), and he is the editor of the anthology *Adventure Vol. 1* (MonkeyBrain Books, Nov 2005). Roberson has been a finalist for the World Fantasy Award for Short Fiction, the John W. Campbell Award for Best New Writer and twice for the Sidewise Award for Best Alternate History Short Form (winning in 2004 with his story "O One"). Visit him online at www.chrisroberson.net.

Larry Niven

MAN OF STEEL, WOMAN OF KLEENEX

H E'S FASTER THAN a speeding bullet.
He's more powerful than a locomotive. He's able to leap tall buildings at a single bound. Why can't he get a girl?

At the ripe old age of thirty-one[1], Kal-El (alias Superman, alias Clark Kent) is still unmarried. Almost certainly he is still a virgin. This is a serious matter. The species itself is in danger!

An unwed Superman is a mobile Superman. Thus it has been alleged that those who chronicle the Man of Steel's adventures are responsible for his condition. But the cartoonists are not to blame.

Nor is Superman handicapped by psychological problems.

Granted the poor oaf is not entirely sane. How could he be? He is an orphan, a refugee and an alien. His homeland no longer exists in any form, save for gigatons upon gigatons of dangerous, prettily colored rocks.

As a child and young adult, Kal-El must have been hard put to find an adequate father-figure. What human could control his antisocial behavior? What human would dare try to punish him? His actual,

---

[1] Superman first appeared in Action Comics, June 1938.

highly social behavior during this period indicates an inhuman self-restraint.

What wonder if Superman drifted gradually into schizophrenia? Torn between his human and Kryptonian identities, he chose to be both, keeping his split personalities rigidly separate. A psychotic desperation is evident in his defense of his "secret identity."

But Superman's sex problems are strictly physiological, and quite real.

The purpose of this article is to point out some medical drawbacks to being a Kryptonian among human beings, and to suggest possible solutions. The Kryptonian humanoid must not be allowed to go the way of the pterodactyl and the passenger pigeon.

I

What turns on a Kryptonian?

Superman is an alien, an extraterrestrial. His humanoid frame is doubtless the result of parallel evolution, as the marsupials of Australia resemble their mammalian counterparts. A specific niche in the ecology calls for a certain shape, a certain size, certain capabilities, certain eating habits.

Be not deceived by appearances. Superman is no relative to homo sapiens.

What arouses Kal-El's mating urge? Did Kryptonian women carry some subtle mating cue at appropriate times of the year? Whatever it is, Lois Lane probably didn't have it. We may speculate that she smells wrong, less like a Kryptonian woman than like a terrestrial monkey. A mating between Superman and Lois Lane would feel like sodomy—and would be, of course, by church and common law.

II

Assume a mating between Superman and a human woman designated LL for convenience.

Either Superman has gone completely schizo and believes himself to be Clark Kent; or he knows what he's doing, but no longer gives a damn. Thirty-one years is a long time. For Superman it has been even longer. He has x-ray vision; he knows just what he's missing.[2]

The problem is this: Electroencephalograms taken of men and women during sexual intercourse show that orgasm resembles "a kind of pleasurable epileptic attack." One loses control over one's muscles.

Superman has been known to leave his fingerprints in steel and in hardened concrete, accidentally. What would he do to the woman in his arms during what amounts to an epileptic fit?

III

Consider the driving urge between a man and a woman, the monomaniacal urge to achieve greater and greater penetration. Remember also that we are dealing with Kryptonian muscles.

Superman would literally crush LL's body in his arms, while simultaneously ripping her open from crotch to sternum, gutting her like a trout.

IV

Lastly, he'd blow off the top of her head.

Ejaculation of semen is entirely involuntary in the human male, and in all other forms of terrestrial life. It would be unreasonable to assume otherwise for a Kryptonian. But with Kryptonian muscles behind it, Kal-El's semen would emerge with the muzzle velocity of a machine gun bullet.[3]

In view of the foregoing, normal sex is impossible between LL and Superman.

Artificial insemination may give us better results.

---

[2] One should not think of Superman as a peeping Tom. A biological ability must be used. As a child Superman may never have known that things had surfaces, until he learned to suppress his x-ray vision. If millions of people tend shamelessly to wear clothing with no lead in the weave, that is hardly Superman's fault.

[3] One can imagine that the Kent home in Smallville was riddled with holes during Superboy's puberty. And why did Lana Lang never notice that?

V

First we must collect the semen. The globules will emerge at trans-sonic speeds. Superman must first ejaculate, then fly frantically after the stuff to catch it in a test tube. We assume that he is on the Moon, both for privacy and to prevent the semen from exploding into vapor on hitting the air at such speeds.

He can catch the semen, of course, before it evaporates in vacuum. He's faster than a speeding bullet.

But can he keep it?

All known forms of Kryptonian life have superpowers. The same must hold true of living Kryptonian sperm. We may reasonably assume that Kryptonian sperm are vulnerable only to starvation and to green Kryptonite; that they can travel with equal ease through water, air, vacuum, glass, brick, boiling steel, solid steel, liquid helium, or the core of a star; and that they are capable of translight velocities.

What kind of a test tube will hold such beasties?

Kryptonian sperm and their unusual powers will give us further trouble. For the moment we will assume (because we must) that they tend to stay in the seminal fluid, which tends to stay in a simple glass tube. Thus Superman and LL can perform artificial insemination.

At least there will be another generation of Kryptonians.

Or will there?

VI

A ripened but unfertilized egg leaves LL's ovary, begins its voyage down her Fallopian tube.

Some time later, tens of millions of sperm, released from a test tube, begin their own voyage up LL's Fallopian tube.

The magic moment approaches. . . .

Can humans breed with Kryptonians? Do we even use the same genetic code? On the face of it, LL could more easily breed with an ear of corn than with Kal-El. But coincidence does happen. If the genes match. . . .

One sperm arrives before the others. It penetrates the egg, forms a lump on its surface, the cell wall now thickens to prevent other sperm from entering. Within the now-fertilized egg, changes take place....

And ten million Kryptonian sperm arrive slightly late.

Were they human sperm, they would be out of luck. But these tiny blind things are more powerful than a locomotive. A thickened cell wall won't stop them. They will *all* enter the egg, obliterating it entirely in an orgy of microscopic gang rape. So much for artificial insemination.

But LL's problems are just beginning.

VII

Within her body there are still tens of millions of frustrated Kryptonian sperm. The single egg is now too diffuse to be a target. The sperm scatter.

They scatter without regard to what is in their path. They leave curved channels, microscopically small. Presently all will have found their way to the open air.

That leaves LL with several million microscopic perforations all leading deep into her abdomen. Most of the channels will intersect one or more loops of intestine.

Peritonitis is inevitable. LL becomes desperately ill.

Meanwhile, tens of millions of sperm swarm in the air over Metropolis.

VIII

This is more serious than it looks.

Consider: these sperm are virtually indestructible. Within days or weeks they will die for lack of nourishment. Meanwhile they cannot be affected by heat, cold, vacuum, toxins, or anything short of green Kryptonite.[4] There they are, minuscule but dangerous; for each has supernormal powers.

---

[4] And other forms of Kryptonite. For instance, there are chunks of red Kryptonite that make giants of Kryptonians. Imagine ten million earthworm size spermatozoa swarming over a Metropolis beach, diving to fertilize the beach balls...but I digress.

Metropolis is shaken by tiny sonic booms. Wormholes, charred by meteoric heat, sprout magically in all kinds of things: plate glass, masonry, antique ceramics, electric mixers, wood, household pets and citizens. Some of the sperm will crack lightspeed. The Metropolis night comes alive with a network of narrow, eerie blue lines of Cherenkov radiation.

And women whom Superman has never met find themselves in a delicate condition.

Consider: LL won't get pregnant because there were too many of the blind mindless beasts. But whenever one sperm approaches an unfertilized human egg in its panic flight, it will attack.

How close is close enough? A few centimeters? Are sperm attracted by chemical cues? It seems likely. Metropolis had a population of millions; and Kryptonian sperm could travel a long and crooked path, billions of miles, before it gives up and dies.

Several thousand blessed events seem not unlikely.[5]

Several thousand lawsuits would follow. Not that Superman can't afford to pay. There's a trick where you squeeze a lump of coal into its allotropic diamond form. . . .

IX

The above analysis gives us part of the answer. In our experiment in artificial insemination, we must use a single sperm. This presents no difficulty. Superman may use his microscopic vision and a pair of tiny tweezers to pluck a sperm from the swarm.

X

In its eagerness the single sperm may crash through LL's abdomen at transsonic speeds, wreaking havoc. Is there any way to slow it down?

There is. We can expose it to gold Kryptonite.

Gold Kryptonite, we remember, robs a Kryptonian of all of his supernormal powers, permanently. Were we to expose Superman himself to gold Kryptonite, we would solve all his sex problems, but he

---

[5] If the pubescent Superboy plays with himself, we have the same problem over Smallville.

would be Clark Kent forever. We may regard this solution as some-what drastic.

But we can expose the test tube of seminal fluid to gold Kryp-tonite, then use standard techniques for artificial insemination.

By any of these methods we can get LL pregnant, without killing her. Are we out of the woods yet?

XI

Though exposed to gold Kryptonite, the sperm still carries Krypto-nian genes. If these are recessive, then LL carries a developing hu-man fetus. There will be no more Supermen; but at least we need not worry about the mother's health.

But if some or all of the Kryptonian genes are dominant...

Can the infant use his x-ray vision before birth? After all, with such a power he can probably see through his own closed eyelids. That would leave LL sterile. If the kid starts using heat vision, things get even worse.

But when he starts to kick, it's all over. He will kick his way out into open air, killing himself and his mother.

XII

Is there a solution?

There are several. Each has drawbacks.

We can make LL wear a Kryptonite[6] belt around her waist. But too little Kryptonite may allow the child to damage her, while too much may damage or kill the child. Intermediate amounts may do both! And there is no safe way to experiment.

A better solution is to find a host-mother.

We have not yet considered the existence of a Supergirl.[7] She could carry the child without harm. But Supergirl has a secret identity, and

---

[6] For our purposes, all forms of Kryptonite are available in unlimited quantities. It has been esti-mated, from the startling tonnage of Kryptonite fallen to Earth since the explosion of Krypton, that the planet must have outweighed our entire solar system. Doubtless the "planet" Krypton was a cooling black dwarf star, one of a binary pair, the other member being a red giant.

[7] She can't mate with Superman because she's his first cousin. And only a cad would suggest dif-ferently.

her secret identity is no more married than Supergirl herself. If she turned up pregnant, she would probably be thrown out of school.

A better solution may be to implant the growing foetus in Superman himself. There are places in a man's abdomen where a foetus could draw adequate nourishment, growing as a parasite, and where it would not cause undue harm to surrounding organs. Presumably Clark Kent can take a leave of absence more easily than Supergirl's schoolgirl alter ego.

When the time comes, the child would be removed by Caesarean section. It would have to be removed early, but there would be no problem with incubators as long as it was fed. I leave the problem of cutting through Superman's invulnerable skin as an exercise for the alert reader.

The mind boggles at the image of a pregnant Superman cruising the skies of Metropolis. Batman would refuse to be seen with him, strange new jokes would circulate the prisons...and the race of Krypton would be safe at last.

LARRY NIVEN is the author or co-author of over three dozen books, and his short stories have won a total of three Hugo and Nebula Awards. His novel *Ringworld* won both the Hugo and the Nebula for best novel, as well as an Australian award for best international science fiction.

ACTOR
AND SUPERACTOR

THE INTERPRETATIONS OF Superman in dramatic form since his comic-book conception in 1938 are legion: from Bud Collyer's voice both on radio and in the Max Fleischer animated shorts in the 1940s to Brandon Routh in the 2006 Bryan Singer–directed feature film, with dozens of stops in movie serials, television, feature films and even musical theatre along the way.

Writing in late 2005 prevents me from dissecting Routh's performance, but it might be both instructive and amusing, as he becomes the tenth actor to don the cape and tights (or at least provide voice for same), to compare the performances of his nine predecessors.

Of particular interest is how each of these thespians managed the inherent duality. One of the more interesting challenges of playing this particular part is that it's really *two* people in one: Superman and Clark Kent. Anyone taking on this role has to play both the mild-mannered reporter from the *Daily Planet* and the world's greatest superhero.

(For the purposes of this essay, we're sticking with Super*man*. There have been four people who've played the younger role of Superboy: Johnny Rockwell in an abortive 1961 pilot, John Haymes

Newton and Gerard Christopher in the 1988–1992 syndicated *Superboy* series, and, after a fashion, Tom Welling in the current series *Smallville*. There are a variety of reasons for this, but I have to confess that a total lack of interest in the character of Superboy—or not-Superboy, as they're doing on *Smallville*—keeps me from sitting down with these three interpretations. I never liked the concept of young Clark Kent posing as Superboy in Smallville, and was always grateful to John Byrne and his editors at DC Comics who wiped Superboy from the mainline DC continuity when Superman's history was overhauled in Byrne's *Man of Steel* miniseries in 1986. To my mind, the character always took the wind out of the sails of Superman's arrival in Metropolis, if he was just the grown-up version of an existing hero. Plus, I never bought that he could keep his identity a secret in a small farm town in Kansas where everybody knew him.)

The list includes, in alphabetical order:

- Kirk Alyn (in the movie serials *Superman* in 1948 and *Atom Man vs. Superman* in 1950)
- Dean Cain (in the *Lois and Clark: The New Adventures of Superman* TV series from 1993–1997)
- Bud Collyer (voice only, on the Superman radio adventures and the Max Fleischer animated shorts in the 1940s, and Filmation's *The New Adventures of Superman* in 1966)
- Tim Daly (voice only, in the *Superman* cartoon and animated movies in the 1990s)
- Danny Dark (voice only, in the *Super Friends* cartoons in the 1970s and *The Super Powers Team* cartoons in the 1980s)
- George Newbern (voice only, in the various *Justice League* cartoons in the 2000s)
- Christopher Reeve (in four *Superman* films between 1978 and 1987)
- George Reeves (in the movie *Superman and the Mole Men* in 1951 and the TV series *The Adventures of Superman* from 1952–1957)
- David Wilson (in the 1975 TV-movie version of *It's a Bird, It's a Plane, It's Superman!*, the theatrical musical)

(I'm including voiceover actors for two reasons, one historical, one personal. The former is that Collyer was the first person ever to provide a personal presence for Superman on the two media that were the most popular in the 1940s: radio and movies. To discuss dramatic renditions of Superman without Collyer would be ridiculous—which means that Daly, Dark and Newbern get their moment in the sun as well. As for the personal reasons, Daly and especially Collyer are two of my favorite interpretations of the role.)

BUD COLLYER

Probably the most long-lived of the Supermen—by virtue of never playing him in person, and so not affected by the aging process—he was also the first. Collyer's deep voice became *the* voice of Superman for anyone who listened to his adventures on the radio or saw the Fleischer shorts before a movie—the former more so, since the animated pieces were rather short on dialogue. It was the radio drama that gave us many of Superman's signature phrases, including "Up, up and away!" to denote to the radio audience that Superman was flying, which is still used in the comics periodically. (The concomitant, "Down! Down!" for when he was coming in for a landing never really caught on beyond radio.)

Collyer had to do more work than most to differentiate between Clark Kent and Superman, as he couldn't rely on the costume and a different hairstyle to do the job for him. As a result, Superman had a deep, terse voice, where Clark's was higher-pitched and more pleasant, less sharp. Amusingly, Superman's voice was actually Collyer's natural voice; it was Clark that he had to "put on."

Collyer was asked to reprise the voice role he was best known for in 1966 when Filmation Studios produced *The New Adventures of Superman*. Where the Fleischer shorts are works of art, with gorgeous animation and gripping stories, Filmation's work was much more pedestrian, with clunky animation and stories straight out of the cliché handbook. Filmation did animated versions of several DC characters, and Collyer was one of the few voice choices that worked; most of the incidental voices, and the narrator, were provided by Ted Knight, and the majority of the other voices were forgettable. Not the best legacy for Collyer, more's the pity.

KIRK ALYN

Movie serials were all the rage in the 1940s and 1950s. Many superheroes were adapted into serials divided into ten-minute installments shown each week at the local theatre, including Batman and Captain Marvel. In 1948, Supes got the treatment, with former vaudeville performer Alyn in the role.

Alyn had the right look for Superman, and gave him a mischievous, youthful quality that no other onscreen interpretation has ever given him—a reflection, at least in part, of the way the character was written in his earliest days in *Action Comics*. (The World's Biggest Boy Scout image that Superman has carried for most of his career didn't really solidify in the comics until the days after the institution of the Comics Code Authority in the 1950s.) He was a bit slight of build, but reportedly Columbia, the producers of the serials, couldn't find someone with the same build as the comics artists gave Superman who could actually deliver lines with any skill.

Generally, Alyn did a mediocre job of differentiating Clark from Superman. Then again, the standards for acting in these movie serials was never particularly high. The episodes were churned out quickly, often with two directors in order to save time. That Alyn did any serious acting work at all puts him one up on many of his colleagues in the serial business. If nothing else, he made more of an effort to differentiate between Clark and Superman than either Robert Lowery or Lewis Wilson managed to do with Batman and Bruce Wayne in the two Batman serials.

It's easy fifty years later to look at the serials and laugh. For one thing, the flying effects were incredibly cheesy. Alyn would make as if to take off, and then an animated Superman—one that was, frankly, inferior to what Fleischer did in the animated shorts—flew through the air, later to land behind a wall or a bush, which the live-action Alyn would run out from behind. And the acting generally is dreadful, which makes Alyn's efforts look even better, since he was trying harder.

The two Superman serials were immensely successful, so much so that Alyn couldn't walk down the street without people recognizing him as Superman. Feeling he'd been typecast, Alyn refused the role when it was decided to do a Superman movie and TV series, paving the way for Reeves—who would make the same complaints about typecasting—to take over. Alyn relented in later years, agreeing to make a cameo as Lois Lane's father in the 1978 *Superman* film.

GEORGE REEVES

With Alyn frustrated at being typecast, Reeves was cast in the movie *Superman and the Mole Men* in 1951, and he starred in the follow-up one-hour TV series *The Adventures of Superman*, which lasted for five years and was immensely popular.

Reeves played the role as a prototypical 1950s hero—tough, square-jawed, always the center of attention. However, what I'm describing is his Clark Kent. It applied to his Superman as well, but the biggest flaw in Reeves' performance was that there was absolutely no distinction, none—not in personality, not in presence, not even in hairstyle—between the two identities.

Having said that, there's no denying Reeves' charisma in the role, even though he, like Alyn, was limited in his ability to fly convincingly. Instead of an animated Superman, Reeves simply lay on a table that was rendered invisible while a background sped along behind him. He was also limited by dull action-adventure plots that made no use of Superman's comic-book origins, and didn't really move much past the radio dramas in their scope.

The show's popularity couldn't be denied, though. Reeves became even more identified with the part than Alyn was, and as it was with Alyn, it was a source of irritation to the actor.

DANNY DARK

In many ways doing a third-rate Collyer, voice actor Dark (his non-Superman roles are generally "Announcer") was the lone voice of Supes in animation throughout the 1970s and 1980s on the various incarnations of *Super Friends*—later renamed *The Super Powers Team*. Dark reflected the blander Superman of the post-Code time period, one who had lost the New Deal–era edge, not aided by storylines that were simplistic in the extreme, and designed to appeal mainly to little kids without requiring them to think much. Still, Dark's authoritative voice left no doubt as to who was the leader of the Super Friends, and everything definitely flowed from him.

Because of the ensemble nature of the cartoons, secret identities were rarely even acknowledged, much less portrayed, so the issue of differentiating between Clark and Superman rarely came up for Dark.

DAVID WILSON

The least-known name on this list, and with good reason. In 1966, in the wake of the success of the Adam West *Batman* TV series, a Broadway play was launched based on the Man of Steel called *It's a Bird, It's a Plane, It's Superman!* Starring Bob Holiday as Superman, it only lasted on Broadway for four months, but in 1975, ABC decided, for reasons passing understanding, to do a television version of the play. Wilson, an unknown who, as far as can be determined, hasn't worked as an actor since, played Superman with all the verve of a high school kid doing a class play. (More than one Web site describes him as looking like "a deranged Ted Koppel.") His style fit the story, however—the music was awful, the plot asinine, the acting abysmal. The TV movie is best remembered as the part of *M*A*S*H* star Loretta Swit's career she'd prefer to forget.

CHRISTOPHER REEVE

I still recall the day in 1977 when they announced that this unknown actor named Reeve was being cast as Superman in the upcoming live-action movie. My first thought was amusement that they cast someone whose name was so similar to that of the guy who played him in the 1950s.

But what most impressed me was that this guy *looked* like Superman. Unlike Alyn or Reeves, who looked like actors playing the role, Reeve looked like he stepped right out of the four-color pages of the comic book.

The trailers for *Superman* in 1978 told us we'd believe a man could fly, mainly because technology had advanced far enough to make Superman's flying a bit more realistic. Although the wirework used on Reeve looks primitive now, it was beyond state-of-the-art at the time, and gave Superman's abilities a verisimilitude they'd never had before. Reeve's charm and sense of both mystery and nobility shone through even in the much weaker third and fourth films.

What Reeve did best, though, was something Alyn tried to do, something neither Reeves nor Cain ever managed to accomplish: he made us believe a man could disguise himself with a pair of glasses. Reeve didn't just throw on spectacles and re-comb his hair, his entire persona changed. He altered his posture, his voice changed timbre, his body language became completely different when he was Clark. Only Collyer came close to matching Reeve for pulling off the dual identity trick. Perhaps Reeve's finest legacy to the pantheon of actors who've donned the role over the decades is his extraordinary facility for differentiating between Clark Kent and Superman.

DEAN CAIN

The most recent live-action Superman until Routh, Cain was cast more to play a super-powered Clark Kent than he was to play his costumed alter ego in *Lois and Clark: The New Adventures of Superman*, a one-hour drama that focused more on the relationship between Kent and Lois Lane than superheroic exploits.

Cain did very little to differentiate between the two roles, mostly counting on the costume, his glasses, and a different hairstyle to do the job. He was aided by the script for the pilot, when he first models the costume for his mother, who assures Clark that, in that outfit, nobody's going to be looking at his face.

The show's focus on Clark helped Cain, because he wasn't really called upon to be Superman as often as his predecessors, and the show did a fine job of showing how Clark's everyday life was affected by being super-powered—and having to hide it. That latter aspect would have been better served if Cain had done more to keep the two alter egos distinct, but at least he made Clark an interesting character. Once again, the live-action version took its cue from the comic books. Clark had evolved from the milksop that Reeve played in the 1970s into an interesting character in his own right, and that's who Cain was playing.

One of the show's best moments came during one episode in which Clark is shot. Cain did a tour-de-force here: in the space of less than a second, we see him shot, looking down at his chest without any physical response, remembering that he's not in his Superman suit, and only then falling down and pretending that he's really been hurt. It was probably Cain's best moment of doing the secret identity thing, and the show needed more moments like that.

TIM DALY/GEORGE NEWBERN

Andrea Romano has done the casting for Warner Brothers' various animated endeavors over the past fifteen years, ranging from *Tiny Toon Adventures* and *Animaniacs* to the recent spate of DC Comics cartoons: *Batman, Superman, Batman Beyond* and the *Justice League* series. Her most impressive feat on the latter is often casting as a voice actor someone who could just as easily be playing the role in a live-action version. (I mean, c'mon, can't we all easily see Dana Delaney as Lois Lane? Clancy Brown as Lex Luthor? Robert Costanzo as Bullock? Gina Torres as Vixen?)

In that vein, Daly was cast when, on the heels of the tremendous success of the *Batman* animated series in the 1990s, Warner produced a *Superman* series (as well as a Batman/Superman crossover movie, called *World's Finest*, after the old DC Comic that often paired the two characters up). Daly's all-American features could easily work as Superman, and his voice managed a combination of the Boy Scout affect that the comics version had taken on—and that Reeve embodied on film—but with a hint of the mischievousness of Alyn's portrayal. As with the others, Daly's rendition reflected the comic-book version, which was much more emotionally vulnerable than the perfection machine of the post-Code era. Daly's Superman was, like Cain's, one who was not always perfect, and who also was willing to open up to Lois Lane rather than constantly lie to her about his life.

When commitments to other live-action television shows—both the short-lived revival of *The Fugitive* and the even more short-lived *Eyes*—prevented Daly from reprising the Man of Tomorrow's voice on the *Justice League* cartoon, Newbern was cast, primarily for his ability to impersonate Daly.

Neither actor did as much to differentiate Clark and Superman as their Bat-winged counterpart—Kevin Conroy, who has done the voice of Batman on *Batman, Batman Beyond* and *Justice League*, does as Collyer did, using a higher, softer voice for Bruce Wayne, as opposed to his natural, deep voice for Batman—both preferring to count on the costume change to do the trick. (Newbern, like Dark, isn't often called upon to do Clark in any case, for much the same reason.)

What's most interesting in looking at these actors is that, with the obvious exception of Wilson, each of them defined Superman for whatever generation grew up with them. To many, there is no Superman but Collyer. To some younger people now, the idea of anybody but Daly or Newbern as the voice of Superman is unheard of. To my own generation, either Reeve or Dark is the definitive Supes.

Tellingly, Alyn, Reeves and Reeve were all identified primarily as Superman when they died.

Here's how I rate the gentlemen listed above:

1. **Bud Collyer.** Something about that voice just always defines Superman for me. Plus, he did Superman at a time when he was most interesting (to me) as a character.
2. **Christopher Reeve.** Close to a photo-finish here, and I came *this close* to ranking him first, but decided to give Collyer his props. Still, gets points for looking so perfect, and doing best at differentiating between Clark and Supes.
3. **Tim Daly.** In a Collyer-free world, he'd be the best voice for Superman ever.
4. **Kirk Alyn.** Rose above his wretched source material to create the first live-action version of the character.
5. **Dean Cain.** Was the best Clark Kent by far, which mitigated his mediocre Superman.
6. **George Reeves.** Limited by weak stories, weak effects and poor differentiation between alter egos.
7. **George Newbern.** Hasn't really put his own stamp on it, simply impersonating Daly, though he does that well.

8. **Danny Dark.** Adequate, but nothing spectacular, rather like the cartoons he was voicing.
9. **David Wilson.** An embarrassment.

So there you have it. As to where the tenth actor to portray the character will fit into this pantheon, we'll just have to wait and see. Routh certainly has some competition to live up to. . . .

KEITH R. A. DECANDIDO really did sit through the TV version of *It's a Bird, It's a Plane, It's Superman!* He'd like to thank Orenthal V. Hawkins for showing it to him, an act for which he may someday be forgiven. Keith, who is a best-selling novelist and prolific editor, has contributed to three prior Smart Pop anthologies, *Finding Serenity, King Kong Is Back!* and *The Unauthorized X-Men.*

Lou Anders

A TALE OF TWO ORPHANS:
THE MAN OF STEEL vs. THE CAPED CRUSADER

BATMAN AND SUPERMAN: together, they are the ur-superheroes. Created in 1938 and 1939, they set the standard for all superhero comics. At one time portrayed as the best of friends, they even appeared together in a joint comic book, *World's Finest Comics*, teaming up to fight crime and injustice every month from 1941 to 1986. But 1986 coincidentally saw the publication of Frank Miller's historic miniseries *The Dark Knight Returns*, with its revamping of the two heroes' relationship. Since then, things have been a little strained to say the least between the two superheroes. But to ascertain whether this is an unfortunate imposition of the grittier, more adult comics that characterized the 1990s, or an inevitable break arising from fundamental differences woven into their disparate characters, one has to look at their respective origins.

While it is true that both Batman and Superman are orphans, everything about their individual character and nature diverges from this one shared characteristic. As a small child, Bruce Wayne watched as both his parents were brutally gunned down in front of his eyes. Before he had reached maturity, he was present for a horrible, bloody and violent double murder. His life, previously one of privilege—the

only son of the wealthiest family in America's biggest city; essentially
the closest to royalty we have over here—is over in a heartbeat. The
arbitrary and transitory nature of our existence is brought home to
him with crushing reality way before he's prepared to handle it. I remember as a teenager hanging out with friends and driving our car
around a tight mountain curve, seeing how close we could come to
a retaining wall without hitting it. We thought we were immortal.
Years later, I almost swooned when I remembered the incident and
how close to death we'd voluntarily (idiotically!) been. The realization that I could die at any time didn't hit me as a *reality* until I was
exiting my teens. Now imagine having that knowledge thrust upon
you at the age of seven or eight. Basically, it shattered Bruce Wayne's
world. He realized in an instant that *there is no security*. No matter
who you are, death can come at you. You can be Donald Trump and
the world is your oyster, but step outside and be struck by lightning,
and spend the rest of your life as a cripple despite all your billions.
Your life can turn upside down in an instant. And there is absolutely
nothing you can do about it. Call it fate or chance, but your whole
world can be shattered like glass in a single moment without any
warning. This knowledge *terrified* the young Bruce Wayne to the
depths of his soul. And, just like Herman Melville's famous Captain
Ahab, who is crippled—and emasculated if you read between the
lines—by Moby Dick, Bruce Wayne set out to prove to himself, and
to the arbitrary universe that struck at him, that *you can't do this and
get away with it*. Just as Ahab selected the brute animal that injured
him, Batman picked the criminal class that struck at his parents as
his white whale and within a defined territory (Gotham City), decided to prove that in whatever manner death might approach him
again, it would not catch him unawares. It was a decision made when
he was still a child, and at that instant, his childhood ended. From
that point forward, although he did not know it yet, he ceased to be
Bruce Wayne and became only Batman. He never again played as
other children did. Every waking moment was spent in preparation
and learning, mastering physical skills, martial arts, chemistry, fo-
rensics, weaponry, computers and a host of other skills, so that when
he was ready, he could face the enemy on any battlefield and always
emerge victorious. Legendary artist Dick Giordano once said of Bat-

man, "Batman does what he does for himself, for his needs. That society gains from his actions is incidental, an added value...but not the primary reason for his activities." Batman's whole life was a drive to prove—for his own selfish purposes—that *you cannot do this to me again*. It's very much a Nietzschean Will to Power, a human being pushing himself to perform at his absolute mental and physical peak, to impose his will upon the world and force it to make sense. No law but his law, which is why it is vital that he protect his identity. The mask is there as much to protect him from the police as it is from the threat of retaliation from the bad guys. The mask *is* his face, as every definitive portrayal of the character has understood. (But more on masks later.)

By contrast, Clark Kent was raised in the heart of Middle America, on a farm in Kansas where I am sure the farmer still milked his cows by hand and tilled his fields with an actual plow. There were no cattle hooked up to mechanical milking machines here. Kent was the product of a vanishing America, the Jeffersonian ideal of small farms owned by individual farmers. Early to bed and early to rise makes a man healthy, wealthy and wise. Bacon and eggs, and football games, and town socials, church on Sunday and be sure to say your prayers at night. And while the legend will inevitably have to be modified as the world marches on, you can bet Smallville will be the last place on earth to have drug problems, street gangs, or teen pregnancies. While it might have been representative of a lot of Middle America in the '40s or '50s, there is no way to view Superman's hometown today without nostalgia for a simpler time, as indeed its very name suggests. Growing up there, with two very loving parents as role models, Clark Kent was completely shielded from much of the larger, uglier world, but especially from the type of fear that drove Bruce Wayne. Far from feeling the fragile, ephemeral nature of human existence, the young Kent never got sick, never had a runny nose, never even skinned his knee. Before Kryptonite came on the scene—well after his formative years—he would have thought himself impervious to all harm. Can you wrap your head around that? Think what it would do to the developing psychology of a teenage boy? In fact, whereas Bruce Wayne's entire motivation is one of forcing his will upon the world, and thus forcing a merely human body to attain superhuman levels, Clark Kent's adolescence was one of completely opposite motivation. For a boy who could survive a nuclear blast, his problem was in *concealing* what he could do, holding back when he ran, holding back when he played, constantly restraining himself so that he did not appear exceptional but merely average. If Batman is the embodiment of the Nietzschean Superman, then Superman himself is a Greek god masquerading as a mortal man. In short, the one pulls all his punches. The other has never pulled a punch in his life.

Nor is the Man of Steel racked with guilt and fear. Although he is an orphan like Bruce Wayne, Superman does not learn of his extraterrestrial heritage until adulthood (or late adolescence, depending on the version of the myth). Although he can appreciate his role as the sole survivor (or one of the survivors, again depending) of an entire planet, he has a lifetime of experience as a well-loved and well-cared-for child of good parents to counter this. His loss isn't that of, say, J'onn J'onzz the Martian Manhunter, who was yanked from his wife and child and torn from out of his doomed world in the prime of his life. And while the loss of a planet outweighs just the loss of a parent (or does it? Psychologically, doesn't the loss of a parent feel like the shattering of a world?), an adult is much better prepared to deal with this loss, and its inherent responsibilities, than a child could ever be.

Which brings us to costumes. Both men are in dark tights. Both have yellow belts. Both have symbols on their chests. Both wear boots and capes that color coordinate with that bizarre underwear they wear on the outside (What is that? Can we get rid of it?). The only significant different in their respective outfits is that one wears a mask and gloves and the other is bare-handed and bare-faced. And this is a *significant* difference. It's the difference of protecting an identity and revealing an identity. Batman hides his face from the world, presenting the mask as the only face he has. Superman displays his face openly. *This is who I am*, he says. *I'm not hiding behind anything. You can trust me.*

I'm just like you, his face seems to say. So maybe bullets bounce off me, and I can leap tall buildings in a single bound, and I could probably take over the planet in a heartbeat if you thought about it, *but don't think about that.* I'm just a regular Joe like you. I grew up in a town even smaller than yours, and all the laws that you have to obey, I obey them too. This is why, while the Dark Knight has no problem with breaking and entering, removing evidence from a crime scene, stalking, harassment, assault and, uh, battery (no pun intended), the Man of Steel doesn't even litter or cross the street anywhere but the designated crosswalk. Like the Son of God, born to live a man's life and fulfill the law to the letter, the Son of Jor-El has come from heaven to show us that we can all just get along. *Hey, I could take over the planet if I wanted to, but I don't. I obey all the same rules you do, and if I can do it, so can you.* He's leading by example, a symbol to the whole world that there is a better way.

Of course, Superman, that's easy for you to say. Bullets bounce right off you, you've never been sick, you've never even been stuck in rush-hour traffic, and if that cowlick on your temple gets the slightest bit greasy, just fly through the sun to take a quick bath. And that bare face you so handsomely display—it doesn't tell us anything. Or does it really say "Superman" on your social security card? You're not a human being, buddy. You're an *alien*. You're a god slumming it by pretending you're less than you are. And you're not fooling anyone. The rest of us have to live in the real world. We have to struggle against those rules you patronize us by condescending to obey. For us, it's not a choice. We all come up by the school of hard knocks. And some of the knocks are pretty damn hard, let me tell you.

Now, maybe that's being a little harsh on the big S, but at least two people in Superman's world think about him in exactly these terms. The first should be obvious: Lex Luthor. Like Bruce Wayne, Superman's arch-enemy is another adherent of the will to power. Luthor rose up through the cutthroat world of global business to the position he is in by the sweat of his back, don't you forget it, and every time he looks at the alien who *never breaks a sweat at all*, it just sickens him. In his eyes, the Man of Steel was effortlessly given, by a mere accident of birth, the kind of power Luthor knows you have to fight for *in the real world.*

But the other person to understand the difference between inherited and earned position is Bruce Wayne, who has experienced both. Wayne, while he's also another wealthy scion of a corporate empire (WayneTech as opposed to LexCorp), knows firsthand what the universe can do to you when you turn your back on it. Batman understands that Superman wears a mask too, just reduced to a pair of reading glasses, and that what lies behind those nerdish shades is the most powerful force on Earth, a power not from this world at all. And the basis of that understanding is a crack in their friendship that must inevitably widen.

To understand this we must look at the very deliberate religious symbolism inherent in the Superman story. From the start, we have the only (begotten) son of a father from outer space (heaven), sending his child (down) to Earth to serve as a shining example of the good to which we can all aspire. In his role as Superman, the Last Son of Krypton seeks, as we have discussed above, to always do the right thing, to obey every law, to live a perfect life, one might say.

The 1978 film made good use of this. In scripture, Christ says, "I and my Father are one" (John 10:30) and "he that hath seen me hath seen the Father" (John 14:9). These words are quite deliberately invoked in the scene in the Fortress of Solitude when Jor-El (Marlon Brando) says: "All that I have, all that I've learned, everything I feel...all this, and more...I bequeath you, my son. You will carry me inside you all the days of your life. You will make my strength your own, and see my life through your own eyes, as your life will be seen through mine. The son becomes the father, and the father becomes the son. This is all I can send you, Kal-El."

If any more proof were needed that Superman was the "light of the world," there is the line from the Richard Donner film quoted in the trailer for the new movie, "They can be a great people, Kal-El, they wish to be. They only lack the light to show the way. For this reason above all, their capacity for good, I have sent them you...my only son."

Frank Miller made use of these allegorical connections between Superman and Christ several times in his graphic novel, *The Dark Knight Returns*. That Superman hides his powers from a world grown timid, "We must not remind them that giants walk the earth," he thinks, but his divine aspect is made clear when the President (clearly Ronald Reagan) says, "We have God on our sides, or the next best thing." Finally, when Superman diverts a nuclear bomb, and is caught in the blast, he almost dies, withering to a skeletal frame all the while beseeching the earth to save him. "Mother, mother, why hast thou forsaken me" indeed! In the story's only supernatural/magical scene, the stored sunlight of a rainforest is transferred to Superman, the forest wilting in order to facilitate a magical revival. This is nothing short of the death and resurrection of Christ, thematically necessary to establish the Man of Steel as the Son of God.

Sadly, the DC comics storyline, "The Death of Superman," fails to make as good use of the parallel, but that Jerry Siegel and Joe Shuster had Christ in mind when they created their orphaned alien cannot be ignored. One only has to look at the name these two Jewish men gave to their creation. Kal-El. Kal meaning all in Hebrew. El meaning God. Literally, "all that God is."

So, given that Bruce Wayne's whole neurosis is an attempt to demonstrate to the universe, i.e. to God, that death can't come at him again, and, in so doing, to *punish* that God for the tragedy it inflicted upon him, the crack in their friendship really is inevitable. After all, when your best friend is angry at God, and you are God, how long do you think it will be before one of you makes the connection?

LOU ANDERS is an editor, author and journalist. He is the editorial director of Prometheus Books' science fiction imprint Pyr, as well as the anthologies *Outside the Box* (Wildside Press, 2001), *Live Without a Net* (Roc, 2003), *Projections* (MonkeyBrain, December 2004) and *Future-Shocks* (Roc, July 2005). He served as the senior editor for *Argosy* Magazine's inaugural issues in 2003–04. In 2000 he served as the executive editor of Bookface.com, and before that he worked as the Los Angeles liaison for Titan Publishing Group. He is the author of *The Making of Star Trek: First Contact* (Titan Books, 1996), and has published over 500 articles in such magazines as *Publishers Weekly, The Believer, Dreamwatch, Star Trek Monthly, Star Wars Monthly, Babylon 5 Magazine, Sci Fi Universe, Doctor Who Magazine* and *Manga Max*. His articles and stories have been translated into German, French and Greek, and have appeared online at Believermag.com, SFSite.com, RevolutionSF.com and InfinityPlus. co.uk. Visit him online at www.louanders.com.

Gustav Peebles

GOD, COMMUNISM AND THE WB

SMALLVILLE, A SHOW on the WB network seducing America's adolescents with visions of an acne- and largely parent-free world, relates the coming-of-age story of two young men: Superman, prior to his days of telephone booths and capes, and his future arch-enemy and global menace, Lex Luthor. Eventually, as we all know, these two will move to Metropolis and become the very yin and yang of apocalypse and salvation. In the tiny Kansan burg of Smallville, however, these future foes are, as yet, shoulder-slapping buddies. By providing American teens with Clark and Lex's saga, the show tries to evoke the antediluvian world of superhero-dom, the world predating the complete separation of God and Satan, before the latter was cast out by God into the dark underworld.

Let's not pull any punches here: the show, quite simply, is suffused with Christian propaganda. Clark appears on a crucifix in the very first episode, after being abducted by a gang of football players on an annual hazing mission. In another episode he is bathed in a halo of light as he rescues a boy from the jaws of a trash compactor. Once, in a graveyard, the camera frames Clark with the wings of an angel

77

who presides over a Smallville resident's crypt.[1] Every time Clark's spaceship is unearthed for inspection or theft, it appears to have a cross imprinted on its battered exterior. Almost every episode has some vaguely apt Biblical citation, such as a throwaway reference to the Holy Grail, three wise men, or Roman barbarism. In the opening credits, the pop band Remy Zero croons the lyrics: "Somebody save me / Don't care how you do it / I've been waiting for you / I'll make this whole world shine for you."[2]

But beneath the more apparent Christian overtones runs a covert propaganda stream of a far more startling and inexplicable sort: dyed-in-the-wool communist rhetoric. If *Smallville* had aired during another era, the scriptwriters would have been blacklisted and tried by the House Un-American Activities Committee, alongside Dashiell Hammett and Lillian Hellman. It is true, in the first few episodes, all evil hails from the meteor rocks that accompanied Clark on his voyage to earth. But in short order, the plot turns its attentions to the dangers emanating from the booming metropolis of Metropolis, whence the devilish effects and demands of capitalism always originate. The nearby burg is constantly threatening Smallville's tranquil idyll with the crude venality of its urban ethos.[3] In its persistent in-

---

[1] Incidentally, it is a time-honored American tradition to think that the Messiah has come for a second time to a small town near you. Prior to Smallville, Waco was perhaps the latest stopover in this hubristic tradition.

[2] The status of the entire Superman corpus as religious text remains to be debated. Personally, I have no doubt as to its obvious Judeo-Christian trappings. Jor-El, father of Superman, sent us "his only son" who then grows up with peasants only to later save the world via miraculous works (after a walk through the arctic desert for about forty days, we learn in the movies). Also, the most fertile evidence for the imagination: the only man with a non-standard name (e.g., Lois Lane, Jimmy Olson) in the series is Lex Luthor, a name which evokes the name of that progenitor of religious battles royale, Martin Luther. Further, "Lex," in Latin, means simply "Law." Thus, the Law of the Protestants is at odds with the first or second coming, a man of miraculous powers. I leave it to you to decide if this Christian figure is the Pope or the Messiah, which would suggest alternate interpretations of the original Superman series as either Papist or Judaic dogma. But sometimes my imagination gets away from me, so I keep this kind of stuff in the footnotes. As testimony, however, to the fact that others also find this sort of analysis compelling, several websites are devoted to the question of parallels between the Superman comics and religious paradigms (see e.g., http://web. archive.org/web/20001029230207/www.tattoojew.com/supermensch.html and http://www.hollywoodjesus.com/superman.htm.

[3] The message is this: America's virtuous villages are fighting the power of its gluttonous and avaricious cities. Of course there have been plenty of shows that take place in small, idealized villages whose moral balance is threatened by a corrupting force. But Andy Griffith or the Beaver's dad never hated business per se; in fact, the latter was a model businessman himself, while Andy was quite at home relaxing with or defending the interests of the business leaders of Mayberry. Eddie Haskell was the troublemaker, not LuthorCorp's strip mall–ification of the cornfields.

dictment of all that is urban, *Smallville* teaches that capitalism should be feared and distrusted. Its residents persistently battle the possibility that all of their cherished human qualities—their desire to work hard, love deeply, be true—can be sold for money. This is the oldest communist fear in the book, arguably the inner drive behind most communist and socialist movements in history.

Perplexingly, these mutually hostile ideological positions—the Christian right (advocates of "family values" over all others) and the radical, capitalist-hating left—have seamlessly joined forces in common cause in Smallville. Here in Kansas, Bill Bennett and Ralph Nader represent the same constituents—an odd dovetailing of ideologies that seems, to our eyes, thoroughly impossible, a full-fledged category error. America's most vociferous Christians are often ardent lovers of commerce and capitalism; there are even self-help manuals written by CEOs and motivational speakers that espouse the Scriptures as essential guidelines for business success. Contrariwise, communism is known in the twentieth century for its rank intolerance toward all forms of religion.[4] But, in Smallville, Christianity and communism form a single, cozy alliance.

By presenting this odd fusion of beliefs, *Smallville* recalls a time inverted from our own, when the political left had not yet retreated to its cosmopolitan enclave, and the political right had yet to entrench itself in the countryside. In an earlier day, Christian cults and Commie revolutionaries were both looking for ways to fight the "godless capitalism" that was gaining power by the day. These forces pursued a romantic myth that the village world was both Christian and separated from the vileness of commerce; today, this myth lies secretly hidden in the heart of America's folklore and philosophy. *Smallville,* in giving new life to the age-old American stance of anti-commercialism, is reminding us of our revolutionary heritage.

---

[4] Communists have fallen on such hard PR times that, today, the Anarchists are considered less extreme and nutty; many a youth considers donning a black mask during an anti-globalization march and subscribing to Adbusters, but not many have learned "The Internationale" of late. Communism is just so déclassé.

LOVING THE COUNTRY

On the threshold of America's industrial epoch, in the days (and even the social circles) of Ralph Waldo Emerson, a host of utopian communities propagated the belief that man's salvation lay in leaving commerce behind and settling in the same Midwestern plains that Clark Kent's parents till on the outskirts of Smallville. These are the communities that, aside from constituting an oft-neglected part of America's history of western settlement, stand as the last wave of people who managed to fuse a leftist critique of capitalism with a rightist embrace of Christianity. These groups were proto-communists at the same time that they were proto-members of Pat Robertson's televangelist network.

There are entire books devoted to this emergence of utopian Christian communities throughout rural America at the time of the Transcendentalists. The Zoarites of Ohio set up a communistic society while they rigorously followed the religious dictates of a stringent form of Christianity, as did the Swedes of Bishop Hill, Illinois, the Amana colony in Iowa and the Bethel colony in Missouri. A group residing in Indiana, known as "the Rappites," followed the communist-Christian cult-of-personality surrounding George Rapp. And then there was that surely festive bunch, the Perfectionists, who settled in Oneida, New York with a peculiar blend of Christian communism.

The heartland of America, in other words, served not only as the dream projection of nineteenth century Europeans seeking the realization of the proverbial capitalist rags-to-riches fable; it was also the dream projection of Europe's incipient communist movement. Some argued that only in this new land, separated from the filthy commerce and old traditions of Europe, could the perfect human community of sharing and brotherly love be built. Along with their contemporaries, America's Transcendentalists, these groups promoted a belief in abandoning the city's profane temptations and digging one's finger's into the more productive and holier dirt of the countryside.

Sprouting out of Europe and America's northeast throughout the first half of the nineteenth century, these sects were propelled by the same forces that influenced the literature and philosophy of the day—the strong strains of utopianism and romanticism that, when coupled with scientific rationality, were developing a critique of nascent capitalism.[5] A peasant lifestyle was endorsed by the likes of Wordsworth and Coleridge even as they feared that such a lifestyle was disappearing because of rapid industrialization and sheep enclosures. The general anxiety of the era—that industry and money were detaching people from the land—led certain extremists to adamantly return to the land, even if they knew little of how to survive there. For example, the "Icaria" settlement was mostly peopled by urban craftsmen who sought to build an agricultural utopia. Lacking vital knowledge, they struggled for many years before they managed to attain relative stability in Iowa.

In practice, each communist society was organized differently. For example, some, such as the Shakers, were completely celibate (or claimed to be), while others embraced free love. (Improbably, Sandusky, Ohio, had a "free love" society in 1857, while the Oneida colony practiced so-called "complex marriage," for its residents held monogamy to be a most transparent example of capitalist selfishness.)[6] Some lived in common quarters, some kept separate houses. But despite these surface differences, the common roots of this trend run deep. Property was held in common, and labor was dispersed equally throughout the population; money could not buy one's way out of the common labor. Thus, class hierarchy was either absent or actively minimized. Trade in general was avoided as much as possible in favor of communal autarky. Often the sexes were announced to be completely equal, certainly a radical notion during the nineteenth century. Sometimes even religious duties were divided up, with no one person controlling the community's access to God. Invariably,

---

[5] In his book, *Escape to Utopia: The Communal Movement in America*, Everett Webber asserts that "in the 1840s, communes erupted at the rate of more than one every three months for the decade."

[6] Many utopian novels published during this era in diverse European languages (e.g., French, English, German, Swedish) espoused the abolition of monogamous marriage in favor of "free love." Aside from being a "bourgeois institution," it was also critiqued because under this system love was traded for money. People used marriage to secure material gain rather than following their romantic or spiritual connections to other people. Examples of this genre include James Lawrence's *The Empire of the Nairs; or, The Rights of Women*, George Sand's *Indiana*, Wilhelm Heinse's *Ardinghello and the Blessed Islands*, and a Swedish author (J.M. Rosén), writing under the pseudonym "Guido," who wrote *Free Love, a Novel of the Future*.

the new towns followed a rationalist architectural order, such as having a common eating and social building that was encircled by equidistant housing.[7]

The most colorful of these utopian plans (many weren't so colorful, since they were intentionally creating spaces of Puritanical order), however, must be attributed to the massive influence of one Charles Fourier, a foundational author in the history of communism.[8] At one point in the 1840s, more than forty "phalanxes" existed in America, communities that were inspired by Fourier's combined hatred of commerce and the city and his almost neurotic love of scientific rationality.[9] In the organized phalanx, no one performed work that he or she disliked. Everyone was expected to follow his or her "passions." Once society was thusly organized, in so-called "Association," massive inefficiencies would be eliminated. For example, time wasted reading the news would be minimized, for those who love to gossip would be dispatched at the communal dinner table. Young boys would clean the sewers, for they love grime: "Filth will be their path to glory," Fourier wrote. Each phalanx should also contain a "Court of Love." Utopian plans such as Fourier's were promulgated throughout the land via a host of newspapers devoted to the topic. Emerson recounted the ferment of the times when he wrote: "We were all a little mad that

---

[7] One of these utopian communes has survived to this day, the Amana colony of Iowa. Humorously, however, it has followed the same trajectory as Clark Kent, beginning life as a hater of commerce and then becoming one of its strongest defenders. Initially Amana was a rigorously communistic society, but as it aged, there was a vote in favor of "the great change." Today, the Amana corporation is one of America's most well-known capitalist corporations, producing much-used microwaves and refrigerators.

[8] Marx lived in a Fourierist "phalanx" when he first arrived in Paris. The worker arrondissements in Paris were modeled on Fourier's architectural schemes, just as its Arcades were. Incidentally, this fact led Walter Benjamin to "write" much about Fourier in his *Arcades Project,* which was concerned with the forces that propelled the growth of nineteenth-century cities and the revolutions that reacted against them. As the title suggests, Benjamin thought it all began with commerce, in the newly constructed Arcades of Paris. For Benjamin, the fusion represented such a unique moment in history that it called for the even more unique *Arcades Project* in order to describe it.

[9] Fourier's writing has tinges of mania that were even noted in his own day. He prophesied the existence of "anti-lions" and "seas of lemonade" in the utopian future. More mundanely, people ridiculed his ideas about sex. On his daily rounds, the neighborhood children would apparently taunt him with the words, *Voila, le fou: riez!"* But he was not without his satirical side himself. At one point he writes of the "hierarchy of cuckolds, arranged progressively by category, type and species." A pressing chart for any budding naturalist to complete, to be sure.

winter [1840]. Not a man of us that did not have a plan for some new Utopia in his pocket."[10]

Emerson's words attest to the fact that Americans, not just Europeans, were seized with millennial fervor; abandoning the grubby city and repairing for the blessed countryside was also immensely popular with many of the most important intellectual forebears in our land, the people who laid the groundwork for much American philosophy. Their plans were similarly based on a distrust of commerce and a desire to escape its laws by repairing to the countryside. Even someone as conservative as Emerson, a man who viciously rebuked himself for giving money to a beggar, flirted in his earlier years with the idea that commerce was something sullying, not befitting humanity:

> I content myself with the fact that the general system of our trade...
> is a system of selfishness; is not dictated by the high sentiments of human nature; is not measured by the exact law of reciprocity, much less by the sentiments of love and heroism, but is a system of distrust, of concealment...not of giving but of taking advantage....That is the vice—that no one feels himself called to act for man, but only as a fraction of man....Nay, the evil custom reaches into the whole institution of property, until our laws which establish and protect it seem not to be the issue of love and reason, but of selfishness.

The good Reverend Emerson, in this quote, sounds like nothing so much as a tried and true Marxist.[11] But his elevation of the indi-

---

[10] At least two of Emerson's good friends attempted to start utopian communes in the countryside surrounding Concord, Massachusetts. George Ripley's "Brook Farm" eventually tried to follow the dictates of Fourier (Nathaniel Hawthorne has a roman à clef, *The Blithedale Romance,* that critiques Brook Farm), while Bronson Alcott decamped from the grimy city to his disastrous Puritanical experiment at so-called "Fruitlands." Among other claims to fame, Alcott may well have been America's first vegan: No flesh, eggs, or milk products were consumed at Fruitlands, and the farmers even eschewed the use of manure as fertilizer.

[11] Note too his indictment of the capitalist factory system and elevation of the countryside: "The robust rural Saxon degenerates in the mills to the Leicester stockinger, to the imbecile Manchester spinner,—far on the way to be spiders and needles. The incessant repetition of the same hand-work dwarfs the man, robs him of his strength, wit and versatility....And presently, in a change of industry, whole towns are sacrificed like ant-hills, when the fashion of shoe-strings supersedes buckles, when cotton takes the place of linen....England is aghast at the disclosure of her fraud in the adulteration of food or drugs and of almost every fabric in her mills and shops....In true England all is false and forged.... 'T is not, I suppose, want of probity, so much as the tyranny of trade, which necessitates a perpetual competition of underselling, and that again a perpetual deterioration of the fabric." It is safe to say that he's not only referring to material fabric here.

vidual (and his repeated refusal to join the utopian communes of his friends) bespeaks a strong aversion to communism per se. This, clearly, is the era when elements of the right and the left had yet to bifurcate into the opposing polarity that we know today.

Or turn to the even more widely venerated rhetoric of Henry David Thoreau, also versed in the school of America's "Great Awakening." A few representative quotes from his essay "Life Without Principle":

> I think that there is nothing, not even crime, more opposed to poetry, to philosophy, ay, to life itself, than this incessant business.... The ways by which you may get money almost without exception lead downward.... You are paid for being something less than a man.... There is no more fatal blunderer than he who consumes the greater part of his life getting his living.... [Instead] You must get your living by loving.... It is not enough to tell me that you worked hard to get your gold. So does the Devil work hard.... A man had better starve at once than lose his innocence in the process of getting his bread.

Today, individualism is universally defended as part and parcel of a capitalist ethos (think, for example, of Ayn Rand); further, we currently believe that communist principles perforce threaten individuality. The writings of Thoreau suggest that in another era, neither of these presuppositions held true. Thoreau, in essence, wants to conquer the power of money with love and human dignity. Only then can we be truly human, just like the communists said.

In the nineteenth century, America was awash with this sort of dovetailing deluge of Christianity and communism. Or more precisely, this era's history clarifies that twentieth-century communism has its roots in Christian utopianism. Striking out from the cities and factories of the industrializing world, these groups were in search of a Christian heaven on *this* earth, during *this* life. Such are the neglected origins of communism in America, our long forgotten leftist leanings.

BATTLING THE CITY

And so America returns to this heritage today, in *Smallville*'s similar Christian distrust and fear of all that is urbane. To fully grasp the nature of this moment, the show should be compared to the films and comics from which it was born. In the Superman ur-text, Lex Luthor was painted as merely a madman whose methods evolved out of a megalomaniacal yearning for wealth and power accumulation. In *Superman* the movie, for example, Lex schemes to eliminate the California coast with nuclear weapons because he has bought all the real estate in western Nevada and would make a killing on the newly created beachfront property. In *Smallville,* Lex's father (and the show's recurrent villain), Lionel Luthor, is nothing more than a pedestrian businessman. While a bit callous, he is only so because of his straightforward and purely rational desire to increase the value of his company's stock. In the traditional Superman comics and movies, Lex is portrayed as sick, he is the neurotic extreme of capitalism; in *Smallville,* evil resides much more mundanely in the everyday capitalist, one whose goals and ambitions would be held in the highest esteem by Dick Cheney or your local Rotary Club.

But no one person—not Lionel, not even Lex (who will grow up to threaten the good and natural capitalist order prevailing in Metropolis)—is the whole problem in *Smallville.* Rather, Metropolis *itself* and its governing ethos are the problem; Metropolis is portrayed as an evil gestating ground for virulent plans and actions meant to infect and destroy bucolic Smallville and its communal values. Superman, who worked so hard to save capitalist Metropolis on so many occasions in the comics is, in his *Smallville* incarnation, constantly doing battle with its dark forces.

It is true, Metropolis in the Superman movies represents a sort of urban chaos (there is a mugging; Lois is working on a "sex maniac" story for the *Daily Planet*), but it is an urban chaos that is embraced, loved and worth fighting for. City scenes don't even try to hide the fact that Metropolis is actually New York City. Superman and Lois fly by the World Trade Center and the Statue of Liberty; in the train station, the PA system calls out destinations such as New Rochelle and Poughkeepsie; the cabbies cant in a steady Bronx accent. In the original series, Superman openly equates his proclaimed agenda, "to fight for truth, justice and the American way," with fighting for Metropolis *and* the capitalism that it embodied. But he also needs to save small towns and the California coast. In other words, America was united; no one was worried that these two demographic extremes were undermining each other. America's scattered cities and villages were still working in tandem.

Not so in Smallville. The various vixens who threaten the town's upstanding men always hail from Metropolis. One, tellingly named "Desirée," has come to seduce and marry Lex for his fortune; another arrives to get an angle on Lex for a newspaper story and thereby catapult herself to fame. Both employ their brute sexualities to get at their men. To boot, their debased commitments to one of the seven deadly sins serve as the emotional wellsprings of their plans. Meanwhile, the lovable women of Smallville always wear the most respectable clothes, neither revealing too much cleavage nor baring a millimeter of thigh. The two women who vie for Clark's attention are admired either for their brain (Chloe) or their purity (Lana). While both are attractive, each is eminently wholesome and chaste; though they easily could, they never rely on simple carnal power to achieve their goals in life.

But the real culprit in this battle between the countryside and the city is much simpler: money. In this field, Lionel Luthor reigns supreme. He is a ruthless urbanite, gracing Smallville for short visits in helicopters, firing local workers, hiding behind a team of lawyers. He even cites Roman history as a trove of business knowledge (i.e., the same guys who killed Jesus are the fonts of wisdom needed in order to conquer the world of trade), thus demonstrating his cosmopolitan erudition.

People in Smallville stand opposed to all that Lionel represents, as Lana Lang describes in her contribution to the *Smallville Torch,* the high school newspaper. In an editorial where she discusses her decision to live in Smallville over Metropolis, she writes: "Living in Smallville teaches you that you are part of this close-knit community, and that your actions affect people other than yourself.... We've learned to help one another, and our neighbors' happiness and safety are just as important to us as our own." For the record, this is the identical goal of the educational theories of Robert Owen, a utopian reformer who moved his planned community to Indiana in the early 1800s. It also sounds a great deal like one of the Ten Commandments.

Tragically, this Christian utopian ideal will never be fully realized, for Lionel Luthor and his company are constantly fraying the social and material fabric of Smallville. For example, a young boy who turns into a werewolf every time he sees the light of day has only developed this affliction because of LuthorCorp's pharmaceutical research. Similarly, a worker in the LuthorCorp fertilizer plant becomes the victim of violent and dangerous seizures. He continually asserts that the disease results from his nightly custodial work on the mysterious "Level Three" of the plant. Though most of the town believes him to be raving mad, Clark trusts him, and during a class trip to the plant, he uncovers the precise Level Three whose existence LuthorCorp had been so strongly denying. Or if you've tired of LuthorCorp's research wings, what of its plans for strip malls and corporate office parks? *Smallville's* writers fail to disappoint. Lionel is building a suburban behemoth on Native American holy ground, causing the appearance of a ferocious shape-shifting beauty who munches anyone affiliated with the project.

The many-armed LuthorCorp creates victims everywhere it turns. In many a plot, these victims are initially supposed by the show's protagonists to be the cause of the town's perils. Yet the show teaches that the werewolves and shape-shifters are mere effects of the capitalist system, and it's not even Lionel's fault. Sure, he's heartless, but he's never intentionally evil. He's just a Metropolitan, doing what Metropolitans do best.[12] Thankfully, our favorite Smallvillian, Clark Kent, always manages to save his compatriots from all the evils leveled upon the town by the ravages of capitalism.

It's worth briefly turning to the only other parents who are shown with any consistency on the show: Clark's terrestrial parents, Joseph and Mary, I mean Jonathan and Martha Kent. Mr. Kent is the classic incarnation of a money-hater, a reliable character from the history of many cultures and bygone eras. Not only do we learn that when he proposed to Martha (originally a Metropolitan), he specifically told her that he couldn't promise her much money, but he could promise her enduring love to the end of her days; we also hear incessantly of the economic travails on Kent Farm, which is always teetering on the verge of bankruptcy. Every time Lex tries to help him out with a monetary infusion, Jonathan's pride tells him to say no, though his

---

[12] In a fit of conspiratorial reasoning that some puritanical sect must own the WB, I noticed that the *only* characters ever shown to be drinking alcohol on this show are the two Luthor men.

material circumstances would tell him to say yes. Even when LuthorCorp causes the destruction of much acreage and cattle on Kent Farm, Mr. Kent still refuses compensation.

But Jonathan Kent doesn't only hate the Luthors' money, he hates all money. In another episode, Clark attempts to effect a reunion between Mr. Kent and his father-in-law. It turns out that their entire relationship disintegrated over the question of Mr. Kent's lack of interest in making money (Martha's dad is a suit-wearing corporate lawyer, innately uncomfortable on the rough-hewn farmstead). When Martha's dad tries to help them out financially, Mr. Kent becomes enraged and hands him back his check. Here is a man who finds the facility with which money solves problems odious. He's all about that *old* American love of sweat and sinew. Money is evil because it replaces real physical labor; a true Emersonian American would insist on being self-reliant. Mr. Kent will have nothing to do with it and those who trade in it, and Martha even tells us in one episode that Jonathan refers to Lionel as "the devil."

While he is thus engaged in his heroic labors to save the family farm, Mr. Kent always serves as the dispenser of human wisdom to Clark as he grows up and comes to terms with his increasing powers. There are a variety of rules concerning deep humility (imagine the humility necessary if you're the all-powerful Son of God), personal control, how to treat friends, the value of work and dignity. He never stoops to give Clark business advice, which is Lionel's *only* task with his son, Lex.

Together, Mr. Kent and Lionel set up the simple dichotomy between spiritual values and material ones, between community and business. But people other than Lionel are seeking out the cosmopolitan heights, a cosmopolitanism that is marked as pathologically individualistic and against the community. In one particularly revealing episode, entitled "Dichotic," we meet an ambitious young kid who wants to leave Smallville for Harvard and a future career of wild material successes. It turns out that his ability to have a straight-A report card, to be involved in a stunning array of extracurriculars and to date more than one girl at a time has nothing to do with his own mental individuality, but rather with his own physical idiosyncrasy. This boy can magically produce a double of himself, so that he can produce twice as much work as anyone else. All his evil ambition is pointed toward success in the city, in the world outside Smallville. His entire scheme starts to unravel because of his one and only poor grade, in shop class, which causes him to murder his teacher in a last-ditch effort to get a changed grade. His encounters with the shop teacher—a simple craftsman who does good ol' work with his calloused hands—are riddled with disdain for craftsmen's labor. This youth wants to decamp for the city so that he can pursue success via elite connections and the pushing of paper; these desires are presented as sinister and warped, while the shop teacher is upheld as the admirable victim of this ambition.

Slightly more humorous, but equally telling, is the long-running critique of football in the Superman oeuvre. In the original movie, Clark's Earth father tells him that "I'm not sure why you've been put here, but I do know that it wasn't to score touchdowns," a sentiment repeated almost verbatim in an early *Smallville* episode. Clark's football coach possesses accidentally demonic powers, which enable him to cast actual fire onto anyone who dares to threaten his ability to win games (the unintentional use of meteor rocks in his sauna grants him this capacity). Clark's premier foe for Lana's affections is the high school quarterback, who everyone in town, shallowly, "treats like a god." As mentioned above, the football players play Pontius to Clark's Jesus when they crucify him in the first episode. In a later episode of the first season, the same high school quarterback begins to have doubts about the value of football. He wonders if this is all he wants to do with his life, just as earlier in the season his girlfriend Lana decides that cheerleading for his squad of dishonest beefcakes (they cheated on a test) is a silly waste of time.

All these critiques of football perfectly resonate with a long-standing strain of American Puritanism, a strain that indicts anything that is merely playful as vain and meaningless. If sweat is to be produced, it must serve the common good, not elevate mere showiness for the sake of showiness itself. The Puritans themselves forbade all sorts of "games," wasteful spectacles that failed to direct human labor toward something productive. Just like the city, games should be avoided because they value decadence and superficiality over moderation and spirituality.

JESUS WAS A COMMIE, TOO

What we have to ask is why the same rhetoric and beliefs are being sappily espoused on a television network geared toward a pointedly adolescent demographic. Why do we have a new community of money- and city-haters encamped in those same pure and good Kansas plains, telling us that cosmopolitan capitalism is the source of all danger and evil? Telling us, just like the ministers of the early nineteenth century, that the city was the locus of grime and defilement, the abode of Satan? *Smallville* advocates the same wild-eyed communistic and Christian values of the utopian societies of America's youth. Some of our most reliable intellectual avatars, read in classrooms throughout the country to this day, hated commerce as much as we love it. There's the rub: that America's intellectual roots trace the same arc as Marxism's, but today we are the global defenders of the commerce toward which some of our most important intellectual heroes harbored so much suspicion.

Thus, we might conclude that the traditional left is alive and well in America today (despite endless claims to the contrary), in the form of a teenybopper superhero television show. Unfortunately, however, *Smallville* has removed its leftist concerns to the realm of myth. Unlike the communists, socialists, or Transcendentalists of another era, the residents of Smallville find that they must rely on a supernatural power in order to battle the deleterious effects of capitalism. They never manage to conquer it on their own, and Clark always comes to the rescue; in each episode our faith in humanistic values and their power over money are only restored by the *deus ex machina* provided by Superman's *other*worldly powers. Social change gets removed to the realm of the fantastical, only to be savored in the imagination, while the everyday world becomes resigned to a sort of natural and unchangeable order. Oddly enough, this was precisely Marx's complaint against the faith people placed in Jesus when he referred to religion as an "opiate of the masses."

But maybe there is good reason to be conspiratorially suspicious, as all Smallvillians are, that the city in our times is in fact out to get the countryside. As with all American TV shows, *Smallville* exists, ultimately, to promote the purchasing of a variety of products; in the odd case of this particular show, the same products and commercialism that its protagonists detest. Yet even this blatant contradiction hasn't deterred the producers of *Smallville* from taking crass selling to a higher level still: the show can often feel like an extended rock video (many of the musical artists, not surprisingly, are owned by the AOL Time Warner conglomerate itself). Just in case we would like to buy the song that accompanied Clark as he unleashed his goodly and godly powers upon some monstrous birth of LuthorCorp, the WB recaps this segment—this time, with the song title and the band included onscreen, so that we might readily sustain the selfsame capitalism that Clark spends his days battling. Watching *Smallville*, therefore, serves as a sort of weekly catechism for our consumer religion: We fantasize about the moneyless Eden, but embrace the commercial Serpent.

As such, *Smallville* is the latest in a long line of perfectly hypocritical American founding myths. The writers at WB have hit upon (consciously or unconsciously is no matter) the fact that what sells best is the denouncement of selling itself; the writers in LA romanticize the moral good in the countryside in order to bring economic goods back to their bosses' coffers in the city. According to this show at least, the paths of our countrysides and cities have diverged once again, one locale harboring and nurturing the forces of social-changing Good and the other pro-business Evil.

The absurdity, of course, is that *Smallville's* writers have inverted the election results maps that we've grown accustomed to since at least Reagan's 1980 landslide. They've peopled Smallville with all the left-leaning Democrats while tossing all the pro-business Republicans into the city. *Smallville* shows that America's heartland used to be, and spiritually remains, a naturally progressive constituency. Somewhere along the way, however, Christ became a Republican, and ever since, the Democrats have failed to reclaim his followers. America's rural population has decided to only remember half of its heritage, loving Christ but ignoring the radical teachings that spurred a wave of nineteenth-century dissent and social policy ferment. The seed of anger and action against the power of big business lies dormant in the Midwestern plains; why America's progressive forces have chosen to forget this vital political fact works only to their detriment. In other words, those forces need to rely on someone other than Superman to reawaken America's rural left. Meanwhile, those of us in the city would do well to convince all the Smallvillians that we're not all in league with Satan and his business partners. We might well need to figure out what we're supposed to be fighting, but it surely shouldn't be each other.

GUSTAV PEEBLES teaches anthropology at Columbia University in New York City. Whenever he's not watching *Smallville*, he focuses his research efforts on the history of monetary reform debates and on the history of utopian movements. He is currently working on a manuscript that studies the development of Europe's new currency, the Euro, as part of a long-standing historical trend to discover the "perfect money."

The article "Jesus Hates New York" originally appeared in the November 2003 edition of *The Believer*. The author thankfully acknowledges the permission of the editors of that magazine for the permission to re-print the essay here.

Steven Harper

SUPERMYTH!

TWO MORE WEEKS, and school was out forever—or for the summer, anyway. Senioritis ran rampant, even among my juniors. My fifth-hour mythology class surged into the room, half of them still logy from lunch, the other half jittery from a junk food sugar high. Three or four checked the grades posted on the back bulletin board to see how they'd done on the unit test, while two juniors recounted a play from the previous day's baseball game. A normal day, except for the large box sitting on my table at the front of the room. Several of my students eyed the box warily. We had just finished the unit on Norse mythology and they had done everything from figuring out what Odin would buy the other Aesir for Yuletide to writing tabloid newspaper articles about Loki's exploits. I have a reputation around the school for being a little odd, so a box on my table could mean *anything*.

When the class had settled into their seats, I held up my hands for quiet.

"Good morning," I said, though it was well into afternoon. "I want to welcome my world-famous colleagues to our tenth annual conference on world mythology. This year, as I'm sure you all heard, we have the privilege of examining for the first time a cache of materials from the twentieth century. They were discovered in the ruins of a city once called Troy in a state called Michigan and are in excellent shape. Since the Great Disaster of 2276 wiped out almost all records of that era, these documents will give us some fascinating insights into a mysterious, long-dead civilization."

The class alternated between mild interest and snickers of disbelief. I opened the box, took out a copy of *Action Comics No. 1* and held it up. (It was a reprint I bought on eBay, so peel yourself off the ceiling.)

"This appears to be one of the earliest stories about one of Michigan's greatest mythological heroes, a man called, alternately, Clark Kent, Kal-El and Superman. In this box are several other stories about him." I held up several other comic books. "The stories appeared in a heiroglyphic format called 'comics.' They also appeared in crude live-action formats called 'movies' and 'television.'" I held up a videotape of *Superman II* and a single DVD of *Smallville* episodes. "We will spend this two-week conference examining these materials at great length, learning what stories this once-proud culture told and gleaning clues about their society and how it functioned."

The mention of movies excited a fair amount of commotion, as it always does. Then one student raised her hand. "Superman isn't mythology, is he?"

"A topic we'll have to discuss at great length," I said, staying in character. "We'll need to examine some of the more accepted definitions of mythology first, though. I believe you all have your various notes from previous years?"

Groans mixed with bits of laughter as the class took the hint and got out their notebooks. Out of this teaching legends are born.

Does Superman qualify as mythology? Answer in two thousand words or fewer, using specific—

Oops. Sorry. Old habits and all. Let me break some of the usual essay rules and start by trying to disprove my own thesis.

Superman *can't* be mythology. Myths are *ancient*. Myths are from faraway cultures about people who lived long ago. They're about gods and great heroes and wars and stuff. They're worthy of academic study and analysis. They aren't cheaply printed, mass-produced stories for kids, fuhgodsake.

Okay, maybe. But were stories about Zeus ancient when the Greeks told them around their hearths at night? Did the Sumerians think of Gilgamesh as part of a faraway culture? Did people study the stories as literature back in the time they were created? Obviously not, but no one would classify Zeus and Gilgamesh as anything other than mythic. Why shouldn't Superman get the same treatment?

But still, let's look at some definitions of mythology and the heroes within it. See if we get anything workable. I use this definition of an epic hero in my mythology class and in my freshman English class when we study *The Odyssey*:

> **Epic hero**: a larger-than-life character who embodies the most desirable traits of a people, nation, or culture.

So. Is Superman a larger-than-life character? I don't think anyone will argue with me if I say, "Hell, yes," so he clearly qualifies there. But what about these "desirable traits of a people, nation, or culture"?

First, what do Americans find desirable? I'll stick my neck out and assemble a little list. See if you disagree:

**Characteristics Americans Think
Are Pretty Cool, Even if They Don't Live up
to Them Themselves:**

1. Treat everyone equally.
2. Immigrants made this country great.
3. Obey the law and follow the rules, even when it's inconvenient.
4. Keep your word, even when it's hard to do so.

Objections? No? Okay, then. Let's start at the fourth one and work our way up.

Keep your word, even when it's hard to do so. Superman always keeps his word. I'm not going to dig through my comic book collection to find those specific examples I'm always harping at my students to use, so I'll put it to you this way: can you think of a Superman story in which he deliberately and knowingly broke a promise? Even one made to a villain? Here's another way to look at it. Imagine your worst, darkest secret. Now imagine that Superman knows your secret but he has sworn that he'll never tell a soul. Do you believe him?

I thought so.

Obey the law and follow the rules, even when it's inconvenient. You ever wonder why Superman doesn't just fly Lex Luthor out to a desert someplace, break his neck and incinerate his body with his heat vision? No trace of the crime would ever be found, and no one would mourn the loss. Luthor certainly deserves death after all the people he's killed. But Superman's enemies don't call him "that overgrown Boy Scout" for nothing. Killing is against the law, and Superman doesn't kill. (No, you aren't allowed to count the times he was affected by Kryptonite or under some sort of mind control or hurt someone by accident.) You'll notice that the only time Superman did deliberately kill someone, it was Doomsday, the unstoppable killing machine. And Superman himself was killed in the process. American ethics at work—if you choose to kill someone, you have to pay the ultimate price. Superman obeys the law and follows the rules at all costs.

Immigrants made this country great. Need I mention that Superman is the ultimate immigrant? He didn't just come from another country—he came from another freakin' planet. And he certainly made this country great. In the comic books, anyway. What other country has a hero who can even remotely touch Superman?

Treat everyone equally. From Superman's perspective, every human life is the same as every other. There's no difference, in his eyes, between saving the President and saving a homeless person. It's a principle that hurts him, sometimes. A fairly common tactic among villains is to force Superman to choose between saving Lois Lane or saving millions of lives in Metropolis. ("You can save your girlfriend, Superman, or you can disarm the bomb buried beneath the city. You can't do both! Mwah ha ha ha!") This tactic crops up in the first Superman movie, when he could either save Lois from being crushed in an earthquake or stop Luthor from killing millions on the East Coast. He chooses to save the faceless millions, even though it costs

Lois her life. We'd all like to *think* we'd make the same choice, but would we really? Superman always makes the same choice, and we hold him in awe because of it.

And even though I didn't put it on the list above, let us pause to note that Superman wears red, yellow (almost white), and blue—true American colors.

Okay, it's pretty clear that Superman qualifies as an epic hero for American culture. So let's go a little further and look at mythology.

How do you know a set of stories qualifies as mythology? Well, to paraphrase Joseph Campbell, mythology must fulfill four functions. The *metaphysical function* makes us look at the mystery and wonder of creation and go, "Wow! The universe is just amazing!" The *cosmological function* explains how the hell the universe got to *be* so amazing. The *sociological function* gets us to understand why the laws and customs of our culture are a good and fine body of work. And the *pedagogical function* leads us through the various stages of life, from diapers to independent life and back to diapers again. Does Superman do all that for us?

You can probably bet on the answer I have in mind.

Read Superman comic books and you realize right quick that Superman gets to do all the cool stuff. He gets to fly and meet aliens and travel all over the world. He throws entire asteroids at Brainiac's ship. He travels back in time and fights dinosaurs. He falls in love with a mermaid from Atlantis. It doesn't matter that most of this stuff is impossible. Odysseus stabbed a cyclops in the eye, fought Scylla and Charybdis, and rescued his men from a sorceress. If reading Superman doesn't get you to say, "Wow! Universe! Amazing place!" then you're jaded beyond all help.

Okay, you say, but what about that cosmological function? Superman doesn't explain the universe or how it came to be.

Au contraire. Superman has traveled back in time in countless adventures and saved various historical figures from death. Also, in the first two issues of *DC Comics Presents*, Superman and the Flash learn that the Volkir, a race of aliens, visited both Krypton and Earth when both were just rocks orbiting their respective suns. The Volkir left behind organic material that started life on both planets. But a time-traveling villain plans to stop the Volkir from this noble activity. If Superman and the Flash can't get to him first, life will never have existed on Earth or on Krypton. They succeed, of course, but in the process both heroes end up taking a role in the creation of life itself. Explains where life comes from, doesn't it? Sounds pretty cosmological to me.

I've already touched on the sociological function, but let's look at it from a different angle—a syllogism.

1. Superman obeys the law.
2. Superman is a good guy.
3. Therefore, if you obey the law, you'll be a good guy, too.

Never mind that the logic is flawed—we're talking sociology, not mathematics. To expound a little further, though, Superman also shows the *benefits* of obeying the law. He follows the rules and does the Right Thing (according to American thinking, anyway), and you know what? He always wins in the end. You can win, too, if you do the same thing. Or so the stories hint. Superman clearly upholds the current social system. Plenty of sociological function there.

On the surface, the pedagogical function appears a bit stickier to prove, but it's actually the easiest. Here's the key:

Superman is always there.

He's been there, tall and strong, since you were a kid, and he'll continue to be there, tall and strong, when the undertaker nails down the lid. Maybe you don't think of it that way, but it's true nonetheless. Proof lies in what happened the day Superman died.

In 1992, DC Comics announced that Superman would meet his demise at the hands of a villain named Doomsday. The reason was simple economics. Sales of all four Superman titles—*Superman, Action Comics, The Adventures of Superman*, and *Superman, Man of Steel*—had dropped to their lowest point ever. And no matter what fond childhood memories you may have of puppy dogs, pony rides and comic books, the companies that publish them exist for one cold, hard reason: to make money. No sane publisher will keep publishing something that hemorrhages cash. Also, the writers were complaining. Superman first appeared in 1938. By 1992, people had been writing stories about him for over sixty years. There were simply no stories left to tell, they moaned. Thus the decision was made. Superman would die in a blaze of glory.

And the American public went into collective conniptions. People who hadn't glanced at a comic book in decades wrote, called and staged demonstrations. The offices of DC Comics were buried under a deluge of outraged letters and screaming telephones. In one thunderous voice, they howled, "YOU CAN'T KILL SUPERMAN!"

So DC brought him back to life. (By the way, it's another mythological motif for a hero to die and then return from the underworld. Just thought I'd mention that.)

Like I said, Superman has always been there, a strong, comforting presence, and the idea that he could die is horrifying. Even though you had stopped reading about him, you were sure kids everywhere still pored over his adventures. When you're a kid, you read Superman. When you're an adult, you get to watch your own kids discover Superman. Even if you turn away from him for a while, you know you can return to him whenever you want. You're also left with the comforting feeling that *this* is a safe hero. Unlike various rock stars, movie stars and badly behaved sports stars, you know that Superman is someone your kids can admire, that the world would be a way better place if we lived up to his example. That pedagogical enough for you? Pretty mythological, too, I have to say.

Have I proven my point? Let's look. Superman is indeed a larger-than-life character who embodies traits most admired by American culture. His stories do fulfill metaphysical, cosmological, sociological and pedagogical functions. Mythology? You bet. And more power to it!

STEVEN HARPER lives in Ypsilanti, Michigan, with his wife and three sons. When not at the keyboard, he sings, plays the piano and recorder and collects folk music. In the past, he's held jobs as a reporter, theater producer, secretary and substitute teacher. He maintains that the most interesting thing about him is that he writes books. He is the creator of The Silent Empire series for Roc Books. All four Silent Empire novels were finalists for the Spectrum Award. Visit his Web page at http://www.sff.net/people/spiziks.

Adam-Troy Castro

SIX THINGS THAT PLAIN DON'T MAKE ANY SENSE ABOUT SUPERMAN

I
T'S THE LITTLE things that rankle.

I'm willing to buy any number of impossible opening premises. The jolly, fat guy who spends his year building toys and his Christmas Eve zipping about on a flying sleigh drawn by twelve hovering reindeer: check. The guy who's clean-shaven twenty-nine days out of the month who just happens to sprout hair and whiskers on the night of the full moon: check. The suave, debonair superspy who somehow manages to find and defeat the evil masterminds while carefully introducing himself, by his real name, to just about everybody he meets: check. The ugly one-eyed sailor so in love with the most unappealing woman on land that he regularly defends her honor using super-strength he derives from canned spinach: check.

These premises are all unlikely to the point of impossibility, and yet we're more than willing to provide them with provisional acceptance, because we like where the resulting stories take us.

Similarly, we are more than willing to accept the existence of an alien visitor, seemingly indistinguishable from other human beings, who upon landing on our pathetic little globe gains the capacity to repel bullets, see through walls, fly at the speed of light and spend his days fighting for truth, justice and the American way. We accept these impossibilities wholeheartedly, while making fun of the many other unlikelihoods that we must accept at the same time: among them, the contrivances that provide him with a steady stream of worthwhile foes, or the one that allows him to successfully, and all but impenetrably, disguise himself as a weakling and coward simply by slipping on a pair of eyeglasses. We can debate the logic of these premises from now until the end of time, and nobody will ever give a damn about anything we have to say. Because he won those fights seven decades ago, and arguing them now is a lot like standing outside the White House with a picket sign, protesting the policies of Herbert Hoover. It's a waste of time.

But he has grown a thicket of subsidiary myth over the years, much of which compounds fantasy with outright lunacy, and that we're free to debate. Because that is what really bothers us. Because we can buy changing the course of mighty rivers, and still screech to an absolute halt when confronted with, picking one example at random, Krypto and the Legion of Super Pets.

Thus we present the following elements of the Superman mythos I just absolutely, positively cannot buy.

One note before we proceed: there has been any number of versions of Superman over the years, some of which contradict each other in the most fundamental ways. Some incorporate the elements listed below, and some do not. For simplicity's sake, we shan't worry ourselves untangling the knotted skeins of contradictory continuities, or omit anything particularly juicy just because it's currently fallen out of favor (though we may note when some elements were current). We'll just amble through the attic and emit an eek whenever we encounter something, however dusty and out of favor, that strikes us as just plain wrong.

1
THE PATHETIC INFERIORITY COMPLEX
OF THE KANDORIANS

Kandor, usually pronounced all in one breath as The Bottle City of Kandor, is the last outpost of Kryptonian civilization in the universe.

It survived the destruction of its home planet because the interstellar villain, Brainiac, liked to travel from world to world shrinking cities and keeping them on a shelf in his spaceship. Freed when Brainiac arrived on Earth and attempted to add Metropolis to his collection, Kandor now resides on a pedestal in Superman's Arctic Fortress, still tiny, still trapped in a bottle, still waiting for Superman to find some way to restore it and its millions of powerless citizens to normal size. Much angst is milked from the sad plight of the noble Kandorians, and their devotion to Superman. Powerless inside the bottle, thanks to its simulated red sun, they aid their benefactor from time to time, by the simple expedient of emerging from the bottle to fight by his side as microscopic Supermen.

The obvious question is why they put such stock in being cured.

Think about it. It's not like they have a world of full-sized Kryptonians their tiny size prevents them from returning to. That baseline is gone forever. Superman, Supergirl and the villains imprisoned in the Phantom Zone are all taller, but they're so few in number that they can only be seen as statistical anomalies. As of now, the average size of the remaining members of the species is defined quite well by the people of Kandor, who now face a practical choice between being small and living in a bottle on a shelf, or being small and free to zip around with godlike powers. It seems an obvious choice to me, but the Kandorians remain so self-conscious about being small that they prefer indefinite storage on Superman's shelf.

This does not speak well of Kryptonian ambition.

Even assuming that the average size of civilized races throughout the cosmos is something like five-foot-ten and that anybody shorter is ridiculed, even if they do have godlike powers, the Kandorians still have all the cards. Transplant the entire city to a friendly world under a yellow sun, where they can establish their new civilization in an area comprising less than one square meter, and think of the wealth they have to work with: natural resources in no danger of depletion, endless room to expand, an environment that poses no real threat to them, the vast capabilities of their super-science, an advantageous scale that will allow them to multiply well past the hundreds of billions and into the trillions before they even think of needing some elbow room, and enough super-power to ensure that any off-world visitors who land with evil intent will find themselves stripped naked and flung back into orbit in about as much time as it takes Clark Kent to say, "Great Scott!" By the time it even occurs to the Kandorians to open diplomatic relations with all those self-absorbed big people, the species will be not only replenished in full, but firmly established in a brand-new civilization that will dwarf Krypton the First as much as the Roman Empire dwarfs Dubuque. Except *this* time, with the ability to zip through space at will, and Krypton's fate still lurking in their recent historical memory, they won't put their eggs all in one basket again. They'll establish a host of off-world colonies and thus preserve their future from the prospect of exploding planets.

By then, I promise, nobody with an ounce of self-preservation will make fun of them.

And yet they prefer to live in a bottle, whining about the lost glory that was Krypton, and their fealty to the caped guy who comes by every Wednesday to change their air bottle and clean out their dirty litter.

Seriously. What a bunch of losers!

2

THE FRIGHTENING DESTRUCTIVE POTENTIAL OF SUPERBABY

Most current versions of Superman, including those familiar from comics and the TV series *Smallville*, posit a Clark Kent whose powers begin to emerge in adolescence, and whose teen years amount to a gradual coming-to-terms with the great destiny that awaits him.

'Twasn't always so.

And past versions which establish a toddling Clark capable of lifting tractors over his head, or driving his parents to distraction with super-speed antics, are most frequently treated as cute.

Assuming for the moment that Kryptonian children are all blessed from birth with an innate understanding of right and wrong, and the importance of listening to their parents and the importance of not squeezing too hard when lifting softer, more breakable sentients over their heads—assumptions not at all borne out by the very existence of characters like General Zod—there's still imperfect muscular control, impulse management and just plain naiveté to worry about. Anybody who's ever seen a sweet, affectionate one-year-old tiring of a toy after thirty seconds and discarding it by throwing it as hard as he can knows we're fortunate that toddlers are weak. And anybody who's ever seen a two-year-old, at the full peak of a tantrum, kick and punch the mother she was hugging and laughing with half an hour earlier knows we're fortunate that toddlers can't inflict as much damage as, for that moment at least, they'd like to.

A true Superbaby, with no sense of right and wrong, would do a lot more than (picking one comic-book sequence at random) fly around the neighborhood grocery store knocking cans off shelves while Ma Kent flutters about trying to coax him into his stroller before anybody sees. A true Superbaby would be pure id, following every whim wherever it led him, wreaking all sorts of terror while the adults around him found placating him, at any cost, the only means of survival. Check out Jerome Bixby's short story, "It's a *Good* Life," so memorably adapted from Rod Serling's original incarnation of *The Twilight Zone*. The powers may be psionic instead of physical, but the dangers are much the same, and a neighbor kid tossed four counties for not giving up his ball on demand is every bit as dead as another spitefully wished into a cornfield.

It might even be worse than that. Life on Earth might not survive a Superbaby at all. To Superbaby, the brick and mortar of human structures, the skin and bone of human beings and the stone of the planet where human beings live are all, effectively, as permeable as open air. He would have very little opportunity to learn how to distinguish the qualitative difference between one surface and another. He would have no reason to stop moving when he encountered furniture or people or load-bearing walls. He would have no reason to stop digging holes in the backyard just because he exposed the Earth's molten core and covered all of Kansas with lava. He would enjoy long, delightful Sunday afternoons reversing the Earth's rotation, crying when he accidentally knocked it into the Sun, and napping in space for as long as it took the memory to fade and leave him looking at all the pretty lights in the sky.

Were Ma and Pa Kent lucky enough to realize what they had on their hands before hard looks from Baby Kal-El set their fields and their home on fire, and were they able to salvage a Phantom Zone projector from the rocket while they still had time, they could zap the kid into limbo and raise him from their side of the portal, not freeing him into the physical world until they were absolutely confident of his promises to be a good boy. But if they were smart, that day would never come. Because by then he would have spent his youth in a cold, dark, joyless place with no physical affection at all, and no peers other than the previous Kryptonian despots banished to that terrible place before him. Such treatment, however necessary, qualifies as child abuse. And Kal-El would grow up resenting it. He might even grow up evil and twisted, even more dangerous because his vast destructive potential would now be paired with genuine malice.

So let's be happy there's no Superbaby, and happier still that I didn't even have to get into the diaper issue.

3
THE ODD CONSTRUCTION OF BUILDINGS IN METROPOLIS

This was most in evidence during the comics edited by one Mort Weisinger, during the 1950s.

Metropolis was a city of skyscrapers, much like Manhattan and Chicago, which stabbed majestically upward while rising, sans warning, out of a clean green field.

Midtown had no context. There was no suburban sprawl, no industrial section, no low-income housing, no airport, no surrounding network of highways and highway interchanges converging on the great city center: just that one bunch of skyscrapers, sticking straight up. This is the city which didn't need the "You are Now Entering" and "Now Leaving" signs. Any pedestrian could tell. It just popped up out of that field, like a stand of mushrooms.

And the buildings themselves had all the physicality of cardboard boxes. Superman used to pick them up and fly around with them, for reasons that I assure you made some kind of sense within the stories themselves. To be sure, it wasn't always sense as you or I would recognize it. Indeed, there was one memorable issue, somewhere in my collection, where Superman removed the entire *Daily Planet* building to an undisclosed location, just to mess with the head of Editor-In-Chief Perry White while Allen Funt filmed the inevitable stunned reaction for *Candid Camera*.

Yes, this was an actual Superman comic. Perry White came walking around the corner and the entire building he worked in was gone. Cops at the scene, in on the joke, assured him that there had never been a *Daily Planet* and that the address had always been a vacant lot. Perry raged so incoherently he almost had a stroke. Then Superman flew back with the building and everybody went, "Ho ho ho."

No harm done, right?

In this Superman comic, and in the legion of other Superman comics which featured the guy in blue blithely carrying buildings on his shoulders, buildings had flat bottoms. They were not attached to foundations and they did not have permanent connections to the technological support systems of a modern city. They were sufficiently solid that a man of physically human dimensions could support one on his shoulders, while winking at his practical joke on dyspeptic newspaper editors. They didn't drip sewage from exposed pipes and they didn't trail a thicket of severed electrical wires and they didn't collapse under their own weight, blanketing lower Metropolis in a cloud of dust while the Man of Steel hovered in mid-air looking exactly like an idiot stupid enough to think he could rip buildings from their foundations with impunity. No, these miracles of architecture didn't drop so much as a rivet. And when he plopped the buildings back where they belonged, they were immediately open for business again; they still had electrical power and phone service and plumbing, and all the drawers were still in their filing cabinets and all the framed pictures of Mom and Dad and Suzy and the dog were still neatly lined up on Dad's desk on the seventeenth floor, and not so much as a single pencil was out of place, anywhere, and none of the businesses established in those buildings were disrupted in any meaningful way, thus freeing everybody to wave happily at Superman while he flew off searching for some other pointless thing to do.

I want to know who built Metropolis and why he isn't making a mint in earthquake zones.

4

THE ODD FAVORITISM DEMONSTRATED BY THE VERY EXISTENCE OF JIMMY OLSEN'S SIGNAL WATCH

For a couple of decades, in the comics, Clark's co-worker Jimmy Olsen wore a signal watch he could use to call Superman in emergencies. Falling out of windows, or menaced by thugs, or buried in Egyptian tombs, Jimmy sometimes relied on his own resourcefulness, but just as often reminded the reader for perhaps the ten thousandth time that he had a Superman signal watch, pressed the dial on its side, and sent off a subsonic "zee-zee-zee-zee" that within an instant summoned the Big Guy to his side.

It was, to put things mildly, a wildly useful fashion accessory.

Lois Lane had no such watch. Whenever she fell out of high windows, which was more often than an entire city of financial analysts during an entire year of stock market crashes, she had no recourse other than screaming.

Clark Kent had no such watch. And, really, he should have. Because wearing one would have gone a long way to explaining how come Superman was so often in his immediate vicinity.

No member of the Metropolis police force had such a watch. And, again, it would have saved them a heck of a lot of trouble, for those occasions when nothing but an alien equipped with super-breath would do.

No, the only guy to have such a watch was Jimmy.

He didn't come up with it by himself.

Superman gave it to him as a gift.

And not surprisingly, Jimmy was known to abuse it from time to time.

I can recall one memorable comic-book story where Jimmy was investigating a Metropolis slumlord. That investigation included living for a while in one hellhole tenement. He took a date home one afternoon, with some box lunches they'd picked up at a nearby restaurant, only to discover that those boxes were infested with roaches. Ewwww! So Jimmy pressed his signal watch, sent a subsonic "zee-zee-zee-zee" into the ether, and was within seconds rewarded by the arrival of his caped best buddy. Superman not only killed the roaches with his heat vision, but also cleared the table of all the trash, before flying off.

I'm not kidding.

Jimmy Olsen summoned Superman because of roaches.

Superman not only showed up, but took care of the situation without protest.

Again: Roaches.

That actually happened. And even at ten years old, or however old I was when I read the story, I felt genuine astonishment that the following did not happen. Superman did not stare at Jimmy incredulously. He did not shake his head as if doubting his own sanity. He did not turn to leave, stop at the window, lower his head sadly as he realized that there was no way to leave this place without venting, then whirl and snap, "Roaches? Excuse me . . . pal . . . but there's a famine in Africa and an earthquake in Indonesia and a kinda ominous smoking volcano somewhere out in the Pacific, and there are house fires and mudslides and people being mugged and for that matter mad scientists and supervillains plotting to take over the world, all over the freaking *planet* right now, so many crises and life-threatening situations that even I can't possibly get to them all at once, and I had to be here cleaning up your trash because I was stupid enough to trust a yutz like you with the world's only Superman signal watch!" And then he didn't snatch the watch off Jimmy's wrist and melt it into slag and fly off muttering to himself in irritation.

The signal watch reduced Superman to the status of Jimmy Olsen's genie. It gave this one geeky, accident-prone, disaster-magnet-of-a-cub-reporter the equivalent of superpowers by proxy. And it had no business existing in the first place.

5
STREET-LEVEL THUGS WHO HONESTLY BELIEVE
THEY STAND A CHANCE

We expect supervillains to be slow learners.

Spider-Man has defeated Dr. Octopus a couple of dozen times. But when Dr. Octopus escapes from prison yet again, he has no compunctions about attacking Spidey for the two-dozen-and-first time, ranting as always that the webslinger is about to meet his doom. It's not all that hard to buy this. After all, his past battles with Spidey include any number of occasions where he almost won, and the law of averages is on his side: as far as he's concerned, he only has to win once.

Similarly, the Riddler has no compunctions over taking on Batman for the hundredth time, Dr. Doom has no compunctions over taking on the Fantastic Four for the hundredth time, and Lex Luthor has no compunctions over taking on Superman for the hundredth time. Even though just about every past encounter has ended with those villains unconscious and covered with bruises.

Again, they're maniacs. Obsessive behavior, with limited understanding of consequences, is their lifestyle of choice.

That much makes sense.

But you might expect street-level crooks to show a little more self-awareness.

Assume you're a bank robber in Metropolis.

Even that much is a stretch. You don't want to be a bank robber in Metropolis. You don't even want to be a bank robber in Gotham City. The cops are troublesome enough. You don't want to work anywhere where costumed folks muscle in on your action. If you're a professional, you go to Des Moines or Scranton or Terre Haute or some other nice, sleepy town unpatrolled by superheroes.

But let's say you're stupid enough to be a bank robber in Metropolis.

And you pull off the job and you leave the bank with sacks and sacks and sacks of filthy lucre and you're racing your getaway car through the city streets laughing about how the cops are too slow to stop you and you hear a whoosh and all of a sudden your car is not on the ground anymore, but instead being carried toward police headquarters at skyscraper altitude while a familiar baritone voice just outside your window says something clever like, "Enjoy the view, boys! It's the best one you'll get to see for twenty years or so! Ho, ho, ho."

If you're a bank robber in any city other than Metropolis, you might be expected to consider your prospects a little hopeless, right about now. At least, if you've got anything resembling a brain in your head.

But if you're a bank robber in Metropolis, you snarl something like, "Get him, boys!" stick your machine guns out the window, and waste your time emptying your clips into the famously bulletproof guy's chest.

Now, leaving aside the point that you should know your city's most famous resident is bulletproof and that shooting at him is a rank exercise in futility, there remains the question of just what you hope to accomplish with even the luckiest of all lucky shots. Let's assume you somehow manage to hit Superman in a weak spot. And let's assume he dies. You don't want him to drop dead while he's carrying you at forty stories above the street. Because then he drops you. And it doesn't matter how many bullets you fire after that, because the ground honestly won't mind. Even somebody stupid enough to rob a bank in Metropolis should be able to figure out that much.

But let's scale back the scenario a little. Let's assume you're not a bank robber, but a garden-variety thug, somebody who thought he could earn his dishonest living under Superman's radar. Even Metropolis has more than its share of those. And let's assume the boss of your gang bit off a little more than he could chew, and got involved in a scheme that Superman had to stop. And you find yourself in the hideout, holding a gun on the snoopy girl reporter tied to a chair.

And Superman bursts through the wall.

You empty your chamber firing at his chest.

The bullets bounce off while he stands there, arms akimbo.

Your gun clicks.

Everything you've done up until now can be ascribed to panic.

But then you throw the gun at Superman's head.

I'm not kidding. This was a common occurrence on the old *Superman* TV show with George Reeves. The same thugs who had just seen bullets bounce off Superman's chest always reacted by throwing their guns at Superman's head. They honestly expected the strength of their own right arm to do what gunpowder applied to lead could not.

Talk about clueless.

I sometimes wonder if Superman ever considered playing with them a little. You know. If he ever thought about letting the gun hit him in the head and pretending that it actually hurt him. "Uh...wo w...ouch...that's one hell of a pitching arm you've got there, slugger." And if the crooks who tried that gun-throwing trick ever spent the next twenty to thirty years of their lives in prison embarrassed by the moment. I can just picture a guy gripping the bars of his cell, while shaking his head and murmuring, "Dumb, dumb, dumb, dumb...."

6
THE ABSENCE OF ANY REAL-WORLD
LIMITATIONS TO SUPER-HEARING

Superman's got one hell of a set of ears. He can hear anything he wants to hear, no matter how distant, even if that happens to be signal watches broadcasting "zee-zee-zee-zee" to alert him of unpleasant cockroach infestations. That capability, coupled with his trademark speed, makes him a formidable altruist indeed, as on occasions when he's heard a gun being fired blocks away and was able to reach the scene in time to catch the bullet before it hit its intended target. An extreme example of this might be one recent comic book story in which he heard Lois being shot in a distant war-torn country and reached her in time to get her some much-needed medical attention.

It's one hell of a trick.

Especially since it's impossible even for him.

We began this journey by discussing the difference between the impossible assumption we're willing to accept for the sake of a story and the ridiculous one we reject because it just plain makes no sense. And the phenomenon of Superman's keen hearing is an especially apt case in point. Because while we may be perfectly happy to concede a guy is capable of discerning a single gunshot on the other side of the planet, it's absolutely too much to expect even that guy to react to a sound he hasn't even heard yet.

The bang we associate with a fired gun travels at the speed of sound, approximately 769 miles per hour.

Slower, in fact, than the actual bullets.

Even ears capable of hearing that bang on the other side of a sizeable city won't pick up the sound waves for several seconds, which is bad news indeed for anybody on the wrong end of a firearm in Metropolis. Since Superman is, as we're frequently reminded, faster than a speeding bullet, he can interpose that invulnerable chest of his if he happens to see the gun go off, but not if he's alerted only by his talented ears. In that case, the victim might already be seconds into a bad case of bleeding.

More critically, even ears capable of hearing a bang on the other side of a planet won't pick up the sound waves for hours and hours and hours.

And even if Superman kept his ears focused on Lois Lane's heartbeat, as he did in that story, so he could race to her aid at a moment's notice, he wouldn't have been able to discern the first real signs of trouble to catch her, as he did, before she hit the ground.

Instead, he could have been sitting around Metropolis, listening to the thump-thump-thump of her heart, and feeling totally complacent about her continued good health, hours and hours and hours after she bled out and her heartbeat no longer belonged in the realm of current events.

Which would be all that more annoying to him if he realized he'd spent some of that time cleaning up the cockroaches in Jimmy's box lunch.

The bottom line? Superman would find his information far more current if, like the rest of us, he got his news from television.

ADAM-TROY CASTRO has written four novels and over seventy short stories, including the Stoker nominee "Baby Girl Diamond," the Hugo and Nebula nominee "The Funeral March of the Marionettes" and the Nebula nominee "Of A Sweet Slow Dance in the Wake of Temporary Dogs." Adam-Troy lives in Miami with his long-suffering wife Judi and a collection of insane cats that includes Uma Furman and Meow Farrow.

Adam Roberts

IS SUPERMAN A SUPERMAN?

THE OBVIOUS ANSWER to the question in my title is: no. But in this instance the obvious answer is the wrong answer.

Allow me to explain.

First, I should be clear about the two terms.

Superman is the name of a comic character, created by Jerry Siegel and Joe Shuster for DC Comics (as the old National Comics have now become), who first appeared in the first edition of *Action Comics* in June 1938. I could now list the various attributes of Superman—born Kal-El on the planet Krypton, living as Clark Kent on Earth where, thanks to our world's lesser gravity and the influence of the light of our yellow sun, he possesses extraordinarily enhanced abilities—but, considering the nature of this volume, and the level of knowledge you (the reader) certainly already have about our chromatically vivid hero, I'd only be wasting your time.

It's more than likely that, although you know a great deal about Superman, you may know a little less about superman. Here I can help you:

"Superman" first appeared in English in the 1880s as a specific translation of the German word *Übermensch*, which was coined by the nineteenth-century philosopher Friedrich Nietzsche. *Über* doesn't have a precise English equivalent: it means "over," "above," "more than," "beyond" (*überwindung* means "overcoming," an *übersetzensung* is a "translation"); but it is very well translated by the Latin word *super* (= "above, beyond, on top, thereupon, remaining'). *Mensch* means "man" in the general sense of "member of mankind" or "human being" (not man as opposed to woman). So there you have it.

But since the 1950s (roughly speaking) English-language scholars have stopped translating *Übermensch* as 'Superman,' generally preferring the translation "Overman." Philosophers sometimes talk about this shift as if "overman" is a better translation of the German—it isn't. "Beyond man," or "Super-evolved man" would be closer; "Overman" carries the quite inappropriate implication that this man is *over*, as in finished, done with, exhausted. Nothing could be further from Nietzsche's thinking.

The real reason why the world of English-language professional philosophy changed its translation was the success of the other Superman, the cartoon figure. It's as simple as that. Professional philosophers didn't like the idea of this core Nietzschean concept being associated with the big muscly guy in the tight blue suit and red cape. They thought this demeaned their subject.

They were extraordinarily wrong.

The association of superman with Superman, far from demeaning philosophy, gloriously elevates it. In an important sense, Siegel and Shuster are closer to the heart of Nietzsche's ideas than most philosophical commentaries.

But before I explain what I mean, I need to be clear about something. I am absolutely *not* saying that Siegel and Shuster were secret scholars of Nietzsche and deliberately decided to cartoonize his Superman figure in their own story book. Although Niezsche was a famous figure in the 1930s there's no evidence that these two particular Americans were especially influenced by him. More importantly, Siegel and Shuster weren't trying to do philosophy; they were trying to tell exciting stories, and develop a character that people liked. And they succeeded, too.

But in another sense we can say that Superman *is* a type of superman. He doesn't embody a set of philosophical axioms, but he does represent an over-coming, a movement beyond older, weaker modes of art, something splendidly and heroically new.

NIETZSCHE

Friedrich Nietzsche was born in 1844 not far from Leipzig, in German Saxony. A brilliant young scholar, a kind of Mozart of philology and philosophy, he became a professor at the University of Basel in 1869 when he was just twenty-four years old. Even at this early age his reputation was so high that he was awarded a PhD doctorate without having actually to submit a PhD. (I wish I'd been given that option when I did my PhD.) He soon began publishing a series of ground-breaking philosophical studies, beginning with *The Birth of Tragedy*, a book that changed the way Greek Tragedy, and culture, was studied. With *Human, All Too Human* he began developing a radical new philosophy, one that would change the way people thought about philosophy forever. Nobody who reads *Thus Spake Zarathustra*, *Beyond Good and Evil* and *The Genealogy of Morals* can ever again blithely accept conventional thinking about morals, religion, the individual's place in society or the meaning of life. *Thus Spake Zarathustra*, in particular, had an enormous influence on twentieth-century thought—this is the book in which Nietzsche expands most eloquently about his concept of the superman.

Nietzsche's thought dispensed with Christianity, and with all conventional morality. He despised the common herd of humanity, seeing most people as weak and servile, like sheep. This degenerate mankind would, he claimed, be superseded.

A new sort of man would inherit the earth; not weak and flabby *homo sapiens* but a *homo superior*: strong, creative and un-illusioned.

Then Nietzsche went completely barking mad. After seeing a man beating a horse in Turin he burst into tears and gave the horse a big hug. Instead of continuing to write books of philosophy that changed the parameters of Western thought, he wrote the autobiographical *Ecce Homo*, which has amongst its chapter titles "On Why I Am So Very Clever" and "On Why I Write Such Wonderful Books." He wrote letters to friends signing them "Christ" and "the God Dionysis." After 1888, and until his death in 1900, he published nothing more. He was cared for by his sister and mother (incidentally his sister, Elisabeth, later became a Nazi, and did much damage to her brother's reputation by painting him as a German nationalist and an anti-Semite. In fact Nietzsche hated nationalism of all kinds, despised German "culture," and admired the Jews for their strength and endurance). In much the way that the 1960s produced several high-profile rock-and-roll casualties, Nietzsche was a Philosophy casuality.

NIETZSCHE'S PHILOSOPHY

So did Nietzsche deserve to brag in his autobiography "On Why I Am So Very Clever"?

Well, yes, he did, actually. His insights have had a greater influence on twentieth- and twenty-first-century thought than any other. Great chunks of Modernism, and Postmodernism would not have happened without his influence.

Nietzsche's philosophy began at the moment when he resolved to be un-illusioned. He refused to believe things just because everybody else believed them, refused to do the conventional thing. Instead he tried to see into the way things actually are, no matter how scorching that vision may be.

His first great insight is that values—things like truth, goodness and the American way—are not absolute. They are not fixed, written in stone somewhere, unchanging; instead they mean different things in different places and at different times. This may not seem like a very profound insight—we all know, for instance, that in Muslim countries eating pork is bad, whereas in America (to quote a highway sign I once saw) "*Bacon is Good.*" But Nietzsche understood that this "relativism"—the fact that values are not absolute things but relative to other things—goes much deeper than this. It runs right through the fabric of existence.

In his book *The Genealogy of Morals* for instance he examines the terms "good" and "evil," things that many people have taken to be fixed and absolute terms. We think we know what they mean: "good" means not hurting people, or following God's will: "evil" means harming others, or suggesting in certain Southern states that the actual value of pi is 3.14 instead of 3. But Nietzsche traces the history of these two concepts to uncover what these two words originally meant. "Good" originally meant "aristocratic" or "high born;" "evil" originally meant "peasant" or "low born." The values of human morality, Nietzsche says, are actually related not to the content of a person's character, but to his or her standing in society. The core of human interaction is not essential truth, or Divine fiat, but power. Peel back the veil of appearance, Nietzsche says, and you will discover not God, nor atoms, but instead "the will to power."

This is what is behind Nietzsche's most famous slogan: God is Dead, which first appears in *The Gay Science*, a book whose title may, but shouldn't, make us think of *Will and Grace*. "God is Dead" is probably Nietzsche's most misunderstood phrase, taken by many as nothing more than a personal statement of atheism. But "God is Dead" means much more than this. For a long time in human history God was not only a supernatural divinity who supposedly created the world; He was the benchmark of all values, the lynchpin of all Meaning and Purpose. Then science came along and challenged this idea; and then changes in culture eroded God's place. The death of God means, for Nietzsche, that human beings can no longer rely on some external thing to validate our lives or guarantee our values. It's a scary prospect, that will lead, Nietzsche thinks, to one of two things. On the one hand we might just give up, surrender to despair and nihilism. But on the other there's just the chance that we might move joyfully *beyond* God, beyond good and evil (the title of Nietzsche's 1886 book), and even beyond man. Children need parents to structure and validate their lives; man needed God to do the same thing; but the Superman needs nothing. S/he contains within him/herself all that it takes to live gloriously, creatively and holily.

NIETZSCHE'S SUPERMAN

What did Nietzsche mean by the term Superman?

The term crops up in a number of the great man's books, but most famously in *Thus Spake Zarathustra*. This is a strange and rather exhilarating book to read. Unlike almost all works of philosophy in the

Western tradition it is a novel, a fictional account of the title figure and his quest. He comes down from his lonely mountain-top and announces to the people in the towns lying next to the forest:

> I teach you the Superman. Man is something that should be overcome. What have you done to overcome him? All creatures have created something beyond themselves, and do you want to be the ebb of this great tide? What is the ape to men? A laughing-stock or a painful embarrassment. And just so shall man be to the Superman: a laughing-stock or a painful embarrassment.

In other words it is clear that the Superman is not a refined version of contemporary man, not (for instance) something you or I could become by getting our act in order, or going to the gym on a more regular basis.[1] The Superman is something radically different from, and superior to, man. The Superman is an evolutionary quantum leap.

It's a little misleading to suggest that Nietzsche sees the Superman as "better" than ordinary man, because to talk like that you need still to believe in concepts such as "better" and "worse" (which is to say, "good and "evil"). The Superman is beyond value judgment, beyond conventional morality, beyond the limitations, servility and petty resentment that hem about the lives of people like you or me. He embodies the "will to power" (the true nature of the cosmos) in a direct manner. He has overcome all of man's dangerous illusions, like the belief in a benevolent God, an afterlife, a universal moral code, a purpose to life, a meaning of our existence—none of that is true, or even relevant, to the Superman.

Perhaps you're saying: this doesn't sound like Siegel and Shuster's comic character. Bear with me.

Firstly, the fact that he has abandoned the old codes that define the "Good" does not mean that the Superman has become "Evil." Only people whose thinking is still stuck in that two-way binary of "good"/"evil" would assume so. Similarly, just because he has aban-

---

[1] I know, I know. I've been meaning to get to the gym more often. Or at all. My membership fee is just going to waste. It's just that, you know, other things have kind of gotten in the way lately. . . .

doned the corrosive habit of "pitying others" does not mean he has become cruel. On the contrary, the Superman is a profoundly *creative* figure; he lives joyfully, masterfully, untainted by the unhealthy psychological motivations that prompt cruelty in other beings. He is no more bothered by the fact that God doesn't exist than we are bothered by the fact that there's no such thing as Santa Claus. He is not concerned that there is no afterlife for his soul. He does not look anxiously into the future fearful of individual extinction, or regretfully into the past, wishing he could have done things differently. He lives continually, joyfully, affirmatively, in the present. He doesn't need external validation; he validates himself—he himself is the principle of validation, of the joyous energy of life.

He is, in the fullest sense, a hero.

What else can we say about the Superman? Or, to put it another way, what does the Superman say about *himself*?

- Like Siegel/Shuster's character, he is strong with a strength, both mental and physical, that surpasses human strength. Moreover, he is never afraid of a fight, although only in self-defense. "Entirely hateful and loathsome is he who will never defend himself, who swallows down poisonous spittle and evil looks, to too-patient man who puts up with everything." (*Zarathustra*, 209)
- But at the same time, again like Siegel/Shuster's character, he is self-effacing; he does not thrust himself into the public eye, or seek fame or glory. "My Ego is something that should be overcome: my Ego is to me the great contempt of man." (*Zarathustra*, 65)
- Indeed, he may even adopt a disguise, to hide his true nature and go amongst men as if he were nothing more than a man himself, like Clark Kent. "The noble man resolves not to make others ashamed. If I am compassionate I still do not want to be called compassionate. And I should prefer to cover my head and flee away before I am recognized: and thus I bid you do, my friends!" (*Zarathustra*, 112)
- At the same time, he will create a stir, blasting across the sky in bright colors like the Siegel/Shuster character. "One has to

speak with thunder and heavenly fireworks to feeble and dormant senses…this lightning is called *Superman*." (*Zarathustra*,
117, 45)

- He encounters evil (actions motivated by pettiness, resentment,
the desire to be cruel) without ever despairing of evildoers, always believing that they can overcome their own selves and become *more*. "I believe you capable of any evil: therefore I desire
of you the good." (*Zarathustra*, 141)

- He can fly. Nietzsche is oddly specific on this point, so much
so that commentators are thrown back on the explanation that
he must be being "metaphorical" or "ironic" or something else.
But several sections of *Thus Spake Zarathustra* stress the literal
fact of the Superman's ability in this regard. "O sky above me!"
he announces. "O pure, deep sky! You abyss of light…to cast
myself into your height—that is my depth" (*Zarathustra*, 184).
How is he able to fly? Nietzsche no more goes into specifics
than do the writers of the comics (of course, the original Siegel/
Shuster Superman could "leap tall buildings in a single bound"
but not fly; it was not until the early 1940s that this ability was
included in his portfolio of amazing abilities). In the chapter
of *Thus Spake Zarathustra* called "Of the Spirit of Gravity," Nietzsche seems to argue that only the Superman will be grave
enough to escape gravity. "To fly away—that is my nature now,"
he declares. "He who will teach men to fly will have moved all
boundary stones; all boundary stones will themselves fly into
the air with him, he will baptize the earth anew—as the weight-
less." (*Zarathustra*, 210)

SUPERMAN AS A SUPERMAN

There are obviously some points in which the comic-book Superman
is a different sort of creature to the philosopher's conception. Clearly Siegel and Shuster's Superman is not an evolutionary advance on
ordinary man; he is an alien from another planet. Equally clearly he
has not overcome the urge to pity; his softheartedness to ordinary
humans is, in a sense, his least superman-ish feature; his constant
meddling in ordinary human misfortune, the fact that he has fallen

in love with the annoyingly wet Lois Lane. He really should have fallen in love with Xena the Warrior Princess. Not that she would, necessarily, have been that interested in *him*.

But the point of this essay is not to list a series of parallels between Nietzsche's superman and the comic-book version. That is not, in the end, going to do more than suggest that Siegel and Shuster were interested in Nietzsche's thought (there's no evidence that they were, especially).

There's another sense in which the comic-book and cinema Superman phenomenon embodies Nietzsche's ideals—a more profound sense in which Superman is *Übermenschlichkeit*, "supermanly." Maybe I can best express it as a parable, somewhat in the style of *Thus Spake Zarathustra*. Although only somewhat. A small somewhat.

In the nineteenth-century there was a dominant mode of storytelling. It was called *The Novel*. As the century wore on, a series of great writers refined and polished this medium—Dickens, Flaubert, George Eliot, Tolstoy, Henry James—until it was a thing of almost endless subtlety and sophistication. It painted human beings diligently, prudently, tracing the finest gradations of their psychological interaction.

Many people fell in love with this manner of storytelling. Throughout the twentieth century, certain people—such as Marcel Proust, James Joyce, Virginia Woolf—made novels that passed human life through a sieve of finer and finer mesh, producing works of a finer and finer sophistication and subtlety. And these people came to believe that storytelling should be a manly, and a womanly, business; and that these "novels" were the pinnacle of human art.

But they were wrong. Theirs was a dead end.

Instead of a manly, and womanly, art, a new form of storytelling had arisen; and it was a supermanly art.

This was *Comics*.

In place of prudence, it brought garishness. In place of fine-grained psychological realism it brought bold figures striving and contending, mastering and self-mastering. In place of the sand of over-analysis it brought the boulders of great clashes and staggering ideas. In place of the slavish following of character consistency and linear story development, it brought a glorious disregard for what had gone before in the story, a love of the intensity of *this week's offering* irrespective of how it fitted with the rest of the myth. In place of the universal grayness of the eye blurring over tiny black print on white pages it brought vivid colors and dynamic visuals.

Zarathustra told the people: "For today the petty people have become lord and master: they all preach submission and acquiescence and prudence and diligence and consideration and the long et cetera of petty virtues."

He exhorted them: "Overcome, you Higher Men, the petty virtues, the petty prudences, the sand-grain discretion, the ant-swarm inanity!" (*Zarathustra*, 298)

This is what is so strong and wonderful about comics: precisely the way that they overcome the petty prudences and the petty virtues of the contemporary novel. They smash, joyously, through that clogging silt of received wisdom about how stories can be told. They blast away the fine-grained mud, and the stories flow through in a strong, bright stream.

This is how Superman is a superman. Not that he was Siegel and Shuster's slavish translation of Nietzsche's ideas into comic-book form (for clearly he wasn't). But that he, and all the other Higher Men, and Higher Women, of the comics world, smashed the old pieties and old certainties of how Great Art is made. They overcame the stifling aesthetic certainties and made something new.

Something *Über*, in fact.

REFERENCES

Nietzsche, Friedrich Wilhelm. *Beyond Good and Evil: prelude to a philosophy of the future.* Trans. Helen Zimmern. New York: The MacMillan Company, 1907 (1886).

————. *The Birth of Tragedy.* Trans. Douglas Smith. New York: Oxford University Press, 2000 (1872).

————. *Ecce Homo.* Ed, Trans. Walter Kaufmann. New York: Vintage Books, 1967 (1888).

————. *The Gay Science: with a prelude in rhymes and an appendix of songs.* Ed. Bernard Williams; Trans. Josefine Nauckhoff. New York: Cambridge University Press, 2001 (1882).

————. *Human, All Too Human: A Book for Free Spirits.* Ed, Trans. R.J. Hollingdale. New York: Cambridge University Press, 1996 (1878).

————. *The Genealogy of Morals.* Gargen City, New York: Doubleday Anchor Books, 1956 (1887).

————. *Thus Spake Zarathustra.* Trans. Thomas Common. New York: Boni and Liveright, Inc., 1917.

Siegel, Jerry (w) and Joe Shuster (p, i). *Action Comics* No. 1. National Comics Publications (DC Comics): June 1938.

ADAM ROBERTS was born in 1965. He has a day job as professor of nineteenth-century literature at the University of London and has published a variety of academic criticism; he also writes science fiction novels and parodies. He is married with a young daughter and lives just west of London, UK.

John G. Hemry

THE MIRROR OF GILGAMESH:

THE FOE SUPERMAN FEARS THE MOST AND THE ALLY HE CAN'T DO WITHOUT

YOU'RE SUPERMAN.

Think about that. Think about being the biggest dog among all the superhero big dogs. Maybe not quite the strongest, but incredibly strong. Almost impossible to hurt or kill, and possessing assorted extra powers that you can roll out like a super Swiss Army knife when the need arises. Need heat vision? Got it. Need to see through things? Got it. Need to fly? Got it.

Maybe you're not unbeatable. There are a few vulnerabilities; take that pain-in-the-neck Kryptonite, for instance. And supervillains keep coming up with new ways to knock you down.

But you always get up again. You always win. You never lose.

Most importantly, though, you wake up every morning knowing you can do anything you want to do.

What are you afraid of? More to the point, who are you afraid of? Not just worried about. Not just some supervillain you can rout again like you've done a dozen times already. Who scares you? Who can really endanger you and everything you care about? Is there anybody like that?

And, if you're that super in every sense of the word, who do you need? Do you need anybody? Friends are nice. Allies are nice. But do you really need any of them? Superman doesn't have a sidekick, after all.

It's true that Superman isn't impossible to kill and isn't impossible to defeat, but he's as close as anyone mortal comes to either of those things. We average people may spend our lives worrying about accidents or blows of fate, but Superman can walk down any street with his eyes closed while stray bullets and hurtling cars bounce off of him, and if his super-senses detect danger to a friend he can be there in the blink of an eye.

Superman's exact vulnerabilities vary depending upon which decade's worth of writing you happen to be looking at, but as a rule, anything that threatens Superman other than Kryptonite falls into the Star Trek techno-babble realm. *"Captain, if we modulate the frequencies of the shields and reverse the polarity of the main sensor array it'll interact with Superman's alien DNA just like the rays of a red sun, thereby rendering him helpless!"* That storyline might generate some nice graphics, but why not save us all a lot of time and just admit right off the bat that Superman is going to kick your butt?

Because at the end of the day, or at least that day's episode, Superman is still going to be flying high in defense of truth, justice and whichever way happens to be politically correct at the moment. That happens to be important, and a key to the foe Superman fears the most, because Superman isn't just a mercenary or a morally ambiguous character. He believes in things like truth and justice even when the humans he's defending seem to have forgotten what those ideals mean. He gets up in the morning ready and willing to do what's right, even though he knows that the next day he's almost certainly going to have to do it again, because humans and supervillains are notoriously slow learners.

One of the most impressive things about Superman, who could do anything and get away with it, is that he has a stronger moral code than the average person who has to fear retribution. He does the right thing because he wants to do the right thing. That, and because he's afraid of someone who could ruin everything he stands for.

Does that sound ridiculous? Given the innumerable times that Luthor has lost and Brainiac has bombed, how could Superman really fear anybody? How could anyone make him wake up in the middle of the night, heart pounding under those super-pecs, sweating and staring at the darkness? Who could possibly frighten Superman with the potential to destroy all that Superman believes in?

One guy. The guy Superman sees every time he looks in the mirror.

That's the one person who couldn't be stopped, because Superman can't be stopped. If Superman loses it, if he lets his immense powers corrupt him, if he gets tired of tolerating the fallibility and the failures of the humans he keeps fighting for day in and day out, then he and he alone could shatter the heroic image of Superman, smashing all that Superman holds dear. He and he alone would become his own ultimate foe.

Imagine being powerful enough to do anything, and not doing it. Every single minute of every single day of your life.

Imagine seeing injustice and pain and suffering that could be stopped if only you didn't have to worry about all the laws and treaties and rules that humanity binds itself with in the hope of avoiding even greater suffering.

When you could be ruler of the world, instead. Sure, you'd be a feared dictator instead of a beloved hero, but you'd clean things up. Heads would roll at the flick of your little finger (literally) if someone tried to start a war or build a dam using flawed materials or preach hatred or didn't do what you told them to do for their own good . . .

Although, since even you couldn't be everywhere at once and stop every bad thing from happening, there'd still be problems. Only now they'd be your fault, because you're in charge.

And eventually you'd die, and instead of mourning the loss of its protector, the human race would celebrate its liberation.

Maybe if you just did it a little. Maybe just once. For the best of reasons. Because you could. You're Superman. And it's for the best, the very best, of causes. No one would know. And you wouldn't do it again. Just because you did it once doesn't mean you'd do it again, right?

That's the little voice inside Superman's head that makes him wake up in a cold sweat at night, wondering if someday he'll listen to it.

Because if he does, who can stop him? There's nobody who can keep Superman honest but Superman himself.

That's something nobody else has to live with. Everyone else knows that if they do something wrong, there's someone or something more powerful that can bring them to account. Everyone else knows that if they lose it and start hurting those they love, someone can come in and stop them. Those things help set the world's boundaries for the rest of us, defining what we do and offering a last-ditch reassurance that, even if all is lost, the amount of damage we can do is limited.

Unfortunately for Superman's peace of mind, the temptation to do something he shouldn't by his moral code is never-ending, and the slippery slope is always there. Just a little abuse of his powers, just a tiny misuse of his awesome abilities, couldn't possibly hurt, could it? But it could. Consider the example of an abuse that has probably crossed the mind of almost every boy who's ever read a Superman story. You're a guy. You've got X-ray vision. There are a lot of girls out there. Who could possibly know if you did a little...skin research?

But if you did, what if somehow you let it slip that you'd done that? It could happen easily. Because Superman is indeed a man under all his invulnerable skin, which means he says and does things he doesn't mean to on occasion, and sometimes he even says things that are really dumb when he's trying to make small talk or be romantic with a lady he likes. He knows if the world ever finds out he scoped out a woman, even once, then it'll never trust him again. Lois Lane will spend the rest of her life in lead-lined underwear. And he'll be Supercreep, the jerk who makes every girl nervous and angry, and every boyfriend/husband/father just plain mad.

He has to be perfect. The only way to avoid being caught in any abuse of his powers is never to abuse them, because even the tiniest misuse will prove to the world that Superman, like the rest of us, is fallible to the temptations of power.

It's not fair to hold Superman to that standard, perhaps. After all, the average person doesn't get branded a liar in all things just because he or she gets caught in a little falsehood. But then again, the average person doesn't have the power to rule the world or do anything he or she desires. Superman isn't just awesome in the sense of astounding, but also awesome in the sense of frightening. Even his best friends must sometimes think, *He could squash me right now just by tightening his grip a little bit. He could do it by accident or on purpose if for some reason he snapped.*

Think how most people feel when they see police officers. Police officers are intimidating. They're supposed to be intimidating. That's why they like those mirrored sunglasses that make people think of *Cool Hand Luke* even if they've never seen *Cool Hand Luke*. Even if you've never done anything wrong, even if you're the only person in the United States who's actually driving the speed limit on a highway (there's got to be somebody doing that), when you see a police officer you can't help checking your conscience and hoping there isn't something wrong that's going to get you pulled over.

How would you feel if you're cruising down the street and see Superman staring at you?

That'd be so cool, and so frightening. Does he know you shoplifted a candy bar when you were seven years old? Does he know you drove home once after way too many drinks? Can he tell? Is there something in your wallet that'll make him think you stole something?

Great power brings great burdens. That's been said many times before. But the cruel corollary in the case of Superman is that his great powers permit not even the smallest failures in handling those responsibilities. Always haunting him is the knowledge that if he gives in even once to the temptations that fill his world, it would serve to justify the worst fears of typical humans: that Superman not only can break human laws with impunity, but does break them.

It's worth wondering how anyone can bear up under that sort of burden and stay sane. The answer lies in the person who Superman can't do without, the one ally who keeps Superman on an even keel in the face of everything he could do but can't. One person who holds Superman to a high moral standard and, indeed, makes him human. Because, left to himself, Superman isn't human. Not just in the sense of being from Krypton, but also in the sense of having "powers and abilities far beyond those of mortal men," as the old saying goes.

No, that all-important ally isn't Lois. If anything, Lois is more likely to drive Superman toward that dark side of himself that he fears.

That's not Lois' fault. It's because the mutual attraction between Lois and Superman is in some ways destined to be as happy a match as the one with which Romeo and Juliet ended up. Only Lois and Superman don't get a romantic death scene that ends the frustration of a relationship that can't ever work, given who they are. Instead, they just get to keep living with the knowledge that the person they want most in the world is the person they can't have, even though everybody else gets who they want. And Superman, the guy who keeps the world safe for all of those happy couples, can't share that happiness with the girl he wants to be his main squeeze. I'm sure there are times when he goes out and wrecks planets (uninhabited ones, of course) to work out the disappointment for a while.

The guy who keeps Superman sane, keeps Superman on the same emotional plane as the rest of us typical humans, is named Kent. Clark Kent.

You remember Clark. He's that annoying secondary character who's always having to find a place to hide so he can change into the real hero. His personality has varied some over the decades, but basically he's a wimp. And probably a nerd. Or a geek. You look at him and figure he's probably got a complete collection of vintage *Star Wars* figurines still in the original packaging.

In many television or movie portrayals of the role of Clark Kent, you have to work hard to imagine how incredibly stupid everybody has to be not to realize that the guy with glasses who's acting and looking and talking exactly like Superman wearing glasses is, indeed, Superman wearing glasses. Only Christopher Reeve got it perfectly. When his Superman became Kent he actually seemed to shrink. His mannerisms were different, his voice was different. His hair changed. You could see that this was a different guy.

That's extremely important. Because Clark *is* a different guy. He's not Superman, and Superman knows that. Think how carefully Superman has to control everything he says and does as Clark. It's no exaggeration to say that Clark has to literally be a second, separate personality that Superman turns on and off. Yet this separate personality also has to be fully aware of and working with the Superman personality at all times. That's quite an accomplishment in itself. The physical aspects of maintaining a secret identity (the apartment, the clothes, the job you don't really need) pale next to the mental strain of living as someone else a great part of the time. This isn't something the average mental health professional is likely to recommend.

Why does Superman bother with it? Why is it so worth the effort that he's kept it up?

Most discussions of the Clark Kent secret identity conclude that Superman doesn't really need it, that it's an anachronism or a badly justified story element to create false tension (how will Clark slip away from Lois in time to change into Superman and save the falling baby?). But that misses the real point. The secret identity is ridiculous as a device to protect Superman. He's not Bruce Wayne, worried about keeping gawkers and snipers away from stately Wayne Manor. He's Superman. He can live on the moon. Or in the Fortress of Solitude.

No, Superman needs Clark because Clark is human. Clark doesn't have super-powers. Clark moves among regular people, talks to them, shares things (good and bad) with them. Clark is Superman's connection to everyone else, the tie that lets a being with incredible powers empathize with all the weak, flawed human beings with whom he shares a world.

Clark is the only window Superman has into normal relationships with others. Other superheroes, even those that don't hold Superman in awe, don't count. Superman's closest friendship with another superhero is Batman, and how can a relationship with Batman be defined as normal by any reasonable criteria? But even other superheroes, even the ones who might fit the definition of being normal in the way they think, can't give Superman that same access to the thoughts and feelings of typical humans.

And if Superman had no window into those thoughts and feelings, if he could only look on from outside, if everyone he met treated him like Superman, what would happen to the way Superman felt and thought? Would he still care about humanity? Would he stop looking and acting human? What would he become?

Growing up in Smallville, Kansas, a mythical small town within a real state that embodies hazy concepts of old-fashioned moral rightness and certainty, the orphaned alien Kal-El became Clark Kent. (It's ironic that while big-city people celebrate the virtues of small towns, people in small towns are usually eager to move to big cities, just as Clark does. How you gonna keep 'em down on the farm after they've seen the Fortress of Solitude?)

Superman only understands humans because of that upbringing. He can't remember not having super-powers, can't recall not being as strong as he wanted to be, has never been too cold or too hot, never feared being bitten by a snake or a dog, never been burned, never been cut, never climbed a tree a little too high and wondered how he'd get back down. Never worried about being late somewhere. Never worried about forgetting his locker combination. But his friends went though that. He saw them hurt and scared and worried, and so understands as well as he can how those things must feel.

And thanks to Lana, he came as close as Superman ever could to learning how to have a typical girlfriend, even as he saw his friends in school also grow and develop relationships.

Clark is his human side, his vulnerable side, the reason he can identify with typical people when they need help. Cut Superman loose from that, eliminate Clark Kent from him, and Superman is adrift, his anchor gone, someone too powerful and too remote to grasp what frail and flawed humans are doing and why. Too powerful and remote to care, too powerful and remote to bother wasting time with our pitiful problems.

Who really loves Lois? Superman? Or Clark?

Who rushes to the rescue? Superman. Why does he come to the rescue? Clark.

It's worth wondering just how weak Clark actually is. Can you call a personality who can control the mightiest mortal being "weak"? Because Clark has to be at least as powerful a mental presence as Superman is if he is to keep Superman in check. In times of stress, Clark has to be stronger. There's two men of steel inhabiting Superman's brain, and when push comes to shove, when Superman has every reason to want to literally crush some low-life who has caused misery for others, it's Clark who stays his hand. How many wimps can keep Superman from throwing a punch?

Which finally brings us to the title of this tale. The most ancient myth known is that of Gilgamesh, thousands of years ago in ancient Sumer. Gilgamesh was a mighty warrior and king, two-thirds a god, so strong and powerful that he could do anything he wanted. And he did. Gilgamesh would stroll down the street grabbing things that caught his eye, usually women. This made everyone in his kingdom very unhappy, but Gilgamesh's might made it impossible to stop him.

His people eventually begged the gods for deliverance from Gilgamesh's abuses of his power, and the gods answered by creating Enkidu. Enkidu was as strong as Gilgamesh, and eventually turned into Gilgamesh's fast friend and tamed his excesses. Thanks to Enkidu, Gilgamesh became a protector of Sumer instead of an arrogant, self-absorbed abuser of those weaker than himself.

Thousands of years later, numerous writers have slowly forged Superman into an image close to that of Gilgamesh. The original Gilgamesh, the super-being lacking empathy or human morality, is what Superman fears becoming and what he could easily have been without Clark Kent. Clark is Enkidu, the only one powerful enough to function as Superman's compassionate link to the lesser beings around him. And Superman, of course, is the latter Gilgamesh. Hero and protector.

Graphic novels. Comics. Sumerian epics. The same stories, the same lessons. The same things to think about. What keeps godlike powers in check? The answer hasn't changed.

JOHN G. HEMRY also writes under the name Jack Campbell and is the author of eight novels, including the first and so far only legal thriller military sf series (aka JAG in space), including *A Just Determination, Burden of Proof, Rule of Evidence* and *Against All Enemies*). His latest space opera is *The Lost Fleet: Dauntless* (August 2006) under the Jack Campbell pen name. John was reading graphic novels when they were still comics, and fondly remembers the thrill of plunking down a whole quarter for a DC "eighty-page giant" comic, but also admires the current Teen Titans and Justice League animated series. (If there's a BenBella book on Hawkgirl or Raven, he wants to participate.) John is also the author of the Stark's War series and numerous short fiction stories, as well as non-fiction articles on topics like interstellar navigation. A retired U.S. Navy officer, he lives in Maryland with his incomparable wife "S" and their three children.

Paul Lytle

THE GOLDEN SHIELD:
IMAGE AS SUPERMAN'S GREATEST POWER

FORGET KRYPTONITE. That's not the way to defeat Superman. It's been tried countless times now, and it only makes him mad. After a moment of seeming defeat, he rages forward again to quash the villain. The way to really get him is through the Golden Shield.

No, I do not mean that he has a point of vulnerability on his back, right where the yellow variation of his symbol rests on his cape. I mean the symbol of Superman. I mean his image. His popularity is his greatest power—greater than his ability to fly, his super-strength or his heat vision. And his image is his most tenuous power, for it is one he cannot supplement with another. If Superman's strength fails, he will find another way to fight. If his image fails, he is defeated, at least for a time.

Who is this man, you may be thinking, to declare that Superman could be so easily defeated? Well, I never said "easily." After all, there have been numerous attacks on Superman's character, and since he's still around, we can assume that all of them have ultimately failed. I only suggest that it can be done. But first we must get rid of the notion that it is Superman's powers that make him unstoppable.

ARE SUPERMAN'S POWERS REALLY SO SUPER?

Well, we know that Superman is not really unstoppable. He can, at least, be stopped for a time. The epic *Death of Superman* saga taught us that lesson very well. Doomsday seemingly killed Superman (thus the title of the story-arc). We also know from his return that it was only his exposure to sunlight, the true source of his power, which brought him back. We can infer, then, that had Superman been permanently buried, he would have forever remained in that limbo between life and death.

If that's not close enough to death for us, we can turn to *The Kingdom*, where a new villain, Gog, literally killed Superman hundreds of times. It was only through time travel that Superman survived.

It would be difficult, to say the least, to reproduce either victory of these villains.

But even Superman's powers themselves are not as great as we may think. Those who are not as learned in comic-book lore as others probably think of Superman as the strongest of the heroes. This is not the case. For example, the Martian Manhunter's powers exceed Superman's. While J'onn J'onzz has every power Superman possesses, he also has the added advantage of telepathy and shape-shifting abilities. It is true that his weakness—fire—makes him a touch more vulnerable than Superman, whose weaknesses (Kryptonite and magic) are far rarer, but if anything the greater weakness only evens their general battle prowess.

Meanwhile, Captain Marvel has matched Superman several times, and has also defeated him on more than one occasion. He, too, can at least equal Superman's powers, but since his own powers are magic-based, Superman has a difficult time fighting against him.

We may forget that even Bruce Wayne, a mere human with no superpowers whatsoever, has battled Superman in equally epic fights. Batman reveals to us another of Superman's weaknesses—he has almost no tactical skill at all. When the two spar, Superman, preferring the forward charge, typically runs directly toward Batman, while the Dark Knight, as always, has come well prepared for the fight. In the Frank Miller masterpiece *The Dark Knight Returns*, Batman, using superior tactics and timing, defeated Superman rather soundly. True, he used devices, traps and help from friends—but Superman never considered that Batman, the greatest tactician of them all, would bring any of that to a fight. In other words, Superman didn't know his enemy. He thought he would win with brute strength alone, but he could not.

In the sequel, *The Dark Knight Strikes Again*, Batman beat him a second time, almost in the same manner. This time, Bruce Wayne's commentary on the fight revealed the problem exactly: "You've never been much in the smarts department. And when you're pushing sixty—smarts count" (Miller Vol.1, 76).

It is clear that not only are Superman's powers not unique—they are fallible. It is only his great strength, once again rare but not unique, that brings him out of these sorts of fights alive.

SO WHAT'S SO GREAT ABOUT SUPERMAN, THEN?

All of this must leave us wondering: Why is Superman so popular? What sets him apart from the rest of the heroes? If his powers are not unique, and he is not terribly bright, then why do we love him so much? The answer is simple: It's because of what he stands for. The Golden Shield is as important in the DC Universe as Captain America's own shield is to the Marvel Universe. And that symbol is not only important in the creation of Superman, but in the whole Justice League.

Consider what happens to other superheroes when Superman is not around. His "death" must be our first example, since it is the most obvious.

Four Supermen took Superman's place after his death. Of the four, only one, the Man of Steel, did not have powers at least comparable to Superman's. It is true that the goals of these four were not the same ones that Superman holds, but the fact remains that Metropolis, for a time, was protected with at least three times the strength that Superman boasts alone. But can we say that the city was correspondingly safer? No.

This was partially the fault of the Supermen themselves. Again, they were not all interested in justice, and so some of their adventures went awry. But we cannot say that all of their efforts were futile or misguided. The underbelly of Metropolis rose up in this time to take advantage of Superman's absence, and each of the four Super-men spent a great deal of time fighting against these criminals. What was the change that attracted the criminal element? Superman was dead. It didn't matter that there were now *four* Supermen. The mere image of Superman held the forces of evil back even more than his actions.

Following his "death," Superman was only absent for a relatively short time. What would happen if he had been gone for much longer? Say, a decade?

We can find the answer in *Kingdom Come*, where master writer Mark Waid and legendary artist Alex Ross teamed up to show us a harrowing vision of the future of the DC Universe. At first, all we knew was that Superman was retired, and had been for ten years following some terrible event.

Metahumans, wielding many of the same awe-inspiring powers of traditional superheroes, were terrorizing the world with their petty battles between each other. One of these battles, in fact, led to the destruction of Kansas. Yes, the whole state. Metahumans were mis-trusted and maligned, and the "classic" heroes (those we know, such as Green Lantern and Batman) had either completely withdrawn, like Superman, or adapted themselves to a darker world. Those who remained, such as Batman and the Flash, were subjected to distrust, as well, but they acted for good despite the public's perception. This was not new territory for Batman, and Flash had drifted so far into the Speed Force that he probably didn't even know what was going on. (In fact, *The Kingdom*, Mark Waid's sequel to *Kingdom Come*, de-voted a full issue to exploring the fading humanity in the Flash.)

Superheroes in *Kingdom Come*, as a whole, were splintered and lost. Without leadership, they were causing more harm than good. What was left on the Earth was death and destruction.

But then Superman returned. Many of the exiled heroes returned at once, and Superman steadily recruited the troublemakers into a new Justice League. What is interesting is that it didn't seem that dif-ficult. The whole book could have been about that quest to make the metahumans into heroes again, but it was not. Waid was insightful there, and his understanding of Superman's natural charisma shifts the focus of the story elsewhere.

Readers should take special note of the effect Superman had on people in this volume. At one point, he walked into a bar filled with young metahumans who had been making life difficult for regular people. Instead of fighting them, he invited them into the League. His speech took merely four frames. The following frame was filled with deafening silence, and then the reaction came. One metahuman said, "I feel like I was just asked to become the thirteenth disciple!" (Waid 87). The other statements were similar. Green Arrow then entered to sway some of them back to their old activities, but Superman's mere presence was too much for him to completely overcome.

It was not Superman's brute strength that accomplished this feat. It was not his x-ray vision. It was not his ability to fly. Most of the people in that room had those abilities. Superman saved the day because he possessed strength of a different sort—the power of his image. *That* is the Golden Shield that makes him so ultimately invincible.

We can see the strength of Superman's influence best when we look at where he is not present. In *Kingdom Come* the ten-year absence told us a great deal about his importance. But if ten years was revealing, a world portrayed utterly without Superman made things perfectly clear. Alan Davis showed us this world in *The Nail*. The premise of the story was simple. One night, as they were getting ready to go to town, the Kents found a nail in a tire of their truck. Instead of fixing the flat, they simply postponed their trip. That happened to be the night that young Kal-El fell from space. Superman never was.

Keep in mind, no other hero was missing. The Justice League still boasted both the Green Lantern and Martian Manhunter in its membership. With that sort of strength, the absence of Superman should not have made the League considerably weaker. Batman was there, too, ensuring that the League lost none of its tactical and investigative strength. There really should not have been much of a difference.

But there was. Metahumans were so mistrusted and feared that the ordinary citizens elected Lex Luthor mayor of New York on the platform that metahumans should be completely outlawed. Metahumans still fought for the people, but against the will of the people. They had become more like the X-Men, Spider-Man or the Doom

Patrol. The comparison is especially apt as these other groups or individuals were mistrusted because they did not have such a symbol as Superman. While Wolverine is a really cool character, he does not inspire trust and hope. Neither does Spider-Man, who is only slightly less mysterious than Batman.

Here's the truth of it: The members of the Justice League are trustworthy because Superman vouches for them.

Save Wonder Woman, the Justice League is made up of mysterious and vague characters. Even with Superman's support Batman is not really trusted. Green Lantern literally has alien powers, which is always a touch disconcerting. Martian Manhunter *is* an alien. Aquaman is, in the words of the Atom in *The Nail*, "a target for jokes by claiming to be sovereign of the seven seas" (Davis 15). It's true, of course, but it is silly at the same time.

Superman seemingly has nothing to hide. He always stands up for right, and he is always in the public eye. He is an alien, but not noticeably so (image is what is important, after all), and his victories are clear-cut enough that they can be admired. Also consider his suit. No one else has a uniform that so clearly states that he is a good guy. In fact, it was Clark Kent's expressed goal to make the suit a symbol. In *Superman: Birthright*, he rejected the idea of a mask by saying, "If I want people to trust me, they'll have to be able to see my face" (Waid 82). Already trust was an issue, and he had not even begun. He was not content to simply protect. He also wanted to be a symbol for the people.

When he saves someone, that person feels special and becomes a loyal fan. Superman has an overwhelming charisma. He can speak for four panels and you feel like you saw a god.

But he's not a god. And that dichotomy will bring him trouble.

ENOUGH OF THIS! HOW DO WE BEAT HIM ALREADY?

It is interesting that a preacher called him a god in *Kingdom Come*. A preacher, after all, should know better. But on more than one occasion, people have begun worshipping Superman. It didn't help that he seemingly rose from the dead. Superman has an image that he cannot possibly maintain indefinitely.

And when it crashes down, Superman is defeated every time. At least for a while.

In *The Kingdom*, Gog was created when someone who worshipped Superman learned the truth about him. Superman is great, truly, but he is not what this man made him. The disappointment caused Gog to break down. A little insanity combined with a lot of power is dangerous.

Let's return to *Kingdom Come*. What was it that caused Superman to retire for ten years? A defeat in battle? Another "death?" No. If you have been paying attention, you know exactly what it was. It was the destruction of his image.

Lois Lane was killed by the Joker, and Magog, one of the new "heroes," killed Joker for the crime. Superman, predictably, took Magog to jail for murder. But Metropolis had a new hero, someone who had finally ended the reign of terror that the Joker had brought upon the world. Magog was acquitted and Superman left, having been replaced, not in power, but in the eyes of the people. He was no longer trusted.

Magog did not understand the proper constraints of violence, though, and it was he who destroyed Kansas. Superman was too late to save the day, and he withdrew completely for a decade. None of it was directly his fault, but his failure to stop it proved that he could not live up to his image.

Luthor got a whiff of this sort of idea in the first story arc of *Superman/Batman*, though his plot was too desperate to work. Luthor was drifting into madness there, and he accepted the battle far too soon. A massive asteroid was heading toward Earth, apparently from Krypton. Luthor, then President of the United States, used the occasion to try to declare Superman a public enemy, as though our hero was bringing the destruction himself. No, the cause was too little there. Luthor acted too soon, and the charge did not stick. To defeat Superman, you must have a true cause, for what will make Superman withdraw will be his guilt, spurred by public opinion.

In *Birthright*, Luthor's plan was a little better. When Superman arrived, Luthor immediately challenged his appearance as a human. Then, just as Superman's popularity was slipping, Luthor constructed an "alien" armada to attack Earth. These soldiers and ships were, of course, wearing the symbol of Superman. Luthor used the Golden Shield against him. Nicely done.

The only problem with this plan was that it was too easy for Superman to prove his loyalties. He simply fought the invaders. Had Luthor found a way to keep Superman from the battle (he did have Kryptonite at the time), it would have worked. Still, Superman did not act immediately, but twice contacted his mother (Martha Kent, not Lara) for inspiration. That approach failed, and he left the *Daily Planet*, even after Lois Lane tried to convince him to remain. It was really only the misuse of his people's symbol that caused Kent to once again don the cape of Superman and resume the fight.

Luthor had an even better, and more successful, plan in the fourth season of television's *Justice League Unlimited*. He began with the systematic weakening of Superman's image through small embarrassments. He made Superman think that he was doing evil so that Superman (again with no concept of battle tactics) publicly accused him, only to be publicly proven wrong. Once these small defeats sufficiently unnerved the Justice League, Luthor hacked into the computers at the League's satellite, the Watchtower, and used its binary fusion generator against Earth. Even though the Justice League helped in the aftermath, its reputation was rather soiled at that point.

Again, what happened next should be obvious by now. Superman did not really need public opinion behind him, but psychologically he was paralyzed without it. He suggested that the founding members of the League surrender themselves to authorities until their innocence was proven. Only Batman (of course) refused to go along, calling it "the single dumbest plan [he'd] ever heard" ("Panic in the Sky," 4–11). In a slightly more mature response, he told Superman, "If you're feeling guilty, clear your own name, don't stand on the sidelines waiting for someone else to do it" ("Panic in the Sky," 4–11).

Luthor's plan was almost perfect, failing only because of two factors. First was Batman, naturally. But Batman alone could not have saved the others, except that Luthor backstabbed some of his partners in this endeavor. They, in turn, backstabbed him by exonerating and freeing Superman. Luthor got too greedy, and it destroyed him.

CAN THIS KNOWLEDGE BE USED?

All of this theorizing is fun, but what would it look like if applied to Superman's world? This is the fun part, where I get to play comic-book creator, because I would like to put forth a plot from a fictitious Superman comic that would use the elements from this discussion.

First, a local television news program in Metropolis hires a new producer, whose job is to create a dramatic increase in slumping ratings. His plan to do so is to shock the public, and the easiest way to do that is to add an element of controversy to the Superman story. Superman soon has another major battle, but this news station's coverage is just slightly different than everyone else's: They twist the story to focus more on the damage Superman has caused in his battle rather than his victory over evil.

Clark Kent is, of course, appalled, but the approach works, and soon the city begins to wonder how much it is costing them to have Superman around. The new producer has the answer, carefully researched—billions, primarily the result of the battle against Doomsday.

This trend continues as Superman fights additional foes, and soon the other stations are following the new approach. Eventually, the pressure even reaches the *Daily Planet*, and it must alter the way it has been covering Superman. We need not go with our first instinct to put Kent himself on this story, since his absolute morality would not allow it, but even having a coworker do it will be bad enough for him.

Some politicians suggest suing Superman himself for reparations, but this movement does not get far. Though public support is still behind him, the opposition is louder than his supporters, causing Superman to curb his crime-fighting activities.

The news stories change now. Where is Superman? Metropolis is being overrun, and it no longer has a protector. Villains from all over the country hear the stories and flock to the city, knowing that the police alone cannot stop them. Other heroes come to fill the void, but there are too many villains, and Batman himself is captured.

Well, now we must bring Supes back, of course. It is fun to think of ways to defeat Superman, but it would not be right to have such defeats be permanent. After all, we have next month's issue to fill. Seeing what has happened to his city and his friends, and with encouragement from Lois, Superman puts public opinion aside in one last epic melee between the villains and the heroes. Superman is so obviously in control that the public cannot help but realize his true worth. He rescues Batman, and the city's politicians publicly thank Superman for his help.

CONCLUSIONS

It is always people who drive Superman away, but it is also people who bring him back. He cares too greatly for Lois, his friends and the citizens of his adopted planet to allow them to suffer. At the end of *Birthright*, Lois contemplated Superman's symbol, saying, "It stands for courage. It stands for hope. It stands for Superman" (Waid 285).

Strange that she said "courage," especially after all the evidence we have just seen. It seems that Superman is always running.

But we should not be misled completely in one direction. We cannot doubt that Superman is courageous. He never hesitates when facing death to help others—he only hesitates when he believes that those people he is helping do not desire his help. He does not want to become one of those dark anti-heroes who are hated by everyone.

Perhaps he is simply smarter than Batman gives him credit for. Maybe he knows what an advantage his image is, that losing it means he could no longer do his job effectively. Maybe he knows that turning himself in when he appears to be a bad guy ensures that he will be able to fight tomorrow.

Perhaps it is simply that he believes in Democracy so much that he will step aside when necessary.

Thankfully, we need not worry too much. No retirement will be permanent for Superman, just as no death will be. He is, to borrow a phrase from the title of another Superman volume, for all seasons.

REFERENCES

Davis, Alan, and Mark Farmer. *Justice League of America: The Nail*. New York: DC Comics, 1998.

Jurgens, Dan, et al. *The Death of Superman*. New York: DC Comics, 1993.

————. *The Return of Superman*. New York: DC Comics, 1993.

————. *World Without a Superman*. New York: DC Comics, 1993.

Loeb, Jeph (w), and Ed McGuinness (p, i). "Public Enemies." *Superman/Batman*. Vol. 1. New York: DC Comics, June 2004.

Miller, Frank. *The Dark Knight Returns*. New York: Warner, 1986.

————. *The Dark Knight Strikes Again*. 3 vols. New York: DC Comics, 2001–02.

"Panic in the Sky." *Justice League Unlimited*. Episode 76, Dir. Dan Riba. Cartoon Network, 9 July 2005.

Waid, Mark, and Alex Ross. *Kingdom Come*. New York: DC Comics, 1997.

————. and Leinil Francis Yu. *Superman: Birthright*. New York: DC Comics, 2004.

PAUL LYTLE is an author and musician living on the southwest side of Houston, Texas, with his wife, Anastasia. He earned a Bachelor of Arts from Houston Baptist University in English and political science with a specialization in creative writing, and is currently working towards a Master of Liberal Arts degree. He is an editor and writer for the bi-monthly webzine Primum Mobile and is amassing quite a collection of comic books and gently used paperbacks. More of his writings, as well as news and other projects, can be found at www.paullytle.com.

Evelyn Vaughn

SUPERMAN BY MOONLIGHT:
CAN CLARK AND LOIS BREAK THE CURSE?

ASTER, MORE POWERFUL, able to leap... that Superman, aka Clark Kent, is an impressive guy. His character is such that he's been able to transcend mediums from comic book to TV and incarnations from Clayton "Bud" Collyer (of the 1940s radio show) to Brandon Routh (of the 2006 *Superman Returns*). But through all that, there's been one constant even Superman—especially on television—has trouble defeating.

Nope, not Lex Luthor.

No, not even Kryptonite.

Superman, and the writers of his on-screen adventures, have had to overcome the dangers of his requited romance with Lois Lane.

You may be asking: Don't you mean his *unrequited* romance?

But I mean requited. Superman is a hero. If anyone deserves the girl, it's him. This is as it should be, like truth, justice and the American way. *Superman gets the girl.* But that brings up one glitch about happily ever afters, something that should not affect Superman's actions but certainly affects the ease of his writers and the enjoyment of his audience.

It's referred to on www.jumptheshark.com in two categories that supposedly signal the imminent death of a show: "They Did It" and "I Do." But for much longer, it's simply been called the "Moonlighting Curse."

THE WHAT CURSE?

First, a little TV history lesson. I promise to get back to Superman as quickly as possible.

Once upon a time in the mid 1980s, there was a wildly successful show called *Moonlighting*. It starred Cybill Shepherd and Bruce Willis as mismatched characters Maddie Hayes (a model) and David Addison (a P.I.), forced by sitcom circumstance to run a detective agency together, and the sexual tension was deliciously cut-with-a-knife thick.

See, the whole concept of exploiting will-they-or-won't-they suspense for TV viewership had previously been relegated more or less to the world of soap operas—even children's chapter plays ("Tune in tomorrow! Same time, same station") used danger, not love, for their hooks. Oh, romance certainly seeped into other types of shows, but it wasn't often played for big suspense. We watched Sheriff Andy Taylor's dating foibles. We didn't spend episode after episode wondering if he would ever win over Helen Crump.

Then the late 1970s and early 1980s saw the advent of hugely popular nighttime soaps like *Dallas* and *Dynasty*. Before you could ask, "Who Shot J.R?" primetime genres that used to avoid such blatant, serial hooks, like cop shows or sitcoms, began to invest in them. Heavily. Suddenly, instead of *Barney Miller*, we had *Hill Street Blues*. Instead of *Alice* we had *Cheers*.

And instead of married couples solving mysteries, like in *McMillan and Wife* or *Hart to Hart*, we got the greater suspense of mismatched pairings solving mysteries while flirting outrageously, like *Remington Steele, Scarecrow and Mrs. King*…and the crème de la crème, *Moonlighting*.

Unfortunately, all three of these shows died pretty miserable deaths at the point that "will they or won't they?" became "Yes, they did."

Now, I'm a romantic. I've claimed in the past, and stringently, that this is a fallacious causal analogy. Remington Steele and Laura Holt didn't hook up until the show had pretty much called it quits (drained, in part, by the emotional gymnastics the writers took to justify the characters' continued abstinence). Scarecrow secretly married Mrs. King one season from the last, but it's more likely that the subsequent drop in ratings came from star Kate Jackson's health problems, which kept Mrs. King-Scarecrow from appearing in most of the final-season episodes. And *Moonlighting*? Not long after Dave and Maddie's most excellent consummation, the actors refused to work together. Cybill Shepherd got pregnant—with twins. Suddenly what used to be a campy show about a mismatched couple solving mysteries became a show about a confused and pregnant woman who ran off to live with her parents, leaving the man who loved her pining and trying to solve mysteries, and resulting in far too many episodes featuring their goofy sidekicks, Agnes and Herbert.

Really. Agnes, the secretary, and Herbet, the accountant. Hand to God.

Call me crazy, but I'm thinking that had even more to do with the miserable death of *Moonlighting* than did Dave and Maddie's consummation (which, truly, was one incredibly satisfying episode). So really—should we call it a "Moonlighting Curse?" *Is* there even a "curse" on shows that allow their couple-with-chemistry to hook up?

Coincidentally, the show that finally forced me to believe that there might actually be something about this phenomenon was *Lois and Clark: The New Adventures of Superman*.

THE LOIS AND CLARK CURSE?

See? Like I promised, we're back to Superman—specifically his 1990s incarnation in the hunky form of Dean Cain, flirting with Teri Hatcher's Lois Lane while solving mysteries. *Lois and Clark* ran from 1993–1997, and it made enthusiastic, sometimes genius use of will-they-or-won't-they suspense, on two levels yet. One level was, "will they or won't they get together?" But just as gripping was, "will Lois or won't Lois learn Clark's secret?" Episode 2:18, "Tempus Fugitive"—in which sardonic villain Tempus revealed Clark's secret to Lois—was a particularly fun sleight of hand, giving the viewers all the satisfaction of the big reveal, only to then erase it from Lois' memory by means of an H. G. Wells time machine (hey, no one said it wasn't campy).

But here's the problem with deliberately dangling this kind of carrot in front of the viewers. You're building audience expectation, that's the problem. Sure, it adds easy suspense. When done well, it even adds a great deal of emotional depth, like with Ross and Rachel of *Friends*, or Doug and Carol of *ER*. But the problem that remains is this: *you can only tease the viewers for so long.* By starting a series on a will-they-or-won't-they note, you invite the audience to hope that they will. The better the chemistry, the more impatient we get.

But if the couple ends up together, what happens to all that great suspense?

It's a double-edged sword. Writers can't just take advantage of the inherent drama without taking a little responsibility as well. If there's no hope of Dr. Richard Kimble ever catching the one-armed man, we'll eventually give up on *The Fugitive*. If there's no hope of Mulder ever learning exactly what truth is out there, we'll tire of *The X-Files* (frankly, many of us did). And if there's no promise of an eventual happy ending for Clark Kent and Lois Lane, then why the hell should we emotionally invest ourselves in it, week after week, for all those episodes? There's a promise in that storyline, a promise the audience expects to eventually be kept.

Oh, you can be cynical if you want. It is true that real life doesn't always provide happy endings. But here's something else to consider: *Fiction is not real life.* That's why we talk about escapist fiction, and don't talk about escapist life. And frankly, it's easier to change the channels when things look hopeless for fictional characters than when things look hopeless for ourselves.

So for two seasons, *Lois and Clark* exploited their two will-they-won't-they themes with campy brilliance. But the show couldn't dangle that carrot forever, no matter how it tried. The cliffhanger at the end of season two was Clark's proposal (remember this: what the cliffhanger is about is what the show is about). Then season three became a study in desperate writing. Lois turned Clark down—but by mid-season they were planning their wedding. Clark accidentally married a clone of Lois. Lois got amnesia. Space villains showed up to complicate matters (one claiming Clark was already married to a Kryptonian). Clark got trapped in an alternate dimension.

This was all in one season, people. Instead of a slow build, we had whiplash.

Is it surprising that season four was *Lois and Clark's* last? And is there a chance that their slumping ratings were due as much to the desperate avoidance of season three as to the couple's eventual wedding (4:03, amusingly titled, "Swear to God, This Time We're Not Kidding")?

The answer probably lies somewhere in the middle. But the fate of *Lois and Clark* certainly illustrates the point that this romantic "curse" can be a problem for any version of Superman's story which doesn't keep his romance reined back to mere subplot. Maybe it's not a problem of Lex Luthor proportions (be he mad scientist or corporate mogul).

But it's a problem, all the same.

OF MYTHOS & MOVIES

Another problem—for new Superman writers, in any case—is that a great deal of Superman's mythos is canon. Tradition. This is also one of the more attractive things about him, for fans. Though Superman may be "fictional" (I feel like I'm killing fairies to even write that!) there are many unalterable truths about him. He's an alien from Planet Krypton. He was raised in Smallville, Kansas, by a childless couple, the Kents. He grows up to work as a reporter at the *Daily Planet* (once the *Daily Star*), in Metropolis. His only real disguise is his glasses. All this is as "true" as the fact that Santa Claus wears red. It makes Superman familiar, recognizable, a friend.

And another truth? The love of Superman's life, in many ways the reward for all of his heroism, is plucky "lady reporter" Lois Lane.

It's already established. A done deal. To blatantly contradict the canon is to break the audience's willing suspension of disbelief, and believe me, nobody wants to do that.

So thus established, how can our serialized Superman break the curse?

One way is, indeed, to keep the romance with Lois Lane firmly in subplot territory. That's how it was in the radio show, the 1950s TV show, the comic books and the current animated series. I wouldn't dare suggest that romance wasn't important in these venues. For as long as Clark Kent has been Superman, he's courted Lois Lane—and

I mean that literally, per the 1938 *Action Comics* No. 1, when Clark invited colleague Lois on a date. Even Lex Luthor didn't show up until two years later, in *Action Comics* No. 23! But neither do these aforementioned venues consistently play up the question of whether Clark will finally end up with Lois. They push his adventures more. Saving the world takes priority.

To our post-nighttime-soap-opera tastes, however, that's just foolishness. Viewers want to see the characters' personal lives entwined with their heroics. Saving the world is well and good, but we want emotions!

Another way might be to do one-shots, as in movies. By the end of 1978's *Superman: The Movie*, Superman and Lois' attraction is strong, but nothing has been resolved—and since the movie ends, the viewer can be as optimistic (or cynical) about their future as s/he likes.

But how often is a popular movie a one-shot? As soon as there's a sequel, much less a franchise, even movies run into the curse. Instead of slowly building on the romantic dance begun in the first movie, *Superman II* hurries to answer both "will they or won't they?" questions by the midpoint, as Lois figures out Clark's real identity and they sleep together. Midpoint means this is *not* a happy ending. The story immediately hunts for ways to escape what it just wrought. In this case, Clark must for some inexplicable reason give up his superpowers in order to be with a mortal. I know SF master Larry Niven did the whole "Man of Steel, Woman of Kleenex" theory, hypothesizing that sex with a full-strength Superman could prove fatal for any poor mortal, but I doubt that's what was going on with this movie.[1] The device struck me more as reflecting the creative fear that committed relationship = impotence. Clark Kent tries going mortal, but of course he immediately runs into a lot of mean bullies who make him look bad, and then the world needs him more, so he forfeits his chance of getting Lois, erasing her memory with a magic kiss.

By this logic, even Superman can't have it all.

Superman II was fairly popular, and the adventure elements were as fun as with the first. But it was hardly satisfying to the romantics among us, far less so than the aforementioned H.G. Wells device

---

[1] A reprint of Niven's piece appears in this volume. See Page 51.

of *Lois and Clark*, some years later, because the end of *Superman II* held far less promise that things might yet work out for these crazy kids—and rightly so. *Superman III* was abysmal, sending Lois on an extended vacation and focusing on Clark's relationship with high-school crush Lana Lang (coincidentally played by Annette O'Toole, who would later take the role of Clark's mother on the TV show *Smallville*). After that came the Clark-less *Supergirl*, and then *Superman IV: Quest for Peace*, which went back to hinting at a romance (Lois remembers!) but remains stuck in bittersweet impossibility.

Also, that one's just a bad movie.

AND THEN THERE'S RETCON

But just when things are looking grim for Superman's love life, we get the generally enjoyable TV series *Smallville*, which uses a newer and sneakier technique to subvert the so-called Moonlighting Curse.

It's a little trick called retcon, short for "retroactive continuity," in which a new work fills in details about or even rewrites the established history of a previous work. The extended prequel that is *Smallville* does just that. Its most notable addition is the supposition that Lex Luthor and Clark Kent were great friends in their youth. This goes against established canon...and yet there's always the chance that a huge dose of mutual amnesia will wipe all characters' memory of it. An even stronger argument for it is that it makes for good television. So we the audience go happily along with the change—and, in fact, enjoy the dramatic irony of knowing Lex will eventually become evil even before Lex himself seems to know.

Ah, the power of audience expectation.

In connection with Superman's romantic troubles, however, *Smallville* gives writers another "out" from the Moonlighting Curse—which, by the way, even producer Miles Millar has cited as the "kiss of death" for such shows. Yet I'm unsure even Millar is fully aware of the power given him by the retcon. Because by looking at Superman's past, instead of his future, a major change takes place.

Lois Lane isn't even a factor! Or at least she wasn't until four years into the series—but even then, Lois Lane isn't Clark's love interest. Lana Lang is.

Better yet, the Lana love doesn't contradict canon. She's been established as Clark Kent's high school crush since DC Comics gave us *Superboy*, in the 1950s. But I'm not sure even the creators of *Smallville* were aware of the power they'd tapped by fleshing out this former romantic interest of Clark's. When Millar complained about the Moonlighting Curse, he was referring to his concerns at ever getting Clark and Lana together. But even a consummated Clark/Lana relationship doesn't hold as much power as a consummated Clark/Lois relationship, and do you know why?

Because the viewers already know better.

It's the power of the canon. The audience knows that Lex will turn out evil, so even when we approve of him, that approval is poignant with the knowledge of what is to come. And the audience knows that Clark will eventually end up madly in love with reporter Lois Lane, so no matter what happens with Clark and Lana's relationship, we know not to count on a happily ever after.

Brilliant, isn't it?

The eventual introduction of Lois to *Smallville* in 2005 (as the cousin of Clark's best friend Chloe Sullivan), is an even better example of fun with dramatic irony. Because the viewers know that eventually Clark and Lois are supposed to be together, the fact that their young selves can barely stand each other is all the more entertaining. Of course, there are also fan theories out there that Chloe will eventually "become" the real Lois—Chloe's thus far the only reporter in the group, and has used her cousin's name before. But that's all speculation...which, again, shows the power of audience involvement.

And in the end, isn't this what the so-called Moonlighting Curse is really about?

HAPPILY EVER AFTER

Audience expectation may be a power as vast and unstable, and in some cases as deadly, as Kryptonite.

Love it or hate it, the Moonlighting Curse comes down to a quid pro quo. The audience is being asked to care. We are being asked to care so very much that we will continue to buy issues of the comic, tune in for the newest episode of the TV series, or show up at the box office for the latest movie release. We're being asked to commit time and energy we could be spending on a zillion other entertainments and pursuits.

This interest is not something the audience *owes* anybody. It is earned. If we are asked to buy into a romantic pairing established at the start of an extended story, we may well buy—but eventually we will demand satisfaction for what we gave. That satisfaction may come in two or three years, as with *Lois and Clark*. It may take fifty-two years, as was the case in the comic-verse (Clark and Lois officially married in DC Comics' 1996 "one-shot" called *Superman: The Wedding Album*. This time they weren't kidding). But however long it takes, we want our expectations fulfilled.

As for what happens after that? Some writers assume they must quickly break the couple up, in order to reestablish drama, but they should tread carefully. One of the things powering the will-they-or-won't-they suspense, be it for Clark Kent and Lois Lane or for any fictional couple, is the sense that these two characters are meant for each other. To break them up too easily (as happened with sad regularity on *Remington Steele*) contradicts that belief. There's always the old "kill off the current partner and start with a new one" trick, but again—way to encourage your audience to ever trust you again! Romantic separation-by-death didn't make the viewers of *Beauty and the Beast* (the TV show) happy. It's not likely to sit well with Superman's fans, either. A cable special on comic books referred to a recent plot twist in which Lois Lane dies in the World Trade Center attacks, but so far, I haven't found any confirmation of that—and I'm immensely relieved.

I like my fictions escapist. I like that the curse has proved a non-issue for the comic-verse version of Superman, happily living with his wife Lois Lane in a penthouse at 1938 Sullivan Lane in Metropolis, and I appreciate the nod to fans that went into the creation of that address. It's just one more reassurance that Superman takes care of the people who love him—in this case, I mean his audience.

But as for his on-screen incarnations?

Well it's not as if married couples haven't also had their adventures. The aforementioned *Hart to Hart* and *MacMillan and Wife* were popular, in their own time. Nick and Nora Charles of the old *Thin*

Man movies make a stellar example. Rob and Laura of *The Dick Van Dyke Show* were great fun together, and Gomez and Morticia of *The Addams Family* certainly kept their romance, er...alive. Or how about *I Love Lucy?*

> SUPERMAN: How long have you been married?
> RICKY RICARDO: Fifteen years.
> SUPERMAN: And they call *me* Superman?
> ("Lucy and Superman")

Clearly, Ricky and Lucy Ricardo's relationship didn't kill the adventure in *their* show, even if that adventure wasn't so much about archvillains or speeding bullets. In fact, it's highly likely that a romance, *if deftly handled*, can continue long after sex and even after marriage.

Is it easy to write? Probably not, though I suspect it helps if your costars continue to work together. But for almost every kiss of death related on www.jumptheshark.com, there has been a show that triumphed over it. Some shows have managed to introduce new characters who, instead of ruining a series, revitalized it—who remembers the original Star Trek series without second-season Chekov, or *Melrose Place* without Amanda? Arguably, *Buffy the Vampire Slayer* got on pretty well after the characters graduated from high school, even if *Beverly Hills 90210* did not. And as much as I usually hate character deaths, some shows have done brilliant things with them, such as the tragic loss of Mrs. Landingham on a pivotal episode of *West Wing*, or the merciful death of Mark Greene on *ER*.

If those show-killers could be transcended, why not the Moonlighting Curse? Perhaps it should simply be called the Moonlighting Challenge—or the Lois and Clark Challenge, considering.

I doubt it will take a writer with true super-powers. And if it does...?

I hear that Clark Kent fellow is pretty good with words.

REFERENCES

"I Do." *Jump the Shark* <http://www.jumptheshark.com>.

"Tempus Fugitive." *Lois and Clark: The New Adventures of Superman*. Episode 39, Dir. James Bagdonas. ABC, 26 Mar. 1995.

"Swear to God, This Time We're Not Kidding." *Lois and Clark: The New Adventures of Superman*. Episode 69, Dir. Michael Lange. ABC, 6 Oct. 1996.

Rita Award-winning author **EVELYN VAUGHN** has published fifteen romance and adventure novels (including *A.K.A. Goddess* and *Something Wicked*), and a dozen fantasy short stories in anthologies such as *Constellation of Cats, Vengeance Fantastic*, and *Familiars*. She also teaches creative writing for Tarrant County College, in Texas. When neither writing or teaching... oh, who are we kidding? She's almost always writing and teaching. Sometimes she slips in some TV-watching (being an addict) and quality time with her cat, Brindle, and her dog, Kermit. But that's usually to rest up from the writing. And the teaching.

She loves to talk about what she writes, whether that's attractive or not. Check out her Web site at www.evelynvaughn.com.

SPEEDING BULLETS AND CHANGING LANES

S TEEL IS A funny sort of metal. It may be impossibly strong, but it can also be inflexible, unchanging. And a man of steel must, ultimately, exhibit these shortcomings. In Superman's case, he changes no more than the basic principles of his adopted country. Though the character's pure, idealized consistency is reassuring in a world all too eager to redefine itself with each passing moment, Superman comics, TV shows and movies *have* changed: and in the process they've reflected our changing society. Yet how can one see this when Superman himself remains a constant? The answer comes from looking at another resident of Metropolis, a constant companion to the Last Son of Krypton. I'm speaking about the First Lady of comic books, Lois Lane, whose evolution illustrates the changing role of women in American society.

Lois first appeared, as did Superman, in the first issue of *Action Comics* (*Action Comics*, No. 1), written by Jerry Siegel and drawn by Joe Shuster. We first see her sitting behind a typewriter, hammering out a news story. Clark Kent approaches her timidly....

CLARK: W-What do you say to a—er—date tonight, Lois?
LOIS: I suppose I'll give you a break...for a change.

The next panel shows the two dancing in a nightclub, but their dance is cut short when a thug named Butch insists Lois dance with him. "Reluctantly, Kent adheres to his role of a weakling," the caption tells us, and Clark instructs Lois to dance with Butch. Lois refuses, slaps Butch across the face and storms out of the club, pausing only to tell Clark she's been avoiding him at the office because he's a coward. Butch and his men pile into their car, chase after Lois' cab, abduct her and drive off into the night.

The rest of the story is predictable but luridly thrilling, even after sixty-five years. Superman races after Butch's car, grabs hold of it and—in an image made legendary by that issue's cover—shakes the car like a box of cornflakes, spilling its occupants, Lois among them, onto a rocky dirt road. "You needn't be afraid of me," he tells her, as Lois cowers beneath him, one strap of her red evening gown now dangling provocatively over her shoulder. For the first time, Superman takes Lois in his arms, and flies her back to the city's outskirts.

Superhero comics are, despite their many virtues, often male power fantasies, and this first adventure is certainly no exception. Lois, for her part, is a core component of the fantasy, if not a stand-in for its very impetus. It's no secret that many men regard sexual power over women with at least as much import as physical power over other men. And few fictional characters embody this as well as Superman. So it's tempting to write Lois off as a mere token damsel, a prop, with no significance beyond that which the plot gives her. But consider the times in which she was created.

In 1938, America was experiencing, as it had through much of the 1930s, tumultuous change. The country had survived World War I, braved the Great Depression and begun bracing itself for a future that was—thanks to news reports of Hitler's campaign through Europe—uncertain at best. Comic books were ripe with potential, but had been created as a form of cheap escapist entertainment, like the comic strips that preceded them. *Action Comics*' forebears, strips like *Flash Gordon* and *Tarzan*, had typically featured leading ladies of the prop variety. That Siegel and Shuster would see fit to create a woman

who'd live life on her own terms, who would in fact settle for nothing less than a god, is nothing to be sneezed at. And to make Lois
a reporter, working in an industry overwhelmingly dominated by
men, was nothing short of remarkable.

Then again, there were a few precedents.

Joanne Siegel (Jerry Siegel's widow and the first model for Lois) revealed in Les Daniels' *Superman: The Complete History* that Siegel got
the inspiration for Lois from a film star named Glenda Farrell, who
had "played a girl reporter [Torchy Blane], very fast-talking, and she
always got the story" (Daniels 20). Warner Brothers billed Farrell, in a
series of films released throughout the '30s, as "the Lady Bloodhound
with a Nose for News." But there was real-life precedence, too. After
all, *New York World* investigative journalist Nellie Bly had pioneered
undercover reporting in the late nineteenth century with her exposé
on the women's lunatic asylum of Blackwell's Island. And muckraker
Ida M. Tarbell had exposed the crooked business practices of John D.
Rockefeller's Standard Oil Company in a classic series of articles for
McClure's in 1902. Still, such role models were, in general, scarce. To
the public of the '30s, the idea of a female investigative reporter most
likely remained novel when they encountered it again in movies—in
the character of Hildy Johnson, played by Rosalind Russell in director
Howard Hawks' 1940 screwball comedy *His Girl Friday*.

Hildy, like Lois, was a newspaper woman through whose veins
flowed not blood, but printer's ink. She was quick with the stories,
and quicker still with the put-downs. Like Lois, there was really
only one man she respected: her estranged husband and editor-in-
chief Walter Burns (played by Cary Grant). Though Hildy didn't pre-
date Lois, she may have inspired her first screen incarnation, just as
Hildy's look, with its '40s bob and pillbox hat, could have served as
the visual template—for the Lois of Max and Dave Fleischer's classic
series of Superman animated shorts.

The Fleischers gave us a Lois who was every bit as brazen as Siegel and Shuster's. In her first film appearance, 1941's *Superman*, she
speaks up when her editor instructs Clark to assist her in covering
the story of a mad scientist threatening Metropolis with his "Electro-
thanasia Ray." "But, chief," she says, "I'd like the chance to crack the

story on my own." As Lois' boss considers her request, she thanks him and darts out the door as Clark whimpers, "But, Lois. . . . ." In the next scene we see her don a flight suit and goggles, climb into the cockpit of a one-man plane and soar off to the scientist's laboratory. She eventually requires Superman's aid, but not before she's proven who has the greater guts and initiative.

The later Fleischer shorts would see Superman battle all manner of Nazi spies and saboteurs. World War II was on, and America's young men were heading in droves to Europe and the South Pacific. With so many vacant jobs to fill, the idea of a woman doing a man's work in almost any field grew less unusual, and Lois' personality remained intact through much of the 1940s. She was kinder to Clark, but still the tough-minded gal of 1938. Her persona was validated not only by a world at war, but by the portrayal of women in other media. The '30s and '40s were ripe with actors like Barbara Stanwyck and Lauren Bacall, and a new wave of cinema, "film noir," sprung up to accommodate their tough-as-nails screen images. Bitter and cynical to the point of nihilism, noir portrayed the dark fantasies of a generation grown weary from years of war and corruption. And when television rose to prominence in the early '50s, noir permeated its black-and-white screens, even when they broadcast the soaring image of Superman.

The first season of ABC TV's *The Adventures of Superman* (which debuted in September of 1952) was rich with the trappings of postwar noir. Gone were the mad scientists and supervillains of the comics and animated shorts, and in their place marched an endless procession of mobsters and hit men. The world of Metropolis, so full of color in the Fleischer cartoons, was now rendered in the moody black-and-white hues of such films as *Double Indemnity* and *Night and the City*. Superman found himself battling a grittier, more realistic criminal element, and his adventures demanded a suitable Lois.

Phyllis Coates played her throughout that first season. Coates' take on the character was quick to call Clark or any other man a fool, and she didn't seem all that interested in Superman. Oh, she smiled, and expressed gratitude whenever he rescued her and Jimmy Olsen from gangsters or the occasional collapsed mine shaft, but she always appeared more taken with her work. Efficient, short-tempered and strong-willed, Coates may have let out a scream or two, but she rarely cried. Her Lois could have almost been *too* self-sufficient. Many *The Adventures of Superman* fans prefer that doom-laden first season to what followed, but Coates is frequently overlooked in favor of her successor to the role.

Noel Neill had played Lois before she replaced Coates, who'd left after the first season to pursue other television work. She had starred opposite Kirk Alyn in the two Superman serials, 1948's *Superman* and 1950's *Atom Man vs. Superman*. A competent actress, Neill may have been a tad young to play the world-weary reporter in the serials, but by the time she essayed the role on TV, she'd matured into a suitably older Lois. At least upon first glance.

Neill's Lois was markedly different than Phyllis Coates'. Gone was Coates' self-assured fire, replaced with Neill's soft voice, wide-eyed innocence and inclination to swoon over the Man of Steel. The episodes that featured Neill had also changed from those of the first season, adapting a lighter, more fanciful touch, a decision on the part of DC (then National) Comics. Witness such episodes as the fourth season's "The Wedding of Superman," in which Lois imagined marrying Superman, only to shed tears upon realizing she was dreaming. It's difficult to imagine Coates' Lois breaking down in this manner.

A sort of infantilization was taking place, mirroring the perceived role of a woman in '50s society: one of homemaker, or wife and mother. It was a role defined largely by men returning home from war, anxious to start a new life and family. Lois still lived and worked in Metropolis, but she might as well have hung her pillbox hat in the 'burbs. To be fair, though, Neill was charismatic in her role, arguably more so than Coates. It was evident in the way she energized the show with her vulnerable-but-charming personality. Her portrayal shined brightest in Lois' relationship with Jack Larson's Jimmy Olsen. The two characters shared a kind of brother-sister dynamic, endearing Neill to the countless ten-year-old boys watching the show.

Neill stayed with *The Adventures of Superman* for the remainder of its six-year run, defining Lois, for better or for worse, to a generation of baby boomers.

While Neill's Lois had set herself the ultimate goal of marrying the Last Son of Krypton, the comic-book incarnation's motives were even more questionable. Mort Weisinger had stepped in as editor of the Superman titles upon returning home from the war. Under his supervision, Lois changed from a woman whose greatest concern was getting the story, to a "girl reporter" preoccupied with proving Clark and Superman were one and the same (and then, of course, marrying him). Weisinger also gave Lois her own comic book, with the unfortunate title *Superman's Girl Friend Lois Lane*, in which an endless series of imaginary tales took place, often detailing the courtship and/or marriage of Lois and Superman. As Ellsworth softened the tone of the TV show, so Weisinger lightened things in the comics and introduced other survivors from Krypton, among them Supergirl and her many super-pets. With so many newcomers flying around Metropolis, Lois' personality was stifled, and she became more of a prop. Sure, she had won her own comic, but only to find her glass ceiling replaced with one of lead through which not even Superman could peer.

Things finally began to change when Julius Schwartz replaced the retiring Weisinger as editor of the Superman comics in 1970. Schwartz's Clark found a new day job as a TV anchorman and saw a reduction in his by-then godlike powers. Lois made the switch with him, and, oddly enough, *ascended* in her power. She suddenly sported shorter hemlines and required less help from Superman.

Was it mere coincidence that women's lib was in full swing? The Pill was now commonly used, Gloria Steinem would soon found *Ms.* magazine and, in 1973, the Supreme Court would legalize abortion. The notion that a woman's place was in the home, supporting her husband, was under constant fire. The times? They really were a-changin'.

And so was Lois.

CLARK: My goodness, don't you ever let up?

LOIS: What for? I mean, I've seen how the other half lives. My sister, for instance. Three kids, two cats and one mortgage. I would go bananas in a week.

When Margot Kidder uttered those words in 1978's *Superman*, she could have been speaking for an entire generation of American women, including those who *were* going "bananas" raising their families. Kidder's was the first truly liberated Lois, and her world-weary cynicism and shoot-from-the-hip gutsiness was a perfect match for Christopher Reeve's bumbling Clark and idealistic, naïve Superman. Kidder gave Lois a personality large enough to fill a movie screen, a personality similar to those of the '30s and '40s film stars. She's endearingly flawed (smoking like a chimney, filling her news stories with sensationalism and retaining an inability to spell words such as "rapist"), yet highly professional (in the words of Perry White, she's a "better" reporter than Clark; and above all, she seeks the Pulitzer). She gets herself into as much trouble as her predecessors and still swoons over Superman, yet never puts her blind faith in him. When he first rescues her after she falls from a helicopter, her response is, "You've got me? Who's got you?" And after he, unbeknownst to her, brings her back from the dead at the film's end, she proffers, "That's the problem with men of steel. There's never one around when you want one." As for her sexual liberation, try to imagine Noel Neill's Lois asking George Reeves what color underwear she's wearing and the character's evolution becomes clear.

To a certain extent, the sequels to Kidder's first *Superman* film weaken her character. In *Superman II*, for example, she's obsessed with outing Clark as Superman, prompting him to reveal to her his secret identity. Lois then declares her love, and, for the first time in *any* medium, they consummate their relationship. The fact that the script demands Superman forever surrender his powers in order to do so may add plausibility, but it betrays a subtle misogyny, reminiscent of Delilah giving Samson a trim. *Superman II*'s conclusion sees Lois break down in near hysterics when she realizes she can't share Superman with the world; and his means of resolution, a "kiss of forgetfulness" (an ability fabricated for the film), can be politely described as patronizing.

Kidder's disagreements with the filmmakers resulted in her being all but written out of *Superman III*, and in the misconceived-on-all-fronts *Superman IV: The Quest for Peace* she's but a shadow of her former self. No matter. Her first *Superman* is the one to cherish. However the movies or television have treated Lois, on at least that one occasion they got her right.

By the time *Superman* hit movie screens in '78, the comics show-cased an equally liberated Lois. At one point, she decided she no longer needed a man of steel and gave up her pursuit of Superman altogether to start a romantic relationship with Clark. In "Clark Kent Forever...Superman Never!" (*Superman*, No. 297), the couple shared a moment of discreet Comics Code–approved intimacy (granted, after she cooked him dinner). When DC enlisted writer-artist John Byrne to revamp the Superman universe in 1986, Lois underwent further metamorphosis.

Byrne introduced changes large and small. He altered the color of Lois' hair from its perennial black to its now-traditional auburn and further "de-powered" Superman (who by then had again grown near-omnipotent). He also heightened the tension between Lois and Clark by having Clark scoop her on the *Daily Planet's* first Superman story, for which she never forgave him. But the biggest change occurred when Byrne removed the public's awareness of Superman's dual nature. With her days no longer spent trying to prove Clark was Superman, Lois was free to become her own woman, one no longer preoccupied with marrying Superman. The two *would* soon wed, but only through the machinations of corporate America, the one force in the universe stronger than Superman.

A few of John Byrne's innovations had seemed arbitrary. But his leveling of the playing field shared by Lois and Clark piqued Hollywood's interest, since the characters could once more be shoehorned into a popular television setting—the workplace.

Inspired in part by the romantic comedy of *Moonlighting*, *Lois and Clark* returned Superman to television, albeit as more of a supporting player. The show depicted, as had the Schwartz-edited comics, a stronger Lois and a weaker (at least in terms of personality) Superman. It may have once seemed necessary, this trade-off; but the '78 *Superman* had portrayed the characters as equals, proving they could function as such. Yet on *Lois and Clark*, though Dean Cain was an attractive and very human Clark, his Superman came off as being a bit young, his voice lacking the timbre of past Supermen. Teri Hatcher was the show's true breakout star, her Lois exploding across the screen like a mortar shell with charisma and sex appeal.

When the show's pilot episode aired in September of '93, Lois first appeared sporting a fake beard and mustache (an ironic touch in hindsight, considering Hatcher inspired more Internet worship than any other Lois). She'd just returned from investigating a stolen-car ring, and the thought of a Lois so willing to go undercover and get her hands dirty was intriguing. But after Jimmy Olsen peeled off her disguise, we first saw Hatcher's cover-girl features and were introduced to a frustrating interpretation.

For every moment in which her character was built up throughout *Lois and Clark's* pilot, there was one that tore her down. In an early scene Lois told Clark, "I live by three rules: I never get involved with my stories, I never let anyone else get there first, and I never sleep with anyone I work with." But some time later, when the two were captured, she confessed to having broken every one of these rules. Much was made of Lois' self-sufficiency—we were told she was *The Daily Planet's* best investigative journalist, and her sister told her that to get a man she must "stop being so smart all the time." Lois' response—"Look, I'm just being myself. If they're not man enough to handle it then I guess I'll just wait for someone who is"—put us on her side, until we saw her swoon *three* times during that first episode: over Clark, over Superman and over Lex Luthor, who remained Clark's rival for her affections for the remainder of the first season. Oh, and she cried. More than once.

These bits of business can't be explained as texture. The insecurity of Hatcher's Lois resembled that of *Ally McBeal's* central character, a flighty single lawyer constantly longing for a husband. *Ally McBeal* premiered in '97, *Lois and Clark's* final year, and the debate it sparked prompted the June '98 *Time* magazine cover headline "Is Feminism Dead?" Yet while *McBeal* was the brainchild of a man (David E. Kelley), *Lois and Clark* was developed for television by a woman (Deborah Joy LeVine). Unlike the vast majority of Superman comics, movies and TV shows, which *were* written by men, *Lois and Clark's* problems ran deeper than mere sexism.

In her *New York Times Magazine* essay "What's a Modern Girl to Do?" *Times* columnist Maureen Dowd (herself a celebrated single journalist) described some of the problems facing working women today as they seek relationships with men. Dowd described a "primal fear of single successful women: that the aroma of male power is an aphrodisiac for women, but the perfume of female power is a turn-off for men" (Dowd 53). Alluding to the present state of feminism, Dowd wrote, "It took women a few decades to realize that everything they were doing to advance themselves in the boardroom could be sabotaging their chances in the bedroom; that evolution was lagging behind equality" (Dowd 53).

Dowd's comments go a long way in explaining the character of Lois in *Lois and Clark* and the way in which she was a step back from Margot Kidder's character in the '78 *Superman*. *Lois and Clark* offered a Lois to a generation that, like Dowd, was questioning the feminist principles it had once embraced. The reasons for this backlash go beyond the scope of this essay. But suffice it to say, Hatcher's Lois, like Ally McBeal, like Grace Adler (of *Will and Grace*), like any number of working women depicted on TV in the late '90s, was fractured and filled with self-doubt.

Hatcher's Lois finally married Cain's Clark in *Lois and Clark*'s fourth-season episode "Swear to God, This Time We're Not Kidding," while, after almost sixty years, their comic-book counterparts did the same (in *Superman: The Wedding Album;* December 1996). Much media fanfare accompanied the synergy, but it wasn't enough to save the show—it finished its run at season's end. Since nature (or Time Warner) abhors a vacuum, yet another Superman TV show debuted during *Lois and Clark*'s final season. *Superman: The Animated Series* featured Dana Delaney as the voice of Lois and Tim Daly as that of Clark/Superman. *The Animated Series*, with its emphasis on action and supervillains, was considerably more popular than *Lois and Clark* amongst comic-book fans, and Delaney delivered a credible performance. Her Lois was remarkably similar to Coates': a hard-nosed pro with little time for love. Unlike Hatcher's character, but true to Byrne's comic-book version, Delaney's rarely broke down and *never* swooned. She considered Clark, whom she often addressed as "Smallville," a rival, first and foremost. And if she possessed romantic feelings for Superman, they went largely unexplored during the show's four-year run.

> LOIS: You're amazing, Smallville. You always look for the best in people, even when they walk all over you.
> CLARK: I guess that's why we're friends.

With *Lois and Clark*, Hollywood had demonstrated its willingness to experiment with the traditional Superman formula. But the most radical break occurred when an eighteen-year-old Lois (played by Erica Durance) met a seventeen-year-old Clark (played by Tom Welling) in season four of the WB's *Smallville*, an exploration of Clark's high school and college years.

As in the comics, Clark spent most of the series smitten with his childhood sweetheart, Lana Lang. But with the introduction of Lois (who, in the comics, didn't meet Clark until he joined the *Daily Planet*) greater artistic license was exercised. Suddenly the traditional tension between the two took on a new dimension—that of an awkward high school boy and his more worldly college friend. Unfortunately, Lois' personality shines less brightly in *Smallville* than it has in shows past, since, in a sense, all of the WB's heroines—Buffy the Vampire Slayer, the Gilmore girls, etc.—are her descendents, their snappy, rapid-fire dialogue the legacy of those scrappy dames of the '30s and '40s. *Smallville* is filled with knowing, precocious young people, among them Allison Mack's Chloe Sullivan, Lois' cousin—who displays all the enthusiasm for news reporting that Durance's character lacked (when Lois' college entrance was delayed, she enrolled at Smallville High and, for a time, wrote for the school's newspaper).

Though not without its charms, *Smallville* is programmatic. To placate comics fans, the writers use Durance's Lois to echo those of the past. In her early episodes, she tried to quit smoking, admitted she couldn't spell (shades of Kidder) and continued to address Clark as "Smallville" (after the comics' and Delaney's Lois). Like the show's other characters, her dialogue is filled with foreshadowing, as when she told Clark, "... The last thing I'd want to do is spend my time in a newsroom. With my luck, I'd probably end up across the desk from the most bumbling reporter on the masthead."

While Lois' cocky WB attitude is meant to attract teenage girls, *Smallville* also seeks to win an audience of hormone-ridden teenage boys, who may have outgrown or are simply uninterested in comic books. To that end, it portrays Lois in frequent states of undress—bikinis, belly shirts, and, in one episode, the skimpy garb of a pole dancer. This supports Dowd's belief that "Before it was don't be a sex object; now it's be a sex object." Yet Durance's character is also self-sufficient. Throughout *Smallville's* fourth season, she neither had nor wanted a boyfriend, could out-drink any frat boy at Metropolis University and proved skilled in the art of self-defense.

We're told Lois' independence comes from her father, an Army general, and his belief in raising both her and her sister as though they were his troops. Whatever surface edginess it gave Lois, in developing this back-story, *Smallville* robbed her of the freedom to define herself. Could she not be tough and uncompromising without the excess psychological baggage? It's something of a missed opportunity, and one hopes that if Durance's Lois must continue to shed her clothes she'll lose some of her demons as well.

No matter how great a turn Lois has taken in *Smallville*, she'll take a greater one when Kate Bosworth plays her in 2006's *Superman Returns*—by becoming a single mother.

Fair enough. It's the next logical step. Society is more tolerant of single moms than ever before (it must be if Warner Brothers is allowing Lois, one of their most valued commercial properties, to enter the ranks of unwed motherhood). But America, at present, experiences a cultural divide and an administration in Washington that counts the Christian right among its base. Politicians have often taken cheap shots at single mothers when lambasting the decay of "moral values" (recall former Vice President Dan Quayle's infamous Murphy Brown speech), and they'll continue to do so. A debate will no doubt rage when *Superman Returns* flies into theaters. After all, if a woman having a child without the help of a man is the ultimate sign of independence, how much greater the symbolism when that man is a superman?

Let the politicians and pundits attack. Lois can take it. She's faced greater threats on the road she's traveled. It's the same road she started out on back in '38, the same road all American women have taken. Only the lanes have changed.

REFERENCES

Bates, Cary (w), Elliot S. Maggin (w), Curt Swan and Bob Oskner. "Clark Kent Forever...Superman Never!" *Superman* No. 297. DC Comics: March 1976.

Daniels, Les. *Superman: The Complete History*. San Francisco: Chronicle Books, 1998.

Dowd, Maureen. "What's a Modern Girl to Do?" *New York Times Magazine*, 30 Oct. 2005: 50–55.

"Pilot (One)." *Lois and Clark: The New Adventures of Superman*. Episode 1, Dir. Robert Butler, ABC, 12 Sep. 1993.

Siegel, Jerry (w) and Joe Shuster (p, i). *Action Comics* No. 1. National Comics Publications (DC Comics): June 1938.

Superman. Dir. Dave Fleischer. Perf. Joan Alexander, Bud Collyer. Fleischer Studios, 1941.

Superman: The Movie. Dir. Richard Donner. Perf. Marlon Brando, Christopher Reeve, Margot Kidder. Warner Bros., 1978.

Superman II. Dir. Richard Lester. Perf. Gene Hackman, Christopher Reeve, Margot Kidder. Warner Bros., 1980.

"Swear to God, This Time We're Not Kidding." *Lois and Clark: The New Adventures of Superman*. Episode 69, Dir. Michael Lange, ABC, 6 Oct. 1996.

"The Wedding of Superman." *The Adventures of Superman*. Episode 73, Dir. Phil Ford, ABC, 12 May 1956.

JOSEPH MCCABE is a contributing editor of *Comic Book Artist*, an assistant editor of *Weird Tales* and a frequent contributor to *SFX*. His book *Hanging Out with the Dream King: Conversations with Neil Gaiman and His Collaborators* was nominated in 2005 for both the Bram Stoker and the International Horror Guild Awards. *Superman: The Movie* was the first live-action film he saw in a movie theater; and though he's still not sure he believes a man can fly, his partner, the photographer Sophia Quach, has shown him that a woman most certainly can.

Lou Anders

A WORD OF WARNING FOR BRANDON ROUTH

THE ADVENTURES OF SUPERMAN star George Reeves was only forty-five years old in 1959 when he was found dead in his home from a single gunshot. There was a lot of talk of foul play at the time, though the death was officially labeled a suicide. Depression over his typecasting as the Man of Steel and failure to find other work was the likeliest target, and rumors even spread that, in an alcohol- (or painkiller-) induced state, Reeves had mistakenly assumed he could fly and leapt from a tall building in a single bound. But over the years, many startling facts about the case have surfaced. One, that no fingerprints were found on the gun that fired a bullet into Reeves' right temple. Two, that the discarded shell was found under Reeves' naked corpse, difficult to explain in a suicide. Three, that Reeves had recently been the victim of a months-long harassment from mobster Toni Mannix, with whose wife Reeves had had an affair. Four, that the suicide occurred at a party at Reeves' house, and the guests had waited thirty minutes before alerting the authorities. And finally, five, that Reeves' depression had ended and he was, according to friends, in the highest spirits in ages about his upcoming marriage and the decision by the producers to film another sea-

175

son of *The Adventures of Superman* after a three-year hiatus, and thus unlikely to commit suicide at this time. In the 1980s, both costars Noel Neill (Lois Lane) and Jack Larson (Jimmy Olsen) revived the case with their claim that the man in tights had been a victim of foul play. But whatever the actual events of his death are, they'll most likely remain a mystery forever more.

The next man to put on the tights was Christopher Reeve, who brought Superman to the silver screen in four adventures, two of them excellent and two of them abominable. But whether the plots supported or undermined his efforts, Reeve's acting magically captured Superman for millions of moviegoers worldwide. No one could deny that Reeve *was* the character, born to play him with a dignity and humanity and small town naiveté that still defines the Last Son of Krypton to this day.

But then in May of 1995 (and here please note that 95 is the reverse of 59), Reeve's thoroughbred, Eastern Express, pitched him forward during a cross-country and jumping "eventing" in Culpeper, Virginia. Reeves fractured his uppermost vertebrae and was instantly paralyzed. Now, this writer has absolutely no interest in demeaning the dignity or importance of the life that the late Christopher Reeve led in his final decade prior to the accident. His work with the Christopher Reeve Paralysis Foundation was a tireless crusade worthy of a real-life superhero, and work perhaps more meaningful and laudable than his previous career as an actor. (In fairness, Reeve was a dedicated activist before his injury and remained a consummate actor after it.) But it can't be glossed over that it was this injury which began the idle speculation that something supernatural existed called the Superman curse. Perhaps man isn't meant to reach too high, the thinking goes, and daring to take on the role of such a *super* man tempts the gods too much. Of course, for *Lois and Clark* star Dean Cain, the only injury done to him after donning the red cape was to his career. Still it is worth pointing out that Dean Cain's initials are D. C., the name of the Warner Communications subsidiary that has reigned over Superman's exploits since his debut in 1938.

But leaving Cain aside, there's a third player that can legitimately be linked with Metropolis' favorite son, who shares some very peculiar similarities with his two big-screen predecessors. Keanu Reeves,

who as Neo, the martial arts superhero of *The Matrix Trilogy*, is chosen to be "the One," is told that he "doesn't have to" dodge bullets,
leaps across tall buildings in a single bound (albeit not so successfully in his first attempt), and, finally, even flies. Writer/directors the
Wachowski brothers' affection for comic books is well documented,
and, in fact, the project was initially sold to Warner Bros. (part of the
same conglomerate that owns DC) when they had famous comic-
book artists storyboard the script as a visual aid. But if any more proof
of who Neo was modeled on were needed, in the final moments of
The Matrix, Keanu even exits the unlikely prop of an old-style phone
booth (long a staple arena for Clark Kent's costume changes) before
taking off into the sky. What played first as subtext and metaphor
in the initial film was front and center in *The Matrix Reloaded* when
Nebuchadnezzar crewmember Link strips the veil of subtlety away,
proclaiming when asked about Neo's whereabouts, "He's doing the
Superman thing again." Neo's aerial rescuing of his own Lois Lane,
the leather-clad Trinity, as she is falling off a skyscraper in the film's
climax, is straight out of the pages of a hundred *Action Comics*.

What is so striking, however, is that if we count this metaphoric
Man of Steel as one of only three big-screen appearances of Superman, then the synchronicity between all three actors becomes un-
bearably obvious. All have the same last name, minus the S on one of
them (S for Superman?). Reeves. Reeve. Reeves.

Interestingly, a quick Internet search for the etymology of the
name Reeves returns the information that it is derived from the word
"reeve," and means "a bailiff, provost or steward." In his Christ-like
assumption of responsibility for the whole of humanity, both Superman and his computer counterpart Neo certainly shine as the greatest steward the Earth has produced. But let us not dally on these
minor synchronicities, mere breadcrumbs to lure us deeper along the
path that lies ahead.

Like the inverse of our next subject's own career path, we'll be jumping out of Hollywood and into politics (dare I mention that DC initial
again?) to pull a strange analogy from the life of an American President—that of Ronald Reagan, who sports the double initial alliteration
prevalent in Superman comics, and whose apparent nemesis (at least
in his mind) was also a bald supervillain. Soviet President Mikhail

Gorbachev even sported a James Bond evil genius–style scar on his chrome dome. And if one manages to suffer through *Superman IV: The Quest For Peace*, it becomes painfully obvious how the Kryptonian's heavy-handed dealing with the nuclear proliferation of the Arms Race and the film's feel-good ending mirrored (and was directly inspired by) Reagan's gradual about-face transition from viewing the USSR as the "evil empire" to advocating a cessation of the cold war. More of the Reagan/Superman connection was made in Frank Miller's landmark graphic novel, *The Dark Knight Returns*, but that's for another time. We're concerned here only with the assassination attempt on Ronald Reagan's life by lone gunman John Hinckley, Jr.

But before we get there we have to go back to 1840, and an Indian curse leveled on President William Henry Harrison. The legend is a fairly well-known one. How the brother of the slaughtered Native American chieftain Tecumseh cursed Harrison for the death of his sibling, proclaiming that if or when he became the "Great Chief" Harrison would die the following year. He went on to proclaim that every twenty years, each person elected to the Highest Seat in the land would suffer a similar fate. True or not, on April 4, 1841 Harrison passed away due to pneumonia, the first U.S. President to die in office. The curse resurfaced two decades later when President Abraham Lincoln, elected in 1861, was shot by John Wilkes Booth in 1865. It returned to claim President James Abram Garfield. Elected in 1880, he failed to prove "faster than a speeding bullet" when he was shot the following year by Charles Guiteau. Elected to his second term in 1900, President McKinley was shot by an unnamed assailant in 1901. Warren Harding died of a heart attack two years into his term, after being elected in 1920. In 1945, President Franklin Delano Roosevelt died in office of a cerebral hemorrhage. Elected four times, his third term began in 1940. If you believe the Warren Commission, it was another Lone Gunman who took the life of President John F. Kennedy. Elected in 1960. Died 1963. But by the Gipper's time the curse must have diminished in power. Elected in 1980, Ronald Reagan was shot in 1981 getting into his car by John W. Hinckley, Jr. with a bullet that burrowed to within one-fourth of an inch of his heart. As 2000 came and went uneventfully, we can infer that Ancient Indian curses have a potency of exactly 140 years, after which time they fade.

But what of our Costumed Crusader and the curse that is supposed to follow those with the hubris to assume the role of this god among men? George Reeves died in 1959 by a gunshot to the head. Christopher Reeve suffered paralysis from the neck down from a horseback-riding mishap in 1995. And unlikely Buddha-figure Keanu Reeves? In a puzzling situation for the star of an action movie to be in, Keanu Reeves was actually seriously injured when he committed to filming the first *Matrix* film. Similar to Christopher before him, Reeves had suffered an injury to his cervical spine requiring surgery prior to his four months of intensive kung fu training. Whatever critics have to say about the depth of his performance, no one can fault this actor's dedication. The one-third-of-a-year exhaustive work with fight choreographer Yuen Wo-ping, as well as the actual filming of the fight scenes itself, was a risk that could easily have landed Keanu with permanent and serious injuries to his spine. One could almost suppose that, like the dwindling pattern breakdown of the Indian curse that began with Harrison and fizzled out with Reagan, the Superman curse that killed George Reeves and left Christopher Reeve a paraplegic made its play for Keanu Reeves and was rebuffed. With *Superman Returns* due from Warner Bros. in 2006, time will shortly tell if the curse has finally run its course. But looking back on the long, strange screen life of the most famous of comic-book icons, one wonders what infernal forces could orchestrate such a Sea of Synchronicity. One could even go so far as to speculate that we must be living in some unimaginably complex, artificial, scripted reality. Dare we say it? A Matrix perhaps...

Of course, if our world really were illusory, every bit as scripted as the comic books that Supes stars in, wouldn't the programmer have left us a few more clues, those odd bits of synchronicity and déjà vu that say "this just can't be real; somebody's got to be behind this"? Well, let's look back at the real-life people and things in the lives of the men to portray the Man of Steel and we'll see that synchronicity—that Jungian term for *meaningful* coincidence—is truly at work here. Look back up and notice the name of George Reeves' co-star: Noel Neill. And the horse that threw Christopher Reeve? Eastern Express. N N, E E. Notice the repetition of the first letter in both names. Well, any aficionado of the Big Blue Schoolboy worth his salt knows that all the significant people in Kal-El's life sport a double letter: From his first Smallville puppy love Lana Lang, to the lesser-known ill-fated Atlantean Lori Lamoris, to his long-time paramour and eventual wife Lois Lane. And, let's not forget, (and I suppose there are Freudian implications here) his number one arch-enemy Lex Luthor. Of course, these all play off a certain letter—a double L. But remember that one of the reasons cited against George Reeves' having committed suicide was his upcoming marriage. And just what was the name of his intended? Why, it was Lenore Lemmon. L. L. Reeves' attraction to a real-world lover with the same name alliteration as his counterpart's girlfriend may have been an identification with his alter ego on a subconscious level, or it might be a tip of the hat to the casual observer that the whimsical universe is up, up and away to its old tricks again.

LOU ANDERS is an editor, author and journalist. He is the editorial director of Prometheus Books' science fiction imprint Pyr, as well as the anthologies *Outside the Box* (Wildside Press, 2001), *Live Without a Net* (Roc, 2003), *Projections* (MonkeyBrain, December 2004) and *FutureShocks* (Roc, July 2005). He served as the senior editor for *Argosy* Magazine's inaugural issues in 2003–04. In 2000 he served as the executive editor of Bookface.com, and before that he worked as the Los Angeles liaison for Titan Publishing Group. He is the author of *The Making of Star Trek: First Contact* (Titan Books, 1996), and has published over 500 articles in such magazines as *Publishers Weekly, The Believer, Dreamwatch, Star Trek Monthly, Star Wars Monthly, Babylon 5 Magazine, Sci Fi Universe, Doctor Who Magazine* and *Manga Max*. His articles and stories have been translated into German, French and Greek, and have appeared online at Believermag.com, SFSite.com, RevolutionSF.com and InfinityPlus.co.uk. Visit him online at www.louanders.com.

Peter B. Lloyd

SUPERMAN'S MORAL EVOLUTION

SUPERMAN IS A mirror to American society. He reflects the moral and technological expectations of Americans. And the American public re-absorbs the ideal that Superman represents. It's a two-way exchange. As American society has changed, Superman has changed. In the Golden Age, Superman had a robust view of justice that reflected the opinions of the average American citizen. If there were to be superheroes, this was how they would behave. The superhero tackled clearly bad people with straightforward force: he used violence to thwart their misdeeds, to extract information, to punish and rehabilitate them. Superman's moral universe at the time is nicely illustrated by this exchange with Lois Lane in *Superman* No. 18:

> SUPERMAN: *(striking suspects)* Need I remind you boys that crime doesn't pay?
>
> LANE: Your fists should convince them better than a dozen sermons!

Things are different now. The American citizen has a more nuanced picture of the threats to orderly civilian life. Social convulsions of the 1960s etched a deeper appreciation of civil rights, and alerted people to the fallibility of law enforcers. Later decades have instilled an awareness of the sometimes intractable problems of social conflict. The changing behavior of Superman reflects this increased sophistication of public understanding. In recent years, Superman has faced the moral tension of serving a democratically elected President who had formerly been a key player in organized crime, namely Lex Luthor. This is a deeper conundrum than Superman had to face in the Golden Age.

Superman has undergone evolution, not revolution. There have been pointers along the way, tracing Superman's growing maturity. Consider this example from the 1960s, where Superman's simple response to crime runs up against the checks and balances of the law. In April 1968, Metropolis Mailbag leads with the following letter from a Mr. Tom Smith of Eugene, Oregon (*Superman* No. 205).

> Dear Editor,
> I have just read Superman no. 103 [*sic*], and I was profoundly saddened by "Superman's Black Magic." I was under the impression that Superman was sworn to combat crime, seek justice and uphold the American way of life. In doing so, it is obvious that such a course must of necessity result in a balanced approach. And yet, in this story, Superman is so over-zealous in his pursuit of criminals that he is willing to cut the very foundations from under our American institutions. The suspected guilt of any individual is irrelevant to the protection of his basic civil guarantees. To destroy such rights with the methods used by Superman—misrepresentation (pretending to be the Devil), forcing them to list their crimes and confederates to escape a fake hell, and then using this as "proof" of their guilt, is to discredit the Man of Steel and set a dangerous precedent. God protect us from such superheroes.

DC Comics' response was:

> If the police suspect someone, don't they go all out to prove his guilt or innocence? Maybe Superman was a bit over-zealous...but when this happens someone like you will always 'horn in' and give us the Devil!
> —ED.

There was evidently a dialogue going on within DC Comics about Superman's moral position on the spectrum that runs from the well-intentioned vigilante at one extreme to the obedient officer of a democratically controlled police force at the other.

The biggest shift in Superman's moral stance happened when he relinquished the use of lethal force. In *Superman* No. 172 (p. 182) Jimmy Olsen says to Superman's temporary successor, Ar-Val, "Don't kill them, Ar-Val! Remember Superman's Oath! Turn them over to the police!" And, in *Superman* No. 205 (p. 120), Superman himself says, "Now I sentence you to death!" but then "I... can't do it! My code against killing... I simply can't break it... not even to crush a monster like you."

It would be interesting to trace Superman's moral evolution over the full span of his career, but that would require a bigger space than this essay. Here I will limit myself to the earliest years of the Golden Age, 1938–1943. This reveals a big contrast with the Superman of today, as will be clear to anyone who is acquainted with modern Superman comics.

CIVIL RIGHTS VS. "THE TWO-FISTED DYNAMIC MAN OF TOMORROW"

(*Superman* No. 17, p. 75)

DC Comics told us—from the very beginning in 1938—that Superman is committed to defending the American way. This must include the fair and open enforcement of a written legal code under an elected executive. Whilst on active service, however, Superman exempts himself from this limitation. He has a secret life apart—a secret society of one man, above the laws and conventions that bind his fellow citizens. He was not elected, nor was he given his authority by an elected body. No elected body can remove his authority. Superman claimed these rights for himself—and he decided to use his *own* ideas of truth and justice. To paraphrase Nietzsche, for him the only truth is *his* truth, the only justice *his* justice. But the truth and justice that DC Comics gives him are a reflection of the American perceptions.

When Superman arrested suspects in the Golden Age, he bypassed the constitutional rights that make up one strand of the American way of life. He smashed through legal safeguards with the same casualness that he smashed down doors. Let us take a look at two ways in which he used to do this: his treatment of evidence, and of suspects.

Superman relied on his own personal observations, which he didn't jot down as contemporaneous notes. (A rare exception was *Superman* No. 9 (p. 19), where he makes a dictograph recording of an incriminating conversation.) Such notes are more than aids to memory. They are assurances of objectivity. How can a court of law trust that Superman is not modifying his recollections to suit his own agenda—either wilfully or unintentionally? Without written records or recordings of his super-perceptions, how can any court trust his unaided memory? Superman says he cannot lie. But how can a neutral court accept that assertion? And Superman never said that he cannot deceive by other means—by selective reporting, or being "economical with the truth."

Where Superman's evidence is gleaned from super-vision and super-hearing, its credibility could be questioned on the grounds that juries have no direct acquaintance with such super-powers, and so have no firsthand view of its reliability. By Superman's own admission, he cannot see through lead. What if a barrier were not pure lead, but some admixture of lead and other substances? For example, the lead component in car exhaust fumes? Precisely what effect would that have? Would it merely dim the vision, or could it distort it too? How does super-vision interact with substances of different kinds, and with gravity? What reflection and refraction does it suffer? Do the rays of super-vision bend in high temperatures—as light does as in a mirage when it is bent by desert heat? Does it suffer interference with physical energy fields such as radar? How much does Superman's mind fill in gaps in his super-vision?

Terran science has no answers to these questions, so how can juries accept Superman's evidence, and how can Superman act legitimately, on the basis of his super-observations? What about possible problems like the following? At an airport, Superman sees a woman pull a gun on a seemingly unarmed man and, with super-speed, he disarms her. What he didn't see was that she was aiming at a terrorist who had in his hand an automatic weapon—which Superman could not see because a lead box blocked the relevant line of sight. Superman would have been acting with good intentions but recklessly because of the imperfection of his super-vision.

Almost certainly, any lawyer defending someone against Superman's abduction and imprisonment would be able to call expert witnesses to discredit Superman's evidence in the eyes of the jury. Look what happened with the CIA's twenty-five-year project in remote viewing! (Hyman 31).

Furthermore, surely Superman's super-perception is an invasive form of surveillance that breaches citizens' right of privacy? He will say that he uses his super-sense only to observe criminal acts. How so? If he is to detect such acts, he must scan citizens at large. Whilst on patrol, and indeed even in his disguise as Clark Kent, he must be sweeping his neighborhood with super-sight and super-hearing, scanning for anything to do with crime. But, since most people are doing legal things most of the time, most of what Superman spies on is legal. Sometimes Superman even eavesdrops on Lois Lane's private life and stalks her (*Superman* No. 9, p. 11; No. 21, p. 45), or spies on her grief (*Superman* No. 21, p. 54). Commentators on Superman claim that he resists the natural temptation to use his x-ray vision to look through women's clothes. But surely, in his scanning the world for crime, he would have to look through women's handbags and clothing for concealed weapons? Only in recent years has this aspect of Superman's surveillance of the American public been raised as an issue with the comics.

So much for Superman's treatment of evidence. How did he treat suspects? In law, force and violence are permitted when a suspect resists with violence or threatens to use it. A cop can shoot a man dead who is brandishing a weapon. But if neither the officer nor any bystanders are in danger, then it is neither legal nor moral to assault the suspects. As Superman is bulletproof, any one-on-one encounter with a suspected villain poses no danger to Superman or bystanders. Yet, in the Golden Age Superman never slapped the cuffs on. His procedure for arresting American citizens was to punch them in the face with a steely fist (*Superman* No. 22, p. 107), which he refers to with satisfaction as "a good old-fashioned sock in the jaw" (*Super-*

man No. 11, p. 169), or throw them aside with concussive force (*Superman* No. 23, p. 149), or knock their heads together (*Superman* 23, p. 181), or throw guns at them (*Superman* No. 24, p. 197). Any cop who behaved in this way would face disciplinary action. Yet in the 1930s, this was considered an ideal for America's youngsters to look up to.

Let us look at some typical arrests, which happen to involve suspects who are innocent or at least have no evidence against them. First, in *Superman* No. 21 (p. 13), he notices gas entering his cab, assumes it to be poisonous, and feigns unconsciousness. When the limp body of Clark Kent is rescued from the cab, he guesses that the two men carrying him are going to kill him, and violently attacks them. When they use their handguns to try to defend themselves against Superman, he responds with a right-hook, causing them to fall on a vial of cyanide, leading to their deaths. Yet, the idea of non-violent arrest is not unknown to him, for later in the story, he saves a suspect from falling from a plane (p. 22), and carries him to a police station. At another point, he captures an illegal militia by electrifying the fence around their compound—but not before assaulting the troops with his fists and boots (p. 20).

Second, in *Superman* No. 21 (p. 30–31): whilst searching for the kidnapped Lois Lane, he breaks into a house, and assaults two men who—as the reader ironically already knows—were innocent of any involvement with the kidnap. In the rescue itself, after putting Lois Lane out of harm's way, Superman concusses the two suspects whom he could have handcuffed (p. 35).

Third, in *Superman* No. 18 (p. 99), he beats Count Armaund senseless in the dark, in the mistaken belief that he is attacking Lane's assailant.

A frequent arrest tactic for Superman is to shake suspects out of a car in which they are riding (*Superman* No. 17, p. 53), or to destroy it outright (*Superman* No. 22, p. 100), or sometimes he just casually trashes the vehicle with the likely death of its occupants [1]. A variant on this tactic is his destruction of a plane carrying Lex Luthor, apparently with the death of all the crew (*Superman* No. 5, p. 54), although in later stories we discover that Luthor somehow survived. After an arrest, he often threatens his prisoners with beatings [2] or with summary execution [3], or he may physically torture them by dangling them from a great height [4] or by more vigorous means [5]—in order to obtain a confession. In some cases, citizens will be sent to the electric chair on the confession squeezed out by Superman's use of deception or coercion.

In most stories, Superman first assaults the suspects, then hands them over to the cops. Sometimes, he takes the law into his own hands and metes out a punishment complete in itself: see the series of beatings in *Superman* No. 5 (pp. 30–35), or his tossing three suspects into a lake (*Superman* No. 7, p. 170), or his death threats (p. 183).

The exuberant use of visually engaging violence is part of the warp and weft of life in the comic-book universe. It's the standard package that you buy into when you pick up a comic. So, am I criticizing Superman for being a comic-book character? No, just noticing how his use of that violence has evolved in response to society's sensibilities.

By the way, we do not observe legal niceties for their own sake. There are two key downsides to abusing prisoners. First, the results of torture are unreliable; second, a policy of accepting such confessions encourages the use of torture on innocent suspects. Confessions that have been obtained under coercion—using threatened or actual violence—are well known to be unreliable. People will 'fess to anything to escape death or a pounding by the Man of Steel. If courts were known to accept confessions gotten by torture, then they would give a green light to unscrupulous operatives to use torture on anyone they don't like.

Sure, Superman sincerely believed in what he was doing, and that the end justified the means. When he believed that an individual was up to no good, he would do whatever was necessary to get them to 'fess up. What he overlooked was that the initial suspicion may be wrong, and an innocent person may be abused.

Even where a suspect is guilty, the legal code of America does not permit arbitrary ill-treatment. The law dictates that a person must be presumed innocent until and unless proven guilty; and, when found guilty, subject to the specific punishments laid down by law and sentenced by a judge. The early Superman inflicted whatever pain he deemed appropriate on suspects, and he saw nothing wrong in it.

These were not one-off aberrations, done in the heat of the moment. For Superman's violence toward suspects was consistent. Almost every arrest he made in the Golden Age involved assaulting the suspect, but he rarely killed anyone (although see *Superman* No. 13, p. 50 for an exception)—in fact, on several occasions he rescued suspects from accidental death [6], so that they could be tried and probably sent to the chair. To one pair of rescued thugs he said, "You're really not worth saving...but you are human beings!" (*Superman* No. 5, p. 38) and for another villain he thought, *I can't stand by and let someone be killed, no matter how much he deserves it* (p. 65). In these early years, Superman's violence was deliberate and systematic, but usually calibrated to a sub-lethal level.

What did the police make of this? Most stories end with Superman delivering suspects into the hands of the police, so we do not see any response. In one incident, though, he is reprimanded by a judge: "As to your kidnapping a citizen and bringing him here against his will ...!" (*Superman* No. 22, p. 94) but in this case the victim, the Prankster, does not press charges. Largely, Superman's irregularities were hidden by his rhetoric, as when he declared "I won't flout justice at any cost!" (*Superman* No. 22, p. 96).

Superman was then in denial of his extra-judicial violence. But he has moved on from this stance, in the course of his moral evolution.

FOREIGN ADVENTURES FOR METROPOLIS' FAMOUS SON

Late in his career, Superman had a code of not killing people. But his earlier adventures sometimes led to loss of life, and during World War II, he occasionally partook of total war. In one of his few combat operations, he destroyed a military airship with its crew (*Superman* No. 2, p. 109). Twice, he dropped a pair of bombs on a munitions factory, killing the civilian workers (*Superman* No. 2, p. 109; No. 21, p. 24). His biggest body count was in *Superman* No. 8 (p. 236) where he attacked a private militia in America, saying, "A ticklish situation! If I attack the munitions works I'm sure everyone in the neighborhood will be killed, but I can't allow that menace to the US to exist!"

after which he allows one of the militia's own shells to hit the factory, and concludes, "Completely destroyed—including the plotters responsible—not a soul left alive—except myself!"

Superman goes through an intermediate phase, where he lets villains die, rather than actively killing them: on one occasion, he allows a villain's plane to crash to the ground—"I can't look!" says Lane (*Superman* No. 11, p. 154); on another, he throws back at them a stick of dynamite, rather than simply extinguishing the fuse (p. 184). Later, as he becomes more concerned about loss of life, he captures German and Japanese troops without killing any of them (*Superman* No. 24, p. 208).

His refusal to kill is another strand of his moral evolution.

HARD CASES FOR THE MAN OF STEEL

As Superman acts independently of the legislature, we are at his mercy when it comes to disputed parts of the law. In the Golden Age, DC Comics steered Superman away from contentious legal points. So, to illustrate my point, I will suggest a purely hypothetical thought experiment. Imagine Superman flying through the skies of America after the Supreme Court's 1972 ruling on the abortion case of Roe v Wade. What does the Man of Steel do? Consider these two opposite scenarios:

a. Superman sees a gynecologist about to perform an abortion. He swoops down and drags away this would-be murderer of an unborn child—or, in Golden Age style, he may simply punch the abortionist in the head, causing him to fall onto a skull-puncturing needle and die. Enraged by the idea of killing innocent, unborn children, Superman then flies around the whole nation at super-speed, systematically wrecking every abortion clinic.

b. Alternate scenario: Superman sees an anti-abortion campaigner training a high-velocity rifle on the gynecologist. He swoops down and hauls off the would-be assassin. Enraged by the terrorist campaign to undermine American women's lawful right to abortion, Superman flies around the whole nation at super-speed, apprehending other would-be assassins of abortionists.

There will always be irreconcilable convictions on abortion. America handles this through the democratic election of representatives who create and repeal laws. But we have no democratic leverage over Superman. He will carry out whatever actions seem to him personally the right thing to do, irrespective of the democratically expressed will of the people.

As a further illustration, let us look at something that actually made it into the comics in the 1960s, but did not become a legal problem until recently, when it became scientifically possible. Playing God with artificial life has been morally contentious ever since Frankenstein (Shelley), and now the Bush administration has forbidden the cloning of humans—the nearest that modern science has come to creating people. But these considerations did not stop Superman creating a golem—"a synthetic android" with "artificial nerves" who nevertheless had a mind, with consciousness and emotions (*Superman* No. 174, "The End of a Hero," p. 5–6) and a "conscience factor." In his fortress, Superman carries out whatever scientific experiments he wants, without regard for any ethical committees. So, where does the buck stop?

SUPERMAN THINKS...

In recent years, Superman has thought more about his own potential abuse of his power [7], and has entrusted Batman with a ring of green Kryptonite, so that if he ever lost his reason, Batman could defeat him with the ring. This only partly addresses the issue of the superheroes' position outside the institutions of democratic power. Handing the green Kryptonite to another metahuman does not give us, the people, any power over Superman. If Superman and Batman were to agree among themselves that, for the sake of homeland security, all foreign nationals living in Metropolis must be subject to indefinite internment without trial, then the government would be powerless to stop them. The problem cannot be fully resolved by Superman's submitting himself to another superhero. He would need to hand over the green Kryptonite to a Terran institution. Only that would bring full compliance with the republican ideal that forms the basis of the American way of life that Superman defends. But then, what if the designated Terran institution goes bad?

When Lex Luthor was elected President of the United States of America (*Superman: President Lex*), Superman faced a deep dilemma. Reluctantly he concluded that his loyalty was to the President, not to an abstract ideal of justice. When Luthor is arrested by the Atlanteans for crimes against the sea-dwellers, Superman fetches him back in defiance of the laws of the ocean. Here Superman regards the presidential authority as absolute. (Yet, it is still Batman who holds the ring of green Kryptonite. So there is still a part of Superman that refuses to submit to Terran authority.)

THUS SPOKE NIETZSCHE

Sometimes, it's helpful to take a philosophical perspective on things. We can see Superman's ethical stance as putting into practice the ideas of Scottish philosopher David Hume who said you cannot deduce an "ought" from an "is." You cannot start with the objective facts about the world and arrive at a conclusion about moral values—about what you should or shouldn't do. Facts just give you other facts. They don't give you values.

Hume was the first big philosopher to say clearly that moral statements are personal expressions of subjective value judgements. There are no moral facts, only opinions. We make our own moral judgments with our own free will, ultimately without reference to any higher moral authority. To be sure, we are influenced by a great many things, including our schooling and upbringing. But when you are born into a culture that has always held certain tenets, you still have to choose whether or not you personally will endorse them. The buck stops with your conscience.

Later, Hume's insights were brought to a pop audience by Friedrich Nietzsche. His most famous sound-bite was "God is Dead" and, by this, he meant that taking our morality from a deity was over. In place of God, Nietzsche put the "Superman" (or "Überman" in German). He recognised no ethical code, no mores, no cultural limitations: instead he regarded his own will as the sole arbiter of what he should or shouldn't do.

A hint at moral relativism came in *Superman* No. 22 (p. 101), where the intro discusses a latter-day Robin Hood robbing the rich to give to the poor: "That type of justice may have been necessary in those dark days, but in the present-day world any form of thievery, no matter how lofty the motives inspiring the crime, is frowned upon." In other words, stealing is not intrinsically bad: you have to decide whether it is right or wrong depending on the circumstances. Clark Kent expresses the opposite view: "You'll have to admit that Robin Hood is only robbing those who deserve it!" (p. 110) and even Superman lets the criminal go free because he had helped Lois Lane (p. 109). Robin Hood is eventually shot by the crooks, saving Superman the moral dilemma of finally arresting him, but not before revealing the ambivalence of Superman's adherence to the letter of the law. The flexibility of Superman's notion of justice was also illustrated in *Superman* No. 17 (p. 34), where suicide bombers are allowed to go free on the grounds that they had been hypnotized. Superman's verdict: "These men are guiltless of the crimes they may have committed. They were completely dominated by Watkins' will!"

Conversely, Superman's concept of lawfulness allows him acts of petty criminality: in *Superman* No. 10 (p. 79), he rips up a water hydrant; in *Superman* No. 13 (p. 33) he resists police arrest; in a later story (p. 45) he rips up mature trees to amuse a baby.

The buck stops with Superman. His moral values are forged in the crucible of his own conscience. Superman has always been thus, although nowadays he peers into the depths of that crucible with a more penetrating gaze than he ever did in the Golden Age.

"RANDOM ACTS OF HEROISM"
(*Superman: Red Son*, p. 24)

Superman has always been a loner, not a team player. Rather than joining any national or international coordinating body, he keeps his metahuman activities firmly under his own, sometimes quirky, personal control. This is as true now as it was in the 1930s. But nowadays the comics evince an awareness of the moral issues involved in this policy. In 1943, when Superman joined U.S. forces for a training exercise, he ends by declaring:

SUPERMAN: Our nation's secret weapon [is] the unflagging courage of the men, no matter what the odds, and their indomitable will to win! Against that, Hitler and Hirohito haven't a ghost of a chance! (*Superman* No. 23, p. 126)

This would have been an opportunity for DC Comics to raise the question of whether Superman should be drafted into the armed forces and play an active role in combat. But the issue is glossed over. In contrast, in recent years President Luthor has voiced concerns about Superman's refusal to slot into the well-oiled machinery of the administration. When Luthor accuses him of not playing a part in Terran post-war reconstruction in 2001, Superman's revealing reply is:

SUPERMAN: I definitely could have contributed to the reconstruction. I could've handled the entire thing. And maybe you're right. Maybe I should have. . . . But I wasn't put here to solve all of mankind's problems. That's not what this is about. (*Superman* No. 596, p. 19)

This level of thoughtful self-examination could not have taken place in the simpler times of the Golden Age.

Superman's emergency jobs are those that he happens to hear about—mainly through his day job as a newspaper reporter. But Max Millar's Soviet Superman ceaselessly monitors his purview for disasters, and systematically rushes off to each and every incident. A systematic approach need not be so exhausting. As his father told him, there is an infinite reservoir of potential jobs for Superman to do, and he must ration his time to avoid exhaustion. A "service-level agreement" could ensure that Superman worked only a fixed number of hours a week on metahuman duties.

In contrast to the imagined Soviet Superman, the real Superman prioritizes his "jobs for Superman" in an *ad hoc* way. Sometimes he happens to spot a crime whilst glancing with x-ray vision through a wall (*Superman* No. 14, p. 85; No. 22, p. 84). More often, his courtship with Lois Lane determines what incidents he encounters. Check out these revealing comments in *Superman* No. 17, p. 19:

LANE: Why should I worry when Superman has made it his full-time activity to look after helpless me!

and in *Superman* No. 24, p. 204:

LANE: Look—Superman!...If it wasn't for me, I'll bet he wouldn't be here!

and p. 205:

KENT: How is it that he [Superman] always shows up where you are?
LANE: Can I help it if he finds me intelligent and attractive?

A side effect of his personal style of monitoring is that he is rarely aware of more than one emergency at a time. (See *Superman* No. 24 (p. 202), where he hears a ship's SOS whilst saving a stricken plane in the Arctic.) If he were to relinquish his sole control, and place himself under institutional command—as President Luthor has urged in recent years—a system of triage could be put into effect, to manage Superman's time better.

It may seem pedestrian to criticize a superhero's time management. But this is linked to a deeper aspect of Superman's attitude to his role. Superman gained his ingrained moral outlook from the culture of Smallville. He likes to keep within small horizons of distance and time, limiting himself to what he encounters within the compass of his own daily life, and shuns any grand strategy.

Superman is not alone in regarding the small-town ethic as a touchstone of moral integrity. Because the alternative—the global perspective—is seen as being too dangerous. For how do you maintain your moral intuitions in the face of problems whose size and complexity put them outside everyday life?

Within our daily lives, we have visceral intuitions about right and wrong. You see some thugs beating up on an innocent person, and you just know it's wrong without thinking about it. But when you leave the day-to-day world, and address large-scale problems, such as how to run the world's economic and political systems, you find that intuition doesn't work anymore. Instead, you have to distill abstract, general rules from those intuitions, make sure the rules are internally consistent, and then work out how to apply them in the big picture. Your moral intuition is your starting point, but then you have to do a lot of theoretical work to see where you're going to from that initial starting point. The vast disciplines of ethics, and political philosophy, and jurisprudence open up before you. And—here's the crux of the whole problem—when you've done all that theorizing, how do you really know that you've arrived at the right answer? How can you be sure that you've not been hoodwinked by some beguiling ideology?

Isn't this what happened in the authoritarian dictatorships such as the Soviet Union? Didn't they become so convinced of the rightness of their ideologies that they sacrificed decency and humanity for the sake of their political ideals? And isn't this the reason that Americans cling to the touchstone of small-town morality—because it protects them against the risks of becoming ideologues? And isn't this why Superman interiorizes his Smallville perspective—it ensures that he never becomes enchanted by some well-meaning but ultimately destructive ideology.

In his penetrating *Elseworlds* story, *Superman: Red Son*, Max Millar imagines Superman landing in the Ukraine instead of Smallville—and he grows up embracing precisely the systematic and global thinking that our American Superman finds rebarbative. *Superman: Red Son* is Superman's worst nightmare come true. What Superman is afraid of is this: if he starts to think in big, global terms, then he will lose touch with personal one-on-one morality. And he could end up dominating the world like a Super-Stalin.

But—and here we hit the equal and opposite crux—the small-town perspective is itself a rigid creed. By trying to insulate himself from ideologies, Superman has become an ideologue. By limiting himself to his small horizons, and his idiosyncratic, reactive stance, he defines himself by an abstract rule—namely the ideology of small-town thinking.

This is a fundamental dilemma that the early Superman just wasn't up to thinking about. But Superman has evolved into a more reflective being, who can and does address such deep questions.

SUPERMAN: ICON OF WHOSE AMERICA?

The present-day War on Terror has heightened public concern over the balance between preserving legal checks and balances, versus fighting internal and external enemies. It is a concern that has long roots. In Oliver North's opening speech to the Iran-Contra commission, he said it was "mind-boggling...to criminalize policy differences between co-equal branches of government" (Crovitz). The law was not, for him, an abstract thing above all people. It was, rather, a manmade obstacle above which he could rise, rather like Superman. While some applauded, others were appalled.

Superman has developed as a mirror of the troubled American psyche, far beyond the "two-fisted man of tomorrow" of the 1930s. As such, he has come to reflect this public concern.

In his commentary on *Superman: Red Son*, Mark Millar wrote, "Superman, to me, was always a representation of everything great about America." The morally simplistic Superman of the Golden Age represented the purity of the American moral instinct. He has evolved into an introspective Superman who represents a reflective moral response to an irreducibly complex world.

REFERENCES

DC COMICS

Binder, Otto (w) and Al Plastino (p, i). "The Man Who Destroyed Krypton." *Superman* No. 205: Apr 1968. In: *Superman: The Man of Tomorrow Archives*, Vol. 17, pp. 111–134.

Casey, Joe (w), Mike Wieringo (p), and José Marzán (i). "Shipbuilding." *Superman* No. 596. DC Comics: Nov. 2001.

DeMatteis, J. M., Joe Kelly, Jeph Loeb, Greg Rucka, Mark Schultz and Karl Kesel (w). *Superman: President Lex*. Paperback edition: DC Universe, 2003. [Comic book edition: 2000–2001.]

Hamilton, Edmond (w), Curt Swan (p), and George Klein (i). "The New Superman." *Superman* No. 172. DC Comics: Oct. 1964. In: *Superman: The Man of Tomorrow Archives*, Vol. 11, pp. 177–200.

Millar, Mark (w), Dave Johnson (p), Kilian Plunkett (p), Andrew Robinson (i), and Walden Wong (i). *Superman: Red Son*. Paperback edition: DC Comics: 2004. [Comic book edition May–July 2003.]

Millar, Mark, "Red Son (2003)." 28 Aug 2005. <http://theages.superman.ws/History/redson/>.

Siegel, Jerome (w) and Joseph Shuster (p, i). *Superman* Nos. 2 & 4. National Comics Publications (DC Comics): 1939. In: *Superman Archives*, Vol. 1, DC Comics: 1989.

———. *Superman* Nos. 5, 7, & 8. National Comics Publications (DC Comics): 1940. In: *Superman Archives*, Vol. 2, DC Comics: 1990.

———. *Superman* Nos. 9–12. National Comics Publications (DC Comics): 1941. In: *Superman Archives*, Vol. 3, DC Comics: 1991.

Siegel, Jerome (w), and Leo Nowak (p, i), and John Sikela, (p, i). *Superman* Nos. 13–14. National Comics Publications (DC Comics): 1941. In: *Superman Archives*, Vol. 4, DC Comics: 1994.

———. *Superman* Nos. 17–20. National Comics Publications (DC Comics): 1942–43. In: *Superman Archives*, Vol. 5, DC Comics: 2000.

Siegel, Jerome (w), Don Cameron (w), Joseph Shuster (p), George Roussos (i), Leo Nowak (p, i), Pete Riss (p, i), John Sikela (p, i), Ed Dobrotka (p, i), and Sam Citron (p, i). *Superman* Nos. 21–24, National Comics Publications (DC Comics): 1943. In: *Superman Archives*, Vol. 6, DC Comics: 2003.

Siegel, Jerome (w) and Al Plastino (p, i). "The End of a Hero Part II." *Superman* No. 174: Jan. 1964.

Siegel, Jerome (w) and Al Plastino (p, i). "Superman's Black Magic." *Superman* No. 203: Jan. 1968 [This was mis-referenced as No. 103 in Tom Smith's letter in No. 205. Note that this story is a reprint from *Superman* No. 138: Jan. 1960, whence it was reprinted in *Superman: The Man of Tomorrow Archives*, Vol. 4, p. 114.]

Smith, Tom. Letter, *Superman* No. 205: Apr. 1968.

Superman II. Dir. Richard Lester. Perf. Gene Hackman, Christopher Reeve, Margot Kidder, Warner Bros., 1980.

OTHER

Gordon L. Crovitz, "Crime, the Constitution and the Iran-Contra Affair." *Commentary* 1987:84(4). Online archive: <http://www.commentarymagazine.com/Summaries/V84I4P25–1.htm>.

Hyman, R., "Evaluation of a Program on Anomalous Mental Phenomena." *Journal of Scientific Exploration.* 1996:10:31–58.

Nietzsche, Friedrich. *Thus Spoke Zarathustra.* [Translation by R.J. Hollingdale from the German original, *Also Sprach Zarathustra*, 1885.] Harmondsworth: Penguin, 1961.

Shelley, Mary. *Frankenstein, or the Modern Prometheus.* [London: Lackington, 1818.] Modern reprint of third edition. Harmondsworth: Penguin, 1992.

NOTES

(i)   Page numbers in comics refer to the DC *Superman Archives* compilations if the comic story is in those compilations, otherwise to the individual story.

(ii) Although Joe Shuster was headlined alongside Jerry Siegel throughout the Golden Age, I have followed the attribution for pencilling & inks that is given in the DC *Superman Archives*.

DC COMICS REFERENCES

[1] Superman trashes suspects' car: *Superman* No. 4, p. 259; No. 5, p. 102; No. 9, p. 70; No. 10, p. 109.

[2] Superman threatens physical violence to gain confession: see *Superman* No. 5, p. 39; No. 6, p. 119; No. 14, p. 76; No. 21, p. 88.

[3] Superman threatens summary execution to gain confession; *Superman* No. 2, p. 134; No. 8, p. 229, 238; No. 10, p. 102/3; No. 12, p. 248; No. 13, p. 23; No. 14, p. 90; No. 23, p. 173.

[4] Superman tortures suspects by dangling them from a great height: *Superman* No. 5, p. 24, p. 73, p. 86; No. 10, p. 118; No. 11, p. 200; No. 19, p. 146.

[5] Superman tortures suspect more directly: *Superman* No. 7, p. 190; No. 8, p. 249; No. 9, p. 51; No. 14, p. 92; No. 18, p. 81, p. 93; No. 19, p. 151; No. 20, p. 206.

[6] Superman rescues suspects from death: *Superman* No. 5, p. 38; No. 9, p. 22; No. 20, p. 212; No. 21, p. 22.

[7] A three-part story: *Superman* No. 44 (2nd series), *Adventures of Superman* No. 467, *Action Comics* No. 654.

PETER B. LLOYD graduated in mathematics at Cardiff University, Wales, in 1981 and did research there in solar engineering. From 1987 he worked as a software developer in a medical research group in the University of Oxford. While in Oxford, he pursued his passion for philosophy in Michael Lockwood's extramural classes. In 2003 he contributed a chapter to Benbella Books' anthology, *Taking the Red Pill*. He regards The Matrix trilogy as a rare vehicle for bringing to a popular audience the concept that the everyday world is a virtual construct—the starting point for his favorite philosophical theory: subjective idealism.

Bob Batchelor

BRAINS VERSUS BRAWN:
THE MANY LIVES (AND MINDS) OF LEX LUTHOR, THE WORLD'S GREATEST VILLAIN

"Luthor—sinister ultra-scientist who plots the enslavement of mankind! He and Superman have clashed on many occasions. Now—once again— the champion of all that is fine and good confronts the Master of Evil!"

—SUPERMAN SUNDAY COMIC STRIP (1941)

A MAN THAT CAN FLY—better yet—an all-powerful hero with good looks, smarts and a red cape! Bullets bounce off his chest, and even death rays and lasers have no effect. He's invincible, right? But who wants to root for a character that has no flaws?

As a little kid, I read every Superman or Batman comic book I could get my hands on. I watched black-and-white *The Adventures of Superman* reruns on Saturday afternoons in my grandparents' living room. George Reeves played Superman with comic flair, but still embodied strength, power and righteousness. As a matter of fact, Superman seemed too good.

I wondered how I would act if I had similar super-powers? My ten-year-old brain weighed whether, given such abilities, I would do only noble things like Superman or use my brawn in ways that would mortify our hero.

The answer seemed obvious back then. I would have used my super-strength to become the Barry Bonds of my little league. A single leap would put Michael Jordan to shame on the basketball court. Let's not even discuss what I would have done with x-ray vision. Yet Superman stood on the sidelines as a youngster. He bumbled about as Clark Kent as an adult, masking himself for the greater good of a race that wasn't his own, both alien and alienated.

By the 1970s, when I discovered Superman, the Man of Steel had moved away from his roots as a "champion of the oppressed…devoted to helping those in need!" (qtd. in Wright 11) and transformed into a patriotic symbol. He seemed somewhat antiquated when compared to the hipper Marvel heroes, almost like your grandfather's superhero, not one that could relate to kids anymore. Looking back, I realize that Superman seemed too invincible to appeal to a little kid in a single-parent home who returned each day after school to an empty apartment and a mind full of fears. Luckily, I had stacks and stacks of comics, which allowed me to forget my surroundings and find a place in a fantasy world.

Like real people, other superheroes wore their frailties openly. They appealed to readers because we knew their covert identities and secret agendas. Revenge drove Batman to become a masked vigilante. Guilt forced Spider-Man into action, after a gunman he could have stopped later murdered his uncle. Wonder Woman fought for the rights of women and children unable to stand up for themselves in a male-dominated world. Superman's personification of "truth, justice and the American way" seemed somehow out of touch. And, as a youngster, I didn't know anything about Vietnam, Watergate, or any of the other national crises that made Superman irrelevant.

Though my friends and I would have never said that Supes stood atop the list as our favorite superhero, we all had a secret agenda too. Despite his aloofness, any one of us would have given anything to become him. But, I also have to admit, just once, I wanted his number one enemy to fulfill the sinister deed promised on countless covers—the ultimate destruction of the Man of Steel.

MORTAL ENEMY

Unlike Superman, who has virtually limitless power, Lex Luthor is a mere mortal. Yet, since first appearing in early 1940, Luthor remains Superman's most dangerous nemesis and, as such, earth's greatest villain. Granted, Luthor is by no means ordinary, but on paper neither his evil genius nor his outsized ego should be much of a match.

From a technical standpoint, much of Luthor's staying power came out of necessity. Jerry Siegel and Joe Shuster had an interesting challenge in keeping readers cheering for a character that has no flaws. They needed a real villain to battle Superman. The early books pitted Superman against a variety of monsters and giants bent on Metropolis' destruction. The notion of an evil genius with unlimited scientific powers gave the creative duo a human character that they could grow along with Superman.

One could argue that no character in the DC universe changed more over the decades than Luthor. In his first appearances, he is a rather two-dimensional villain. He wore white lab smocks or nondescript jumpsuits, a caricature of the mad scientists that appeared in that era's movies. Luthor triggered havoc by creating advanced technologies to battle Superman. As time progressed, the villain gained a back-story, appeared in several *Superman* movies and the early 1990s television show *Lois and Clark: The New Adventures of Superman*, as well as the more recent *Smallville*. Acclaimed actor Kevin Spacey is portraying Luthor in the latest flick, summer 2006's *Superman Returns*.

As the years passed in the real world outside comics, Superman's archenemy changed, too. Luthor morphed from evil scientist to mafia-like crime boss, then later to Gordon Gekko–style corporate profiteer. The world's greatest villain even rose to the exalted position of president of the United States. Despite his career moves and evolution, Luthor's enduring characteristics have been his hatred for Superman and the fine line he balances between genius and insanity. Most often, it is Luthor's own instability that ultimately leads to his downfall. Superman simply waits for the schemes to implode, catching the villain in the ensuing fallout.

A deeper examination into the Superman/Luthor relationship reveals another interesting dynamic at work—the ongoing battle between brains and brawn. Superman, representing power, strength and invincibility, is clearly the hero, while psychopath Luthor with the smarts he can't control is the villain.

THE ORIGINAL MAD SCIENTIST

Early Superman comics portrayed "Luthor" (known then only by the single moniker) as a mad scientist bent on the hero's destruction. He believed Superman was jealous of his scientific genius, keeping him locked up because Luthor chose to use his power for crime. Luthor battled Superman because the superhero repeatedly thwarted the villain's attempts to rule the world, the first step in controlling the entire universe.

However, Luthor wasn't Superman's first evil genius nemesis. When casting about for the perfect villain who could stand up to their invincible creation, Siegel and Shuster first introduced a mad scientist called "Ultra-Humanite." A precursor to Luthor, the wheelchair-bound Ultra used superhuman mental powers in an attempt to rule mankind. He fought Superman using robots, hypnotic powers and even morphing himself into a female starlet's body to carry out his plots. The transformation ended badly for Ultra, though, killed in a volcano at the end of that storyline.

By the time Siegel and Shuster brought Luthor to life (*Action Comics* No. 23, April 1940), Superman had become America's top-selling comic (averaging about 800,000 copies per issue, nearly double its closest competitor) and came to life on a nationally syndicated radio show. Superman literally created the superhero genre, showing other publishers how to reach audiences, but none were able to achieve the iconic status of the Man of Steel. The character also transcended comics by appearing as a marketing tool for various corporations, selling airtime and products, virtually becoming a mini-industry and the public face of DC Comics. What villain could possibly stand up to such an unassailable hero?

The earliest Luthor incarnation sported a full head of red hair. A year later, however, the hair is gone and the bald Luthor took on a more sinister tenor, mentally and physically. Beating Superman or outsmarting him did not satisfy Luthor; he added killing the hero to his goals.

Luthor's appearance also changed. He aged and grew thicker through the arms, neck and shoulders, sometimes looking more muscular than Superman himself. Although his typical uniform was the drab white smock of a lab technician, Luthor's facial structure took on the stereotypical look of a criminal, with a pug, hooked nose, doughy cheekbones and deep-set eyes with thick, furry brows.

Given the pop culture mindset in early Cold War America, Luthor's resilience is hardly remarkable. As he had his entire existence, the villain mirrored the times. Under constant threat of nuclear annihilation, the public both regaled and kept a suspicious eye on scientists. No one had to stretch very far to imagine a Luthor-like character growing incredibly powerful, maybe even strong enough to take over the world or alter history forever.

America's battle between brains and brawn played out as leaders like Eisenhower and Kennedy pumped money into research and advanced technology on one hand, while at the same time maintaining a powerful army constantly on alert.

An unprecedented level of paranoia swept the United States and its European allies. A potential Luthor lurked in every shadow. In the 1950s, teachers ran schoolchildren through duck-and-cover drills just in case nuclear attacks came. The anxiety over atomic weapons must have made their comic books seem more real. By 1964, both Stanley Kubrick's *Dr. Strangelove or How I Learned to Stop Worrying and Love the Bomb* and the film *Fail-Safe* centered on accidental nuclear wars started by unstable characters.

No real-life Superman stood ready to rescue humanity from itself. Did that mean that the Luthors of the world were in command? Since no Supermans appeared, Americans placed their hopes in dashing film stars, such as the superhero-like John Wayne, and suave political leaders, like John and Bobby Kennedy.

In the early 1960s, Superman writers gave Luthor a more detailed background. In the new version of their relationship, Luthor's genius is cranked up several notches, as is his conceit and contempt for Superman.

In 1960, Jerry Siegel wrote a story starring Superboy for an issue of *Adventure Comics* that provided the adversaries with a synchronized past in Smallville. He depicted them as teen outsiders with special secret powers. The story describes their friendship and "Lex" Luthor's hero fascination with Superboy. However, it is "Lex" Luthor who opens the story by saving Superboy's life by pushing a Kryptonite meteor into quicksand before it can kill the hero. "I owe my life to you! What's your name?" Superboy asks. "Lex! Lex Luthor!" Luthor replies. "Meeting you, Superboy, is about the most thrilling thing that ever happened to me!" (Siegel)

Later, Luthor shows Superboy the shrine he built to the hero, filled with mementos of his adventures. In gratitude for saving his life, Superboy uses his strength and speed to build Luthor a lab capable of carrying out experiments worthy of his intellect. Superboy even provided Luthor with rare and undiscovered chemicals. To further repay Superboy, Luthor decides to concoct a Kryptonite antidote. In his excitement over creating the antidote, the young scientist accidentally knocks over a beaker of acid, setting fire to his lab.

Luthor calls for Superboy to help. The superhero decides to extinguish the flames using his super-breath. A cloud of chemical-infused gas engulfs Luthor, which causes his hair to fall out. Superboy apologizes, but Luthor reacts violently, accusing him of being "jealous of my genius." Later, Luthor says, "You deliberately ruined me because you're jealous. You were afraid my genius would make me more famous than you" (Siegel).

Later, Luthor attempts to help the farmers of Smallville by first manipulating the weather to produce summer year-round and then introducing miracle seeds that grow fruit trees to full-size overnight. The young scientist is instantly praised for his brains, but soon the experiments go awry, threatening the town. Superboy intervenes to save the day. Luthor becomes an outcast, one adult passerby telling him, "You're a menace, Luthor! From now on, keep your discoveries to yourself!" (Siegel)

The repeated rejections merely intensify Luthor's rage, so he sets a trap using Kryptonite. Superboy once again foils the plot. Instead of jailing Luthor, Superboy tells him to use his genius for good, stating, "For your own sake, I hope you will straighten out your thinking and use your brilliant mind to help humanity as I do!" As the book ends, Superboy wonders whether Luthor will "become a great scientist? Or...a criminal?" (Siegel)

This scenario plays out over and over in Superman's ongoing fight with Luthor. Just when brains, as represented by scientific genius and innovation, seem to come out ahead, a glitch or unanticipated consequence takes place that threatens the public. Superman comes to the rescue, using his super-strength and otherworldly super-powers to save the day.

Interestingly, Superboy raises Luthor's scientific abilities to the level of his own super-powers, telling Luthor that both of them have the talents to do good for mankind. Placing the two nearly on par in terms of abilities added additional intrigue to their relationship, which had been less personal in the past. The added dimension, based on personal animosity, pushed Luthor out of the stereotypical mad scientist sphere, making him a more complex character.

GEKKO GONE BAD

Just like Superman, Luthor transformed with the times, though always retaining his dual goals of the hero's destruction and control of the universe. In the 1970s and early 1980s, Luthor took on starring roles in books that put him in alternate universes where he acted as a hero, rather than villain.

The inhabitants of a mythical alternate world dubbed Lexor credited Luthor with saving their planet and erected statues in his honor. These "what if" scenarios further built out Luthor's character and showed that science and innovation used appropriately could be the universe's greatest savior, perhaps as much or more than a man in blue tights and a red cape.

In 1986, writer John Byrne changed Luthor's background as part of a complete overhaul of Superman folklore. Byrne made an important decision about what guise would suit a 1980s villain. He transformed Luthor from evil scientist to corporate executive and white-collar criminal, a kind of Gordon Gekko gone bad, even though the revamp occurred the year before Oliver Stone's movie appeared. Byrne must have felt the anti–corporate raider spirit in the air, particularly with the high-profile scandals by real-life Wall Street villains.

According to the "DC Secret Files and Origins," Luthor's parents planned to use his mental gifts to make them rich. The plan backfired. Their manipulations, instead, "bred a sociopath who engineered their deaths to capitalize on their life insurance." In the new storyline, Lex and a young Clark Kent meet in Smallville and fire still destroys his lab. He blames the fire on Smallville, though the fire and subsequent physical and emotional damage it causes on young Lex forever changes him. Rather than confront his pain, Luthor amplifies the evil aspects of his personality—arrogance, hatred and an unyielding desire to rule the universe. The insurance money becomes the nest egg he needs to fund his next venture.

As an adult, Luthor arrives in Metropolis and founds a technology company—LexCorp—as a front to hide his control of the local organized crime syndicate. LexCorp's success not only makes Luthor incredibly rich, but he parlays his notoriety into political power. Soon, he is considered the most powerful man in Metropolis... until Superman arrives.

The Man of Steel sees through the guise and "openly accused Luthor of being a criminal mastermind rather than a benefactor of mankind." The battle begins once again, although neither hero nor criminal seems able to link the other to their shared pasts in Smallville.

The corporate tycoon Luthor is darker and more criminally insane than past versions of the character. The goonish aspects of his earlier appearance have disappeared—no more doughy jowls and hook nose. The new Luthor is buff, with angular features, though a furrowed brow symbolizing his intensity/insanity is a telltale sign of his temperament. Now that shaven heads are in style, the modern Luthor looks more stylish than in past decades. For the first time, the villain seems like he could walk right off the page and into corporate boardrooms in Silicon Valley, New York, or Washington, DC.

Luthor's reputation as a corporate philanthropist and business executive helped him transition to a role that Siegel and Shuster could never have imagined decades earlier—President of the United States. Luthor won the 2000 election on a platform promising that advanced technology would reshape society, including the introduction of flying cars for every household. Even winning the presidency and the power that office holds, however, could not keep Luthor from trying to destroy Superman. Like the early versions of Luthor, his maniacal fascination with the Man of Steel eventually leads to his demise.

In 2003–2004's *Superman/Batman* 1–6, writer Jeph Loeb depicts President Luthor's final fall from grace at the hands of the super-duo. As a Kryptonite meteor large enough to destroy the Earth hurtles toward the planet, Luthor schemes to blame the projectile's appearance on Superman. He hopes that world public opinion will turn against the superhero, enabling him to wipe out Superman for the good of mankind. In a worldwide telecast, the president explains, "As incredible as it seems, we can only conclude it is coming here because he is here…He is an alien. A curse upon this planet." Luthor then offers a $1 billion reward for delivering Superman to federal authorities, "So he can face charges of crimes against humanity" ("Early Warning," No. 2).

Luthor's declaration turns Superman and Batman into outlaws. They fight off numerous villains who want the bounty and a superhero team Luthor assembles to bring them to justice. Superman views the battle as a concluding showdown with his long-time nemesis. The fight is personal, even as dozens of past supervillains ambush the pair on the lawn outside the Washington Monument.

Later, Luthor begins his own preparations for the face-off, injecting himself with a serum that gives him super-strength, but at the same time pushes him further into insanity. Shown bare to the midriff, Luthor is as ripped as any superhero, not unlike the pictures *Fortune* magazine used to show of dot-com paper billionaires working out at the gym at the height of the dot-com boom.

Seemingly on the ropes and at Luthor's mercy, Superman and Batman turn the battle to their advantage, ultimately trapping the president in the Oval Office. With glowing red eyes, Superman clenches Luthor by the throat and contemplates killing him, thinking, "Holding him like this—he's so small. So frail. He would snap like it was nothing." Still baiting his enemy, Luthor demands, "Do it then. Give me what I've always wanted—the end of you" ("State of Siege," No. 5). Although Batman accepts Luthor's fate and tells Superman that they could make his death look like an accident, Superman spares his enemy once again.

Injecting himself with more serum and donning a green and purple battle suit, Luthor prepares to battle Superman after the duo leaves to deal with the asteroid. Green eyes glowing, Luthor outlines another evil thread that plagues his thinking—racism—telling the people, "I find it absurd that an alien can come to this planet, defy the orders of the president of the United States to surrender himself and force me to take this bold step" ("Final Countdown," No. 6).

Superman and Luthor fight it out high above the streets until the hero gets angry. Superman destroys the suit, propelling Luthor into his beloved LexCorp Towers. After a fistfight with Batman, Luthor falls off the tower, setting off a bomb that blows the building to bits. In a scene reminiscent of post-9/11 cleanup, Superman digs through the rubble searching for Luthor's remains, which he never locates. The final panel shows Luthor very much alive, insane, declaring, "There will be a reckoning...A crisis" ("Final Countdown," No. 6).

ARE WE SUPERMAN...OR LUTHOR?

Across the ages, Luthor and Superman have symbolized a war between brains and brawn that continues to conflict us. Luthor, fighting an invincible foe, represents the fears we have against hegemonic power and reflects the forces (science, invention, corporate supremacy) that we can't combat.

In public discourse, the argument is often portrayed as intellectualism versus anti-intellectualism. There are eras, like the early years of the Cold War, when intellectualism held sway. Science and innovation gave the public hope, despite the obvious terrors that technology could deliver. The current Bush Administration, on the other hand, shuns intellectualism. The president's worldview centers on the nation's military power and how that image is fostered across the globe.

During his closing fight with Superman, Luthor sums up the dispute in real-world terms, saying, "Technology is what moved this country leagues ahead of the rest of the world—the universe." Although he doesn't discuss the public's simultaneous fear of technology, Luthor does sketch out the other side of the equation. "If mankind has one common emotion—it's fear. Fear of the unknown. Fear of what they cannot control," he says. "And look how ready they are to believe that you are that thing they fear the most!" ("Final Countdown," No. 6) Luthor remains interesting after more than six decades because he embodies our conflicted feelings about intellectualism, science, technology and absolute power.

Perhaps the American preference to root for the underdog somehow also keeps Luthor around after all these years. He is mortal, yet remains a viable opponent against an invincible force because of his ingenuity. As Americans we are trained to believe that we can overcome any obstacle with smarts and determination, the kind of skills Luthor has portrayed for decades.

Who wouldn't want to be Superman...just for a minute to feel the power of flight or to have unlimited strength? Given that the superhero is so ingrained in modern popular culture, it is easy to imagine. However, in practical terms (if you discount the insanity), aren't we more like Luthor?

Like most people, Luthor deals with his fears and personal pain by adopting different personas to conceal his frailties, but still dwells on past slights. He's adaptable, based on the situation he's in. Luthor uses his brains and ingenuity to get ahead, despite being born into a family with nothing in an environment considered detrimental. He is no Boy Scout and doesn't wrap himself in the flag. Luthor's human. Maybe that is what keeps him interesting after all these years—Superman's ultimate enemy and the world's greatest villain.

REFERENCES

Benton, Mike. *The Comic Book in America: An Illustrated History*. Dallas: Taylor, 1989.

Daniels, Les. *DC Comics: Sixty Years of the World's Favorite Comic Book Heroes*. Boston: Little, Brown, 1995.

Gresh, Lois H. and Robert Weinberg. *The Science of Supervillains*. New York: Wiley, 2005.

Jones, Gerard. *Men of Tomorrow: Geeks, Gangsters, and the Birth of the Comic Book*. New York: Basic, 2004.

Loeb, Jeph. (w), Ed McGuiness (p), and Dexter Vines (i). *Superman/Batman* Nos. 1–6. DC Comics: Oct. 2003–March 2004.

"Luthor, Lex." DC Secret Files and Origins, 14 Dec. 2005.
< http://www.dccomics.com/secret_files/pdfs/lex_luthor.pdf>.

Siegel, Jerry (uncredited, w), Al Plastino (a). "How Luthor Met Superboy." *Adventure Comics* No. 271. National Comics Publications (DC Comics): April 1960. The Superman Web site 14 Dec. 2005. <http://superman. ws/tales2/howluthormetsuperboy/?page=0>.

Wright, Bradford W. *Comic Book Nation: The Transformation of Youth Culture in America.* Baltimore: Johns Hopkins, 2001.

BOB BATCHELOR is an award-winning business writer and historian. He teaches public relations at the University of South Florida. Bob is the author of *The 1900s* (2002), editor of *Basketball in America: From the Playgrounds to Jordan's Game and Beyond* (2005); and co-author of *Kleenex, Kotex, and Huggies: Kimberly-Clark and the Consumer Revolution in American Business* (2004). Bob's forthcoming books include *The 1980s* (2006) and *Literary Cash: Writing Inspired by the Songs of the Legendary Johnny Cash* (2007). Bob graduated from the University of Pittsburgh and received an M.A. from Kent State University.

Paul Levinson

SUPERMAN, PATRIOTISM AND DOING THE ULTIMATE GOOD:

WHY THE MAN OF STEEL DID SO LITTLE TO STOP HITLER AND TOJO

"It is that willing suspension of disbelief for the moment which constitutes poetic faith."

—SAMUEL TAYLOR COLERIDGE, *Biographia Literaria*, 1817

THE NICE THING about Coleridge's explanation of what makes poetry work is that it applies to much more than poetry. Nearly two centuries later, we know that we cry at sad movies, get angry at villains in novels, are thrilled by special effects because we voluntarily suspend our disbelief in all of these encounters, and pretend that what we know to be fiction is real. Unlike a roller-coaster ride in which there is a chance, however slim, that we can really lose our lives, our gasps at a horror or science fiction movie come completely from the success of temporarily believing that we can lose our lives, when we know full well that we cannot. The more effective the presentation in eliciting this grand pretense, the more highly we prize it.

Comic books in general and Superman in particular are no strangers to this wonderful wheeling and dealing with our emotions. A human-like alien from another planet with superpowers is easy for fans to believe. All right, as a kid I always wondered why Superman didn't use his x-ray vision to look though women's clothing, but this super-morality was a minor part of an otherwise convincing catalog of super-strength, super-speed, long-distance seeing and hearing, flying and leaping and weakness to Kryptonite. With one glaring exception.

Why didn't Superman use his powers to stop the German Blitzkrieg and the Japanese fleets during the Second World War?

THE SIZE AND DATES OF MIRACLES

Wallace Harrington put the matter aptly in his 1999 "Superman and the War" essay: "Most every Superman fan has asked at one point or another over the last sixty-one years: If Superman is so powerful, why does he not simply put an end to all wars and suffering?" Debuting in 1938, on the eve of World War II, Superman certainly blew his first big chance. It took D-Day and Hiroshima, and the loss of thousands upon thousands of lives, to put an end to the Axis powers.

Instead of applying himself to this worthy task—a task he could easily have accomplished—the Man of Steel for the most part used his powers during the war years to take out common criminals and petty dictators, and vie with fascinating fictional villains such as Lex Luthor who were not as evil as Hitler. There were a few exceptions.

First and foremost was the two-page "What If Superman Ended the War?" which appeared in the February 17, 1940 issue of *Look* magazine. In this story scripted by Jerry Siegel and drawn by Joe Shuster, Superman flies to Berlin to pick up Hitler by the scruff of his neck (the classic Superman grip on a villain), does the same with Stalin in Moscow and hauls the two to the League of Nation's World Court in Geneva, where they stand trial for crimes against their own people. (In our reality, this court was dissolved by the final League of Nations assembly in 1946 and succeeded by the U.N. World Court in the Hague.) The *Look* story is noteworthy, even controversial, for a variety of reasons:

- It appeared before the United States entered the Second World War in December 1941. It thus was a safe fantasy story, in that it was not presented to the American public at a time in which the nation was actually at war. The story in this way avoided such questions as why didn't the Man of Steel first destroy every weapon that was firing at American troops.

- The story has been incorrectly identified by many comic-book historians—including Harrington—as having been published not in 1940 but 1943. This may well reflect our yearning for Superman to have made an attempt to stop World War II after it had become a fully global war with massive American participation. Of course, the 1940 story is somewhat anachronistic in 1943—why would Superman in 1943 bypass Tojo and Hirohito in favor of Stalin, who while certainly no angel was then an ally of the United States and England?

- More recent anti-war advocates have correctly noted that Superman sought to put an end to the beginning of World War II by bringing its chief villains (Hitler and Stalin had both invaded Poland in 1939, which started the war) literally to justice, without firing a shot. The little story was thus a powerful brief for settling disputes among nations in a world court of law, and for taking the leaders of criminally aggressive nations, not their citizens, to task. These ideals have by and large yet to be adopted by the world, some sixty-five years out from the *Look* Superman story.

- The story was published as a special feature in *Look* magazine—not as part of the continuing DC comic-book series, or newspaper strips—and thus was outside of the normal canon of Superman narratives. This meant that the comic books and strips could continue their accounts of Superman without making reference to the *Look* fantastic tale. Which was a good thing, since the U.S. was soon to enter World War II, and the comic books would have been utterly beyond anyone's suspension of disbelief had they depicted a world in which Hitler (and Stalin!) were in prison.

How, then, did the Superman comic books handle the reality of World War II?

With scant use of the war as a central theme, and certainly no knockout punches to the Axis. "Japanazis" were mentioned in *Superman* No. 18 (September–October, 1942), Superman helped train troops in issue No. 23 (June–July, 1943) and he saves a fictional comic-book writer from the German Bund (Nazi sympathizers in the U.S.) in issue No. 25 (November–December, 1943). That "King of the Comic Books" tale is a spectacularly inventive "meta"-story—the comic-book writer has angered the Nazis because he portrays Hitler unfavorably—but it is hardly a piece with any major or significant relevance to the actual war effort. Meanwhile, Clark Kent, who has been declared "4-F" because of his poor vision (nice touch—he accidentally sees *through* the eye-chart, courtesy of x-ray vision, and reports the letters he sees on a chart in the next room!), helps with Air Force technical training in another memorable story in that same issue. But, again, the Man of Steel, this time in disguise, only helps in training, forgoing the frontline role one might expect of Superman, and which would have been much more inspiring to America.

Harrington accurately notes that, although the stories in the *Superman* and *Action Comics* comic books had little relevance to the main battles and issues of World War II, the covers were often brightly patriotic. (Superman stories appeared in both of these publications.) Wartime covers showed Superman attacking battleships, tanks and enemy positions. He sped to protect our fighting men and (of course) delivered supplies (a valuable but behind-the-scenes activity). The cover of *Superman* No. 17 (July–August, 1942) does have him holding Hitler and Hirohito (no longer Stalin) by their necks and trying to shake some sense into them. And *Superman* No. 29 (July–August, 1944) depicted Lois Lane walking arm-in-arm with a soldier, a sailor and a Marine, saying "You're my Supermen!" But you couldn't judge what was inside those comic books by their covers: as Harrington remarks, "It was actually rare that the action went further than the cover." In comic-book land, as in our reality, the war raged on, and took its course, with no significant impact from Superman.

The war fared about the same in Superman's radio and cartoon exploits, 1941–1945. A Nazi spy appeared as a villain in Superman's adventures on the Mutual Radio Network. Two cartoons produced by the Fleischer studios have Superman engaging the Japanese. Another has the Man of Steel against the Nazis. Although fans held and hold these episodes in high regard, none dealt with decisive events in the war.

WHY DIDN'T SUPERMAN END THE WAR: OF SUPERHEROES AND THE DEITY

We have already touched upon the very practical reason why Superman could not have put Hitler and Tojo out of their misery in 1941: the war in fact would rage on for another four years, and the comic books and radio broadcasts and cartoons would have been totally out of touch with reality had they allowed Superman to play such a conclusive role in the war. In terms of Coleridge's analysis of poetry, we could say that, although Superman's failure to fully confront the evils of Germany and Japan strained the willing suspension of disbelief of his fans, that suspension of disbelief would have been utterly shattered had the comics and broadcasts and cartoons brought us a world in which the war had been ended by Superman.

But there is a deeper, more profound, reason for Superman's inaction. It has to do with the god-like powers that were ascribed to him. A more mortal superhero such as Batman would not have been in the same predicament. Had Batman and Robin devoted all of their energies to stopping Germany and Japan, they at best would and could have played only a minor role. The Dynamic Duo could have worked day and night in high profile to end the war, and the war could have plausibly continued, just as it did in reality, with no jeopardy to our willing suspension of disbelief. But Superman and the suspension of disbelief required to believe in him enjoyed no such luxury. His super-powers were such that if he had applied them to the task of ending the war, it would have been over. We expected more of Superman precisely because he is able to fly at incredible speeds, lift extraordinarily heavy weights, see and hear what no mere mortal can and is invulnerable to bullets, fire, water and all manner of catastrophes except those packaged in Kryptonite.

Indeed, from the vantage point of 2005, we can look back and wonder why Superman did not lend a hand that made a difference in all kinds of disasters, natural as well as of human creation. Why didn't the Man of Steel hold at least one of the levees together in New Orleans with his bare hands after Hurricane Katrina? Why didn't he rescue at least some number of people when the World Trade Center towers were blazing and crumbling on September 11, 2001? His absence that day cuts especially deep, because he is so closely associated with tall buildings. (A poignant September 11th thread on the web which began just an hour after the attacks is entitled "Where Is Superman When We *Really* Need Him?"[1]) Questions such as these may seem unfair to pose about a comic-book character, but Katrina and 9/11 were if anything a lot less destructive than the Second World War, in which Superman did so little to prevent millions upon millions of deaths.

Perhaps we are inclined to ask such questions of Superman because we hold him, and his judgment as well as his powers, in such high, nearly god-like esteem. Similar questions have been asked for millennia, after all, of the Supreme Being. The *Book of Job*, thought to have been written some time between 700 and 300 BC, asks why, if God is good and all-powerful, would He allow such bad things to happen in the world. On an individual level, many who have lost loved ones have had similar concerns. Sometimes entire peoples have been haunted by this question. In the aftermath of the Holocaust in World War II, devout Jews had their faith severely tested: why would—how could—God allow such a thing to happen?

The answer provided in the *Book of Job* is that God sends these monstrous things our way to test us. Other religious teachings suggest that God might not be omnipotent—that God contends with powerfully evil forces, and is sometimes less than completely successful in stopping them. Several religious leaders made this point on the *Larry King Show*, after September 11: It was their view that the Supreme Being sought to sway the hijackers against their terrible acts, but did not prevail. Or perhaps He/She did, and this intervention prevented that tragedy from being worse than it was.

---

[1] http://www.geocities.com/womenofgotham/sept11.htm.

But Superman can be saved by neither of these answers. Surely the Man of Steel did not refrain from helping more in World War II, and from intervening in recent disasters, to test us. And though we can understand that he might not be totally successful in vanquishing evil, surely he could make more of an attempt. While unshakeable belief in the Deity may survive the most unspeakable of evils on this earth, can a willing suspension of disbelief in Superman survive his general failure to even confront such evils?

THE REAL LIMITS OF FICTION AND COMIC BOOKS

Superman fans can at least have the comfort of knowing that all fictional characters who seek to fight evil suffer from this same exquisite problem, in direct proportion to the size and scope of their powers. Where were the wizards in Harry Potter's world during World War II? Or were they checked by evil wizards on the Axis side? The annals of science fiction are chock full of time travelers bent on killing Hitler before he does his damage. The travelers almost always run into some unforeseen complication—sometimes their intervention even ironically enables Hitler. This must happen if the story is to remain consistent with our reality.

Of course, a novel or a movie can posit a new reality, made different from ours by the action of the hero, in which Hitler is never more than a failed painter. But a comic-book series and character would have a very difficult time taking that route. The proximity of comic books to the real world, the pace with which they move, means their characters and stories must toe a fine, demanding line to real events. When I discovered Superman in comic books in the 1950s, they were sold on newsstands and in candy stores, right alongside copies of *The New York Times, Herald Tribune, Journal-American, Daily News, Daily Mirror*, and *New York Post*. The fiction in the comics had to be in just the right doses to thrive next to the black-and-white reality in the papers.

Further, the more horrendous the real disaster, the more careful the fictitious hero needs to tread, lest the real victims of the tragedy take offense at their pain being trivialized or exploited. Television and movie docu-dramas about September 11, announced in

2005, were subjected to criticism that the theme was inappropriate for Hollywood treatment. (I disagreed, and argued in a Reuters article "Third Hollywood Studio Sets Sights on 9/11" by Steve Gorman, August 16, 2005, that such presentations are "part of the process by which we come to understand our own feelings about this.") But any comic-book treatment of September 11th would bear a much bigger burden.

So what's a Superman fan to do? Well, there's always the approach of not pushing such questions of Superman's non-intervention too far, and letting him off the *Book of Job* hook. After all, he is not a deity, he is a just a comic-book action hero, and if his life next to newspapers and chewing gum means he has to be more in touch with reality than does a character in a novel, well, maybe we should also give him the benefit of such casual company, and not hold him to impossibly exacting standards.

No...I don't think so. That's not really very satisfying either. Part of the fun of all fiction, comic books included, is teasing ourselves and the stories against how well they relate to our reality.

Maybe a better answer is this: Comic books are inextricably part of the matrix of everyday life—in the case of Superman, our everyday urban life. These little storybooks work on the premise that, if you happen to look up at the sky for no particular reason, you may see a superhero flying by. Or if you see a thief snatch a lady's purse, Superman may well streak down to retrieve it, and haul the thief—by the scruff of his neck—off to jail. We can expand this thieving villain to the level of a corrupt politician, or even to a mad scientist, also living and working in the city, maybe just around the corner, right under our noses. But the key to all of these characters may be that something about them is intrinsically and irrevocably city-sized. Not bigger than or beyond the city, not world-sized or even nation-sized. City-sized. And that includes Superman, who came of age in the heyday of Fiorello LaGuardia, the larger-than-life, beloved New York City mayor who read comics to the kids over the radio on Sundays. And this may be as good as any an explanation for why Superman is singularly and frustratingly incapable of responding with real effectiveness to larger-sized threats and more pervasive evils. We can gauge him best in terms of intra-city issues and realities. When we get beyond that, we are in unchartable territory for this kind of superhero.

But we can still draw inspiration from Superman's successful urban-sized exploits. We can be awed by his powers. We can bemoan that he has been unable to use them to stop or end the debacles of our day since his first appearance back in 1938. And we can retrieve that noble, lost, impossible potential and do all in our limited, non-super power to help.

REFERENCES

Harrington, Wallace. "Superman and the War." *Superman Home Page.* <http://www.supermanhomepage.com/comics/comics. php?topic=articles/supes-war>.
Siegel, Jerry and Joe Shuster. "What If Superman Ended the War?" *Look* magazine, 17 February 1940.

PAUL LEVINSON'S *The Silk Code* won the 2000 Locus Award for Best First Novel. He has since published *Borrowed Tides* (2001), *The Consciousness Plague* (2002), *The Pixel Eye* (2003) and *The Plot To Save Socrates* (2006). His science fiction and mystery short stories have been nominated for Nebula, Hugo, Edgar, and Sturgeon Awards. His eight nonfiction books, including *The Soft Edge* (1997), *Digital McLuhan* (1999), *Realspace* (2003) and *Cellphone* (2004), have been the subject of major articles in the *New York Times, WIRED*, the *Christian Science Monitor*, and have been translated into eight languages. He appears on *The O'Reilly Factor* (Fox News), the *CBS Evening News, Scarborough Country* (MSNBC), the *NewsHour with Jim Lehrer* (PBS) and numerous national and international TV and radio programs. He is professor and chair of communication & media studies at Fordham University in New York City.

Larry Dixon

THIS IS A JOB FOR...

HAVE A TATTERED old poster from Fort Bragg that lists Murphy's Laws of Combat.

Number one of the thirty-something rules is: *You Are Not A Superman.*

We are not super-beings of limitless might. We are but mortal! The poster means to tell us to watch ourselves so we don't get in over our heads. That's good advice, because sometimes our need to excel can push us well past the point when we should have stopped. A human can only do so much. We can only work for so long, struggle through just so much pain, and give of ourselves only so much effort until we collapse.

But I have seen men of steel.

As I began writing this, it was between long hours of coordinating a Hurricane Katrina relief effort. Men and women were in a serious hazard zone trying to rescue people, clear debris and contain a massive biohazard, and putting themselves in increasing danger to do so. Human strength, ingenuity and willpower were accomplishing superheroic miracles amidst disaster. It occurred to me, while on a supply run taking in clothing, food, medicine, generators and other goods to Louisiana, that they're all doing what Superman would do in the same situation.

Superman would use his super-strength to pull downed trees out of the way so rescue vehicles could get in. Regular people were doing that, using winches and bulldozers. Backhoes run by volunteers were clearing the way for whatever means we could find to carry refugees to shelter. Supes would use super-breath to put out fires. Determined folks were doing that job too, using firehoses, pickaxes, sand, water and rakes. Fire engines and ladder truck crews were working to exhaustion and beyond, to contain infernos and preserve life, limb and property. Supes would use super-speed to dash into buildings to save people. Rescue personnel worked as fast as they could to do the same thing, with trucks, jeeps and police cruisers. Supes would use his powers of flight to swoop in and pick people off of rooftops. We mere mortals were doing that too—with helicopters, boats and anything else we could get our hands on. Soldiers rolled in and eventually, there were destroyers and an aircraft carrier working evac, and everything from tents to cruise ships for housing.

Superman would give his best, but still feel remorse that he couldn't do more than he already was, to help these people in need.

We did too.

Oh, did we ever.

We wanted to do more. We wanted to do so much more, and I don't know if any of us feel like we did enough, and the things we saw will stay with us always.

There's an interesting thing about Superman, to my eyes anyway. One of the things that makes him Super, I suppose, because we mere mortals can't always manage it. Supes can *cope*. He sees violence, destruction, death and misery—and he's so Super Level Headed that he manages to shrug it off. It's a superpower we don't have—he has *invulnerability to horror*.

Ol' Clark has his x-ray vision, his invulnerability and speed. We're just these fragile sacks of meat and bone. He ricochets bullets from his chest! We bleed from a paper cut. Yet, we all can summon awe-inspiring courage when something *must* be done. When there's an overwhelming imperative, we can find the steel in ourselves and push in to confront the danger. Sometimes we are grievously injured doing it. Sometimes, we survive it but never completely recover emotionally. Sometimes, despite our best efforts, we fall in the line of duty and leave our brother and sister firefighters and rescuers to live on with the memories. People can crack, from survivor guilt, post-traumatic stress, nightmares and more. We can be left crippled in more ways than flesh and bone. Steel can break.

Many of us dwell on what could have been—that if we could have mobilized better, if we could have just been quicker—well, truthfully I don't know anyone who doesn't. We know that at some point a second could have been shaved off a response time, or we might have brought surer force to bear on a problem. We know we could have had better equipment, or better communications, or more manpower. We know that there'd be someone still alive and smiling if we just could have been a little more than we are.

We keep trying.

We have to deal with "lifeguard's dilemma," and Superman really doesn't—to a certain point. Have him up against a really supreme supervillain like Darkseid or Doomsday and all bets are off, but generally speaking, he's never in a position where he has to choose between saving someone else and saving himself. One of the toughest things anyone in the rescue biz can do is let go. Lifeguard's dilemma is basically this: you have to keep yourself safe, first, even if it means someone else comes to harm, or else you won't be able to help *anyone*—and you might even endanger your fellow rescuers if they have to come after you. If you drown saving one swimmer who will drag you down, you won't be alive to save the next forty swimmers who wouldn't drag you down. But that *one* always bugs you.

Superman gets to save people with an eyeblink of speed, and gets instant results. We need accountability, but heaven help us, sometimes people die because of the burden of bureaucracy. Superheroes get to be superheroes, and simply get things done. Superheroes have freedom from bureaucratic obstructions to go with their clarity of purpose. I envy them so. We get slowed down by permissions and forms and logistical roadblocks.

We mere humans are stuck with ignorance, graft, corruption, politics, lethargy, denial, pride, posturing, territoriality and indifference as our personal supervillains. Those are a rescuer's Kryptonite. They sap the strength from us and ultimately, they get people killed. Still. Just as Kryptonite can be contained by lead, so can those evils of human nature be overcome. We learn, and with knowledge we gain invulnerability. Education's the core. It's our yellow sun that gives us Kryptonian-level ability.

Children are inherently hungry to *know*. Hungry to learn. Children are taught and what's taught to a child early on sticks the most. It's strengthened when the principles in those lessons are reinforced by the child's own experiences. Someone can be told, like I was—and like Clark was—that to help other people is good. However, it takes a personal connection for a lesson to make that transition into something more than a low-impact abstract.

When there is a sense of disconnection, even alienation, from one's fellow man, there builds up a strong urge to connect. To be a part, and more than that, to be an *important* part. We *want* to be *wanted*. We want to not just be acknowledged, but shown that we are special, and beloved because of what *makes* us special. Consequently, we turn to doing the things that we have been taught are good. When we have a strong personal experience with a life lesson, it can generate the emotional spark that turns a job into a passion. And, in doing something that attracts the attention of those around us, in a positive way, it brings others in, soothing the feelings we have had about standing "outside."

I figure that Clark does his good deeds for two main reasons—to follow the good teachings that the Kents gave him, and to feel a connection to humanity as a result of his deeds. The approval of his adopted planet's people enable him to be a part of something else out there; it de-alienizes him. I know that in the case of many firefighters and rescuers, their "civilian" social awkwardness vanishes when they wear the uniform or the badge, because people will automatically react favorably toward them. The ice is broken.

Clark has seen that people can be very cruel and uncaring—but at an early age, in a bright moment of introspection, he must have had an epiphany. He must have realized that these people, the Kents, who found him at his most vulnerable, could have abandoned him and let him die, turned him over to who-knows-who, from an orphanage to a Shadowy Paramilitary Organization™, and not personally raised and cared for him. They could have been safe and less emotionally stressed—*far more easily* than going to the years of trouble of what they *did* do—by simply doing nothing. The fact that Clark was alive, and on top of that had a pretty good childhood at all was proof to him that going to the effort to help others is an extraordinary thing, and could yield extraordinary results.

Will Eisner observed that superheroes caught on in the early twentieth century because, really, they were always there. Human history has always had characters of superheroic magnitude: Beowulf, Gilgamesh, Robin of Sherwood, Zorro and so on. Superman's story is biblical in scale because, well, it's biblical in content: he's the last survivor of a race, flung into the cosmic river in a rocket ship, brought up to help mankind by strong family values, folks. It doesn't get much more dramatic than that without a Korngold soundtrack and a James Earl Jones voiceover. Like previous generations had theater, storytellers, priests and holy books to give the heavy ideas of their world drama and weight, the early twentieth century had its own, easily accessible popular media. Most people have been raised with legend all around them, thanks to film, TV, books, comics and radio. There's a direct line that can be drawn to hieroglyphics and friezes to sacred text, a ghost story by a campfire, and to our beloved "talking books" with pictures and speech in little bubbles. They're our very own paper movies, with roots all the way back to cave paintings.

So why do superheroes, supervillains and super-adventurers catch our fancy so much? People have also been raised with a sense of reverence for those who *accomplish things*, and without a doubt, one of the core elements in a comic book is that things happen. There are accomplishments. Deeds are done: Dr. Sivana might have a nefarious plan, but it is a plan and things *do* happen. Luthor's a superbrain bald guy, and he *does* things. Big Blue reacts, and *does* something. A friend recently told me that people have a hard time relating to me because I seem like fiction to them: because I actually do things that most people are content to just read about or see in a movie, I don't seem real. Most people want to just let things happen, rather than put themselves in true danger, and so instead they live vicariously through the stories they see. Maybe the alienation I've felt so many times stems from the voice inside that tells me I don't have to just be an observer of what happens in this life. I couldn't look at heroes and see them as something I couldn't be. I saw an adventure hero as something I *ought* to be.

When you're young, and the world's way too big to wrap your brain around, you want to accomplish something. Being a superhero is a child's dream for a lot of reasons. Not only do you make a difference, you might make a difference with a *lot* of special effects. You may choke on the math test in your third-period class in real life, but if you were a superhero, you wouldn't have to worry about something as tiny as that. You'd be busy using heat vision to fuse fallen rock into a dam to save the city, then you'd be off to stop aliens from destroying the moon! And for some of us who grew up poor, the idea that you could do something that would impress *everyone*—even the *rich folks*—was pretty awesome. The wise guidance of my parents, and the books, TV shows, comic books of my youth—and later, role-playing games—inspired me to learn and to take action. I knew that I couldn't do great things just by reading about them, because no lives get saved by someone reading about a hero and doing nothing else.

When I go in on a rescue I am all business, but in my introspective moments I am mindful that the kid I help now may become a great artist or civil rights leader or teacher, because he or she made it through that one day. The kid might be an entertainer, a teacher, and a good, cool parent. The kid might be a musician and rock the house and make the world a better place as an inventor or physician. I think that on some subconscious level, Superman carries a similar feeling with every rescue he does. It isn't the person of the moment that he is saving, it's the person of the future who'll be changed by that day.

Like Kal-El's future was changed for the better by the action the Kents took one fateful day, in a Kansas cornfield.

Impressionable young Kal-El becomes Clark Kent becomes Superman. I think we all go from being impressionable youngsters with broad potential into focused adults, though some might say we aren't so much focused as limited. Certainly Superman is a being of self-imposed limitations, from moral choices to simple powers—control like not crushing doorknobs (or peoples' hands) by mistake. We regular people are like that in our daily lives, too. Someone who learns martial arts knows that they CAN beat someone up, so it becomes an act of responsibility and restraint when we choose not to. Firefighters know how to destroy things very well—heck, part of our training is exactly that—but we choose not to. Usually. Unless it's really called for, or, all right, unless it's really fun. For us, there are serious consequences for property damage. Not for Superman! Supes gets to bust through a concrete wall—blam!—but never stays around long enough to be billed for it.

Smart guy!

Supes gets to do things we rescue types would *love* to do. Superman gets to dive into the middle of trouble without reporting to Incident Command, handing over a dogtag, or signing in. We have to follow procedures so that emergency ops knows where we are—in part, so *we* don't have to get rescued by getting caught in harm's way without anyone knowing we're there. But Supes? He's a red-and-blue blur into the thick, and everyone points. It's a bird! It's a plane! It's an above-accountability civilian! Really, that's a superpower in itself, isn't it? Something to dream about? Even the goodiest of the goody-goody heroes get away with it: they get to show up, perform some quasi-legal act without answering to anyone, and move on. No paperwork or debriefings, no reports or even a memo. A flash of cape followed by a pause long enough for the cameras to get the gleam off their teeth—then a jaunty "My work here is done!" and away they zoom! We poor schmucks in the heavy rubber boots don't get that kind of cool. Sometimes it feels like twenty percent of every incident is spent asking who's in charge and finding where *they* are, and another twenty is spent making sure they know where *we* are. The other sixty percent gets spent trying to figure out what to put in the report. We squeeze in some time for a rescue, too.

Plus, Superman always has good weather and great lighting. In real life, it's always cold, dark and wet. Even if an incident began in mid-summer at noon, somehow it always ends up with clearing debris at night, when it's cold and muddy and probably raining. Hurricane Katrina was kind of one-stop-shopping in that regard. But heck, Superman could have even stopped the hurricane through some combination of super-breath and super-speed and flying against the wind to create sonic booms that would cancel the rotational velocity. Superman can deal with huge-scale things. We're human, and we deal with things on a human level. It always comes down to the human scale, when we consider anything we might be able to do. When I drove a tanker or fire engine, it was twenty tons of weight ultimately steered by one little guy in a chair. Even a supertanker or aircraft carrier, for all its bulk, is directed by just one regular human at the controls. We humans can't control even the smallest tornado, and a hurricane is, basically, a tornado twenty miles wide. It's on a scale beyond us. All we can do is deal with the human-scale reaction to it.

I believe people have far more power than we might think we do, but the slightest amount of power is dangerous without the self-control and education to use it wisely. Sometimes, that wisdom means doing something daring with your power because the results can be so amazing. It'd be a shame not to.

Brighter people than I can go into the psychology of what makes Superman tick, and what his motives are—but I can tell you this opinion of mine. Corny as it may sound, it came home to me during the Katrina work that Clark would feel proud of himself to be as much of a superhero as these regular humans were as they helped their fellow man in this time of need.

A few great comics writers have observed that it's not such a big deal to take on masked gunmen when you know you're bulletproof, but it takes incredible bravery to do it when you're just a human. It can't have escaped Superman that in emergencies all around him, vulnerable people were facing down their mortality for the sake of others, and had no superpowers to back it up—just a hat, some fireproof clothing and hand tools. I wonder if invulnerable Clark ever gets an inferiority complex seeing a bunch of stubborn people in bunker gear face off against a multi-story blaze with nothing but water, guts and determination?

Comics, movies and books taught us that those who dare truly live, and inspire others to dare as well. It uplifts us all. In chatting with fellow firefighters about comic books and about helping others, more than a few observed that even as a child they felt an urge to not be a victim, or as one put it, "another one in a crowd losing their minds and not knowing what to do." They wanted to be someone who knew what was going on and knew how to get people to safety.

In particular I recall that during my second year as a volunteer firefighter, one of my fellow firefighters got a new Dodge pickup and the first thing he did to customize it was put a Superman "S" symbol on the rear glass next to his maltese cross decal. It's not the first time I've seen something like that, and it won't be the last.

I think the Kents would be honored to see it.

When I began this essay, I thought I'd be writing about how much real-world rescue workers want to be like Superman. In the end, though, I discovered that the truth is, Superman wants to be like us.

LARRY DIXON is an acclaimed artist and interior illustrator with work ranging from Harvard Press to Marvel. Son of an extraordinary Okie farm-girl and a Delta Force commando, Larry has been a race car driver, volunteer firefighter, stormspotter and all-around adventurer. His passions are falconry, technology, music history, special effects, custom cars, comedy, games, fashion and model making. Larry was also the Great Eagles reference advisor for the Lord of the Rings films. With Mercedes Lackey, he's credited for popularizing gryphons and has been Guest of Honor at more than 200 conventions worldwide.

He lives in Oklahoma, where he collects comics, odd cars and injuries.